Conversations with Economists

Conversations with Economists

*New Classical Economists and Their
Opponents Speak Out on the Current
Controversy in Macroeconomics*

ARJO KLAMER

ROWMAN & ALLANHELD
PUBLISHERS

Published in the United States of America in 1984
by Rowman & Allanheld, Publishers
(A division of Littlefield, Adams & Company)
81 Adams Drive, Totowa, New Jersey 07512

Library of Congress Cataloging in Publication Data
Main entry under title:

Conversations with economists.

Bibliography: p.
Includes index.
1. Macroeconomics. 2. Economics. 3. Economic
policy. I. Klamer, Arjo.
HB172.5.C66 1983   339   83-17765
ISBN 0-86598-146-9
ISBN 0-86598-155-8 (pbk.)

86 / 10 9 8 7 6 5 4

Printed in the United States of America

CONTENTS

PREFACE

Can the government help to stabilize the economy through active, interventionist policies?

The question is particularly relevant in a world that experiences painful swings in the degree of economic activity and an increase in the levels of unemployment. How do economists answer it?

To seek to know is to court confusion. Listening to neo-Keynesian economists, such as James Tobin and Franco Modigliani, one hears that the government can remedy economic pains. Monetarists Milton Friedman and Karl Brunner, on the other hand, while acknowledging some effect of governmental economic policies in the short run, deny any such influence in the long run. In fact, they attribute most economic pain to governmental meddling in economic affairs. And recently, new classical economists (often referred to as rational expectations theorists) have extended these laissez-faire conclusions. Bob Lucas and Tom Sargent, major protagonists of this group, have stirred the world of economists with arguments supporting the view that stabilization policies are impotent even in the short run. Moreover, at the nonconventional end of the spectrum we hear protests from post-Keynesian and Marxian economists who have little sympathy with the endeavors of conventional economists. Many of them believe that the sickness has progressed too far for the government to doctor the economy in any significant way.

Economists, doubtless, still command respect outside their own world. Their ability to talk about a subject as mystifying as economics can inspire awe at dinner and cocktail parties. There is suspicion, however; and along with unemployment rates, the suspicion may be rising.

People have noticed that economists do not return unanimous, clear and unambiguous answers to straightforward economic questions. The suspicion is well expressed in jokes like the following. Andropov asks the head of the KGB, during the October parade, "Comrade, who are those guys in the plain suits in the parade?" "Oh," the KGB head answers, "they are economists, comrade." And when Andropov raises his eyebrows, he hastens to explain, "Just wait until we let them loose in the US." In Poland, we are told, the Poles tell "economist jokes."

Strong and persistent disagreement among economists is disconcerting. "Who is right?" the onlooker or the beginning student in economics may wonder. "Is there not a way to decide who is right?" One is tempted to pose the question to economists themselves, but their answer does not satisfy.

Economists tend to be scientific optimists. They believe in their discipline, in its methods or tools, and in their ability to deal with major questions. Among themselves they may speak in disparaging terms about psychologists and sociologists, asserting that "They never agree on anything, use imprecise methods, and have no measurements." They then crown economics the queen of social sciences. Economists do acknowledge disagreements, but these are not supposed to be fundamental. Differences in opinion occur, with respect to political issues especially, but a sharpening of the tools will eventually smooth those differences out. Most important, economists insist that empirical tests will determine who is right. Their intent is to reach agreement. Personal and ideological differences may temporarily stand in the way, but, in principle, economists are detached scientists who suppress their "normative" ideas (on what ought to be) in favor of positive insights (on what is). They depict the acquisition of economic knowledge as the outcome of a rational process little influenced by external factors, such as political alliances or personal inclinations.

This picture of what happens within the world of economists is both incomplete and misleading. For one, it does not account for the persistence of disagreements between neo-Keynesian, monetarist, new classical, and other economists. Where are the empirical tests that should arbitrate these disputes? Second, anyone who has had a chance to observe interactions among economists is likely to be struck by the passion and commitment of their arguments. Their communication frequently breaks down, as students may discover when they attempt to be critical inside the classroom. Persistent criticism often meets annoyance and is dismissed abruptly. Detachment does not appear to be a common phenomenon in the world of economists.

Third, the idealized picture does not do justice to the diverse styles of argument in economic discourse. My own first encounter in the world of economists was with econometricians who preferred to speak "econometrics" instead of economics. Later, I met Dutch economists, who tended to discuss economic issues in a critical way, and who were wary of abstract economic theories. My US teachers did not mind theory; as a matter of fact, they loved it. They were dead serious about the assumption of rational behavior, which I had heard criticized so persistently in Holland. When I suggested that the assumption is absurd, as I had been taught before, I was told that I did not understand economics. "Did you ever read Friedman's essay on Positive Economics?" they would ask. "Well, if you do, then you will understand that the realism of an assumption does not matter."

Personal impressions like these suggest that the world of economists is divided into separate spheres among which communication can be difficult. The world of Dutch economists is not the world of US economists. But one can go further. The style of Chicago economists is not the style of Harvard economists; the New School of Social Research, where radical economists prevail, is another completely different story. It is as if economists in these separate worlds speak different languages. Some want to talk in terms of highly abstract models; others opt for historical and institutional discussions. Some like mathematics, others do not. Likewise, while one group of economists may worship a particular analytic technique, other groups may resist or ignore the very same technique.

In this book, I reproduce a series of conversations with new classical economists and their opponents. The obvious way to read these conversations is as a report on what today's leading macroeconomic theorists are thinking about economic theory and the policy questions that dominate both the profession and much of the public debate. On this level, the participants in these conservations are remarkably lucid and enlightening. But an underlying theme is the exploration of the disagreements and problems of communication in economic discourse. New classical economics is a good focus for this purpose. It has taken the world of macroeconomics by storm and recruited large numbers of budding economists. Its claims have penetrated the public domain, and the ideas of Lucas and Sargent are frequently quoted in the general press.

Much of the economic profession at large, however, remains to be convinced. Neo-Keynesian economists and monetarists also (with whom new classical economists are often associated) have produced a substantial literature that is critical of new classical economics. The debate evokes the image of two well-entrenched camps beleaguering each other, neither willing to surrender. This image may be too strong, but that we shall discover by talking with the main representatives of each camp.

I am suggesting that the ways in which economists talk about what they do is unsatisfactory and that a new perspective is needed. These conversations can be used to support such a perspective. Whereas economists generally address the logical characteristics of their theories when they talk about economics, I propose to emphasize the more personal and *communicative* aspects of economics. The difference is between asking "How can we appraise economic theories?" and asking "How do economists argue?" or "Why do they disagree?"

According to my perspective, economics is an art of persuasion. Economists argue to persuade their audiences of the significance of their ideas or claims. My interpretation of the conversations at the end will elaborate on the particulars of the process of persuasion. Here it suffices to say that the emphasis is on the variety of arguments that economists use and, above all, the role of personal judgment. I shall argue that economists are not at all wholly detached, but are committed from the start to a point of view which they will then support with different types of argument. The persuasiveness of their arguments is critical, and whether an argument persuades is often *not* a matter of evidence or logic.

Economic discourse is flooded with articles, but most of them are little read and quickly forgotten. Why did Lucas's work escape this fate and have such a powerful impact? And why are neo-Keynesian economists unpersuaded? We can push the questioning further and wonder why neither neo-Keynesian nor new classical arguments convince Marxian economists. What are the dynamics of these intellectual interactions? We shall see by listening to how they argue.

Most people answer questions by reading and deducing attitudes and intentions from the written word. Why not talk directly with the people whose intentions and judgments one is trying to guess? This radical suggestion, which I owe to my brother, I was able to follow, and the reader is invited to join me as I talk with the main participants in the debate on new classical economics. Let me briefly introduce them here.

Bob Lucas, Tom Sargent, and Robert Townsend will represent the new classical economics. Lucas and Sargent are obvious choices; they stand out as the most influential new classical economists. Townsend speaks for the younger generation of new classical economists. The distinction between the younger and older generation also influenced the choice of neo-Keynesian economists. James Tobin, Franco Modigliani, and Robert Solow belong to the older generation of neo-Keynesian economists, that is, the generation that dominated the world of economists during the '50s and '60s. The importance of each is universally recognized. Alan Blinder will talk about the way he, a leading younger neo-Keynesian economist, views the controversy. I include, perhaps unjustly, John Taylor in this same category. Although he resists the neo-Keynesian label and his work is very close to that of the new classical economists, he still produces neo-Keynesian conclusions. Karl Brunner represents the monetarists here, and David Gordon, the Marxist economists. Leonard Rapping occupies a special position, partly because he worked with Lucas just before the take-off of new classical economics, partly because of his radical views now. But mainly I am interested in his conversion from conventional to radical economics. His story nicely illustrates the importance of personal and social factors in economic discourse.

The conversations are reproduced more or less verbatim; the editing has been kept to a minimum. The intention was simply to listen to the ways in which economists talk about themselves, and about doing economics. There is some structure in the questioning, but in general the questions are adapted to the tone and direction of the conversation. The introductory chapter gives a general overview of the issues that are discussed and will be of special help to students and those who are unfamiliar with the current debates in macroeconomics. Some technical detail is included, but it can be ignored without losing the thread of the exposition. The final chapter draws connections between what was said and the perspective that I adumbrated above. A glossary gives some brief information on the important names mentioned throughout the text.

The conversations have been conducted with several purposes in mind. Most will find the talks entertaining, for these are interesting as well as important people. The informal tone may help to illuminate what new classical economics is all about. Even those familiar with the debate will profit from these accounts by those most involved in it. The discussions may further clarify the significance of the notions of rational expectations and equilibrium in new classical models and the problem of information. In general, the conversations convey a vivid personal sense of what is happening in the world of economists.

This book is, of course, the product of extensive communication. I want to acknowledge the following students, colleagues and friends for their advice, warnings, enthusiasm, criticism, and help: Sue Wagner, Paula D'Amasi, Anne Pitcher, Rob Fisher, Spencer Carr, Sandy Baum, Rod Morrison, Len Nichols, Janet Seiz, Susan MacDonald, Karen Gustafson, Maria Elena Campbell, Phillip Jones, and MaryAnne Gucciardi. Wellesley College has been generous in its financial support. Talking with prominent economists has been a stimulating experience. Bob Lucas, Tom Sargent, Robert Townsend, James Tobin, Franco Modigliani, Bob Solow, Alan Blinder, John Taylor, Karl Brunner, David Gordon, and Leonard Rapping all deserve my deepest gratitude for the time and attention they have given me. The book is dedicated to Janny, Alje, Gonda, Channah, and Ronald, who are responsible for my fascination with the process of communication.

1

A BACKGROUND FOR THE CONVERSATIONS

In 1971 Robert Lucas presented an economic analysis with rational expectations to a conference of economists. He suggested that rational people use all available information and the knowledge of economic models when they anticipate the future. Reaction was, predictably, highly critical, for the analysis constituted a frontal attack on the Keynesian hegemony of that time by suggesting that if expectations are rational, Keynesian theoretical and empirical work is wrong, and so is Keynesian policy. James Tobin attacked the heart of Lucas's argument, the assumption of rational expectations. He wondered how it was possible that our expectations are consistent with the predictions of an elaborate econometric model that most people cannot understand? Despite Tobin's authority and the apparent commonsense nature of this criticism, rational expectations, or what became known as the new classical economics, caught on. The impact on macroeconomic discourse has been dramatic.

Economics textbooks do little justice to the impact of new classical economics. In their picture of macroeconomics, neo-Keynesian economics usually occupies the foreground, with monetarism as the main alternative. New classical economics is depicted as a special and extreme case of monetarism. Its main features are the assumption of rational expectations and the belief that Keynesian economic policy is ineffective. This picture is at least partly misleading. In the academic literature, the new classical arguments predominate; neo-Keynesians and monetarists alike are on the defense. And new classical economics has clearly contributed more than just the notion of rational expectations; it has engendered fruitful discussions on, for example, equilibrium, the role of imperfect information, and the importance of stochastic variables, that is, variables subject to random fluctuations.

The following sketch will add detail to the textbook picture by recounting the recent history of macroeconomics, incorporating coverage of new classical economics. It should serve as a background when reading the conversations.

AN ERA OF NEO-KEYNESIAN CONSENSUS

In the '60s, the world of economics witnessed the massive triumph of the Keynesian Revolution. Neo-Keynesian economics dominated macroeconomic analysis. Its message was conveyed to students as well as to political leaders, and the message was an optimistic one. Although Keynes had dispelled the absolute faith of classical economists in the market forces, neo-Keynesian economists argued that government intervention could remedy market failures. If political leaders only listened to their advice, another Great Depression would never occur again.

Politicians began to listen to Keynesian economists. In the United States, an important symbolic step was the acceptance of the Employment Act of 1946, which assigned responsibility to the government for economic stability and growth. Throughout the 1940s and 1950s, however, politicians paid little attention to Keynesian advice on ways to live up to that responsibility. The tide began to turn in 1960, when President John F. Kennedy appointed a Keynesian Council of Economic Advisors with Walter Heller as its chairman. But Kennedy needed time to adjust to the radical ideas of neo-Keynesians. Initially, he maintained the importance of "sound" fiscal policy, i.e., a balanced budget, against the opinion of his Council that advocated a deficit to stimulate the economy. The victory came in June 1962 when Kennedy, in a speech at Yale University, endorsed the Keynesian position and supported a massive tax cut. In 1964, the tax cut was implemented by Kennedy's successor, Lyndon B. Johnson. In 1966 Heller claimed overwhelming success, observing "an expansion that in its first five years [after 1961] created over seven million jobs, doubled profits, increased the nation's real output by one third, and closed the $50 billion gap that plagued the American economy in 1961" (Heller, 1966, p. 1).

THE NEO-KEYNESIAN THEORY

The optimism of the neo-Keynesians was founded on a confidence in their tools of analysis. They especially relied on the IS/LM framework, which John Hicks and Alvin Hansen devised as a formal interpretation of Keynes's general theory. The framework, which up until now has been the standard equipment for each student in macroeconomics, indicates the relationship between interest rates and equilibrium output and can be used to show the effectiveness of fiscal policies. The IS curve represents the spending or real sphere and illustrates that spending, i.e., consumption, investment, and government spending, increases when interest rates decrease. The LM curve shows that the financial sphere allows an increase in spending only at the expense of an increase in the interest rate. The rationale is based on Keynes's notion of liquidity preference, which states that people want liquidity, or money in the form of cash and checking accounts, in order to make transactions *and* to speculate in the bond market. When spending goes up, people need more money to make transactions. If the total amount of money were constant, they would get that money only when the speculative money holdings decrease. To decrease speculative money holdings, higher interest rates are needed. Consequently, in the financial sphere, more spending is related with a higher interest rate; the LM curve is upward sloping. The equilibrium output and interest rates are determined at the point where IS and LM intersect.

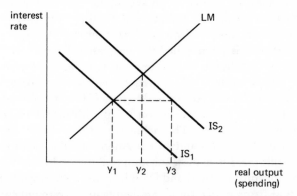

The IS/LM framework illustrates the effectiveness of fiscal policy as follows: A tax cut or more government spending increases the income of individuals and hence induces more spending (IS_1 shifts to IS_2). The increase in spending generates an additional need for transactions money, which pushes up the interest rate. As a consequence, the initial increase in spending ($y_3 - y_1$) is reduced, but the final impact of the fiscal measure remains positive ($y_2 - y_1$).

In the late 1950s, inflation occurred along with unemployment. The Phillips curve offered an explanation. Discovered by the Australian economist A. W. Phillips, it represents an inverse relationship between inflation and unemployment: lower unemployment leads to more inflation. In the 1960s, neo-Keynesian economists permanently added the Phillips curve to their kit of tools. This was important, because the price variable was now included in the Keynesian model. The IS/LM framework by itself did not account for what happens to prices, and initially neo-Keynesians had not bothered assuming that prices remain constant in a state of less than full employment.

Neo-Keynesians assumed that the relationship between unemployment and inflation is stable and asserted its usefulness for government policy. Fiscal measures were considered effective to move the economy along the Phillips curve, setting it at a preferred combination of inflation and unemployment. A tax cut, for example, would induce more spending and a lower unemployment rate, as the IS/LM diagram indicates, but only at the expense of a higher inflation rate, as the Phillips Curve predicts.

Drawing a curve on a blackboard can be an effective pedagogical device, but it does not suffice as an argument. Neo-Keynesians needed theoretical backing for the IS/LM and Phillips curves. For this they drew heavily on neoclassical microeconomics. As a result, neo-Keynesian theory is often called the neoclassical synthesis. The basic motivation is to provide microeconomic foundations for macro relationships, that is, to show that aggregate behavior is consistent with individual maximization. Accordingly, James Tobin demonstrated that the upward sloping LM curve is consistent with individual maximization of financial portfolios. This achievement would earn him a Nobel prize. Franco Modigliani and Albert Ando used the idea that individual households maximize their consumption over a lifetime as the basis for a theory of consumption, and Dale Jorgenson analyzed the behavior of individual firms to determine an aggregate investment function.

The search for microfoundations is also manifest in the neo-Keynesian account of a stable Phillips curve. The interesting development here is the shift of focus toward the supply side of the economy or the labor market. The demand side of the economy, which is captured in the IS and LM curves, was always considered pivotal in Keynesian thinking. Keynes's main message was that a shortage in effective demand is responsible for economic woes of unemployment and recession, and hence demand policies (i.e., fiscal policies) constitute the remedy. The discovery of the Phillips curve required attention for production and pricing decisions of firms and thus for their costs. As labor constitutes the major cost component, economists had to turn their attention on the microeconomics of the labor market to find a theoretical interpretation for the negative relationship between wages and prices, on one hand, and unemployment and production, on the other.

To explain the inverse relationship between inflation and unemployment, neo-Keynesians conceived the labor market to be in disequilibrium. A market is in disequilibrium when demand is unequal to supply, and neo-Keynesians assumed that an excess demand for labor is responsible for rising wage rates, which, in turn, cause prices to go up.

But there were two major complications. Firstly, it is unclear how an excess demand for labor can coexist with unemployment, which indicates an excess supply of labor. Secondly, this excess demand must not only exist, it has to persist to warrant the stability of the Phillips curve.

To solve the dilemma of coexistence, neo-Keynesians characteristically appealed to various imperfections of the market, such as lack of information, heterogeneity of workers, and mismatch of jobs. Because of these imperfections, vacancies are not filled immediately even with an excess supply of labor; adjustments take time but may be accelerated when labor becomes scarcer (in that case inflation goes up and unemployment, down).

The dilemma of persistent disequilibrium was handled with references to the stickinesss or rigidity of nominal wages, which prevents the labor market from clearing. According to the neo-Keynesians, the existence of contracts and of social pressure against tinkering with wages too much are two reasons for such rigidity. They concluded that the Phillips curve was vindicated, as was the government's ability to choose and maintain any combination of inflation and unemployment along the curve.

This was the situation at the end of the 1960s. Neo-Keynesians had bolstered Keynes's claim that demand policies are effective. More importantly, they demonstrated that a vision of market failures is compatible with an allegiance to neoclassical microeconomics. Their achievements had found recognition in the "real" world. Around 1970, however, the neo-Keynesian hegemony broke down.

THE NEO-KEYNESIAN CONSENSUS CHALLENGED

It took a chain of traumatic events to shake confidence in Keynesian economics. In the United States the economic demands of the Vietnam War propelled inflation rates. In 1970, the world witnessed a breakdown of its financial system when Nixon devalued the dollar, which had functioned as a key currency, and canceled its convertibility into gold. National economies faltered. Bad harvests, disastrously low catches of anchovies off the coast of Peru, and the OPEC oil shocks, all in 1973, compounded the problems. The result was an experience of high inflation rates *and* high unemployment rates throughout the 1970s, an experience that seemed at odds with the Keynesian Phillips curve.

Economists had to account for the economic hardships. Some of them targeted the neo-Keynesian approach and advocated radically different answers to economic questions. Post-Keynesian, Marxist, and monetarist economics were offered as alternatives and had to be reckoned with.

What unites *post-Keynesian* economists are a rejection of the neoclassical synthesis, an ambivalence toward Marxist economics, and the belief that the economic discipline is in disarray. Their own positive answers, however, are varied. Sydney Weintraub, for example, stressed rising wage costs as the cause of persistent inflation and proposed an income policy. Paul Davidson accused neo-Keynesian economists of ignoring Keynes's notion of fundamental uncertainty, which points at the impossibility to fully predict future events. Accordingly, expectations, which are often volatile, dominate economic behavior. Partly because of this, Davidson considers the IS/LM framework of little use as a tool of analysis and urges economists to take the original writings of Keynes more seriously. Other fervent opponents to neoclassical and neo-Keynesian economics are located in England and Italy. Among them, Joan Robinson is probably best known. These critics have taken not only Keynes's work off the shelves, but also that of the 19th-century economists like Ricardo and Marx. They make the point that conventional economics has no theory of income distribution and assert that the struggle for a larger share in income among various groups can explain many of the contemporary economic problems. The reactions of neo-Keynesian economists to these criticisms have been tepid. James Tobin and others may have endorsed the post-Keynesian idea of an incomes policy to combat inflation, but there is little explicit discussion of post-Keynesian theory.

A similarly cold reception was accorded to *Marxist* economists who came out of the social turbulence of the 1960s and its concomitant social critique. Young economists consulted the work of Marx and neo-Marxists, such as Ernest Mandel and Paul Sweezy, to find expressions for their frustrations with the capitalist system. They regarded neo-Keynesian economics as ideological and unrealistic, and argued that it perpetuated an unjust system where a majority of the people are denied a fair chance for dignified work and a respectable life. They criticized the neglect of power and class conflict in neo-Keynesian models. David Gordon, Samuel Bowles, Donald Harris, and Thomas Weisskopf, to mention a few young Marxists, view the market system as fundamentally unstable and stress its tendency to generate severe crises. Initially, some conventional economists, such as Paul Samuelson and Martin Bronfenbrenner, felt compelled to take the Marxist arguments seriously, but in recent years interest has subsided. Although the Marxist point of view is briefly treated in most introductory textbooks, Marxist economists are outsiders in the world of economists.

From the other side of the political spectrum, the neo-Keynesian rampart had to endure the *monetarist* critique, which ultimately turned out to be more effective. During the 1950s and 1960s, however, its influence was minimal. Milton Friedman, the eloquent spokesman of monetarism, was considered a heretic. His appeal to the classical belief in market forces, which Keynes had so decisively rejected, and his campaign against Keynesian policies seemed out of place. But Friedman and others persisted and finally forced neo-Keynesian economists to confront their argument. The resulting monetarist debate would dominate macroeconomic discourse in the early 1970s.

A crucial element in the discussions between neo-Keynesians and monetarists turned out to be the distinction between the short and long run. The neo-Keynesians stressed the short run, adhering to Keynes's famous phrase: "in the long run we are all dead." The monetarists contended that Keynesian conclusions falter and that classical beliefs are reaffirmed if the long-run effects of policies are acknowledged.

One of these classical beliefs is in the *neutrality of money*. The idea is that changes in the money supply affect the price level only and are neutral with respect to real output and employment. According to neo-Keynesian economists, money is non-neutral. An increase in the money supply (which causes a shift in the LM curve), they argued, brings down interest rates; lower interest rates induce more spending, and real output increases. The monetarists contested this conclusion and claimed a neutral effect in the long run. Paradoxically, they also argued that money is more important in the short run than the neo-Keynesians acknowledged; they even held fluctuations in the money supply responsible for fluctuations in real output, which constitute the phenomena of business cycles. This needs an explanation.

An important element in the monetarist explanation of their paradox is the *real balance* effect. Real balances, i.e., the amount of money held by the public divided by the price index, should be interpreted as wealth for the public. Monetarists argued that real balances have a strong effect on spending. Accordingly, when the money supply goes up (the LM curve shifts to the right), people want to spend the extra money (the IS curve shifts to the right), and output increases. This is the short-run effect. In the long run, the real effects of the money supply are elim-inated, according to monetarist theory, because of price adjustments in the markets. The increased level of spending generates higher prices, and real balances decrease again. This process continues until real out-put returns to its original level; the only change as a result of more money is a higher price level.

Monetarists concluded from this that the only good monetary policy is the adherence to a constant growth in the money supply. When neo-Keynesians argued acceleration of the money growth to accommodate the oil price shocks in 1973, monetarists resisted such a measure be-cause of the alleged inflationary consequences for the long run. For various other reasons, monetarists opposed the active fiscal policy that neo-Keynesians advocated. Initially, they claimed that the demand for money is insensitive to changes in the interest rates due to the absence of speculative money balances. As a consequence, the LM curve is ver-tical; a change in government spending (i.e., a shift in IS) leaves real output unaltered. In this case one speaks of total crowding out. Empir-ical evidence subsequently showed that the demand for money does re-spond to interest rates, but the monetarists were not discouraged. They continued arguing about the price effects of more government spend-ing, which would realize total crowding out anyway. They also contested the confidence that neo-Keynesians had in their tools. Monetarists simply did not believe that the large-scale econometric models that the neo-Keynsians had constructed to calculate the effects of alternative policies were good enough to guide policy. All kinds of lags interfere, encumbering the timing of measures. If the government is too early or too slow, the consequences could be disastrous. Monetarists concluded that the government did better to keep its hands off and let the market forces work unhindered.

In 1968, Friedman added a significant dimension to the monetarist challenge when he switched the attention to the supply side, i.e., to the Keynesian account of the Phillips curve. Again, the distinction between the long and short run is pivotal in his argument. He asserted that the short-run Phillips curve is highly unstable; whenever the government wants to maintain a low unemployment rate, the inflation rate accelerates, an effect that signifies an upward shift in the Phillips curve. The long-run tendency is toward a predetermined equilibrium rate of unemployment, which Friedman called the *natural rate of unemployment*; no fiscal or monetary policy would be able to keep the economy away from this natural rate. This provocative stance required considerable backing.

Friedman's defense of, in effect, an unstable Phillips curve is as follows: Imagine that the government attempts to reduce unemployment through an expansionary policy (more spending or more money). This results in more production and higher prices. Initially, workers consider the increase in the price level temporary and do not adjust their price expectations. They are induced to work more even though the actual real wage rate does not warrant a greater willingness to work. Employers, getting higher prices without having to pay commensurately higher wages, increase their demand for labor. But the good times for them are temporary, as workers begin to adjust their expectations and demand a higher wage rate. The adjustment takes time, but in the long run the price expectations of workers catch up with the actual price level, and the classical long-run equilibrium situation is reattained. So again, the expansionary policy has only nominal effect.

The monetarist account of the unstable Phillips curve attests to their emphasis on the market mechanism and the equilibrating role of relative prices. Disequilibrium occurs temporarily. Adaptive expectations and not rigid prices, as in the Keynesian story, are responsible for the occurrence for such a disequilibrium; workers need time to adjust their expectations and hence are temporarily fooled. Once expectations are fully adapted the classical situation, which is analogous to the natural rate of unemployment, rules.

The monetarist challenge did not leave neo-Keynesian economics unaffected. They had to acknowledge, for example, the significant role of money in the economy and could not deny the existence of a natural rate of unemployment in the long run. They questioned, however, the length of the long run and maintained that price rigidities bring about a short run that is long enough to warrant government policies. At about this point, with the debate stalemated, the new classical economists entered the debate with the assumption of rational expectations. But before discussing their contributions, one more theoretical comment on Keynesian economics deserves attention. It deals with the notion of disequilibrium and adds a significant dimension to this background.

NEO-KEYNESIAN DISEQUILIBRIUM ECONOMICS

The crux of this theoretical comment is a complaint that neo-Keynesian theory is wrongly based on a notion of general equilibrium and that a disequilibrium theory is more compatible with what Keynes had in mind. The association with general equilibrium springs from the neo-Keynesian pursuit of a neoclassical synthesis. One tenet in neoclassical microeconomics is that an interdependent system of markets tends to a general equilibrium. When one or more markets are in disequilibrium (that is, when the quantities demanded and the quantities supplied are not equal), adjustments in relative prices will "clear" the markets. With such a mechanism, unemployment or a disequilibrium in the labor market can only be temporary. It could be argued that the reasons for price rigidity are unclear, and if they could be found, then removal would suffice to generate full employment. Such a solution would contradict the Keynesian doctrine that the problem is a shortage in total demand. We saw above that neo-Keynesian economists appealed to wage and price rigidities to maintain a protracted short run with disequilibrium in the labor market, but this was not a particularly strong case, certainly not in the context of neoclassical microeconomics. Robert Clower was the first to respond with a call for a reorientation in the neo-Keynesian approach. The result was a lively interest in disequilibrium economics.

Clower introduced the dual decision hypothesis as a rationale for the disequilibrium approach. According to this hypothesis, a household plans both its demand for commodities and its income necessary to buy the commodities. The plans, however, may differ from the actual outcomes. In particular, income may be less than planned because of the lack of available work. In that case actual or *effective demand* falls short of planned demand. A disequilibrium with unemployment results.

Axel Leijonhufvud developed Clower's theme by arguing that an enduring state of disequilibrium does not require rigid prices as neo-Keynesians assumed. He appealed to the authority of Keynes who, allegedly, did not resort to rigid prices or irrational behavior to account for a chronic state of unemployment, as was commonly believed. Leijonhufvud interpreted Keynes as saying that coordination failures in the market are responsible. In other words, information problems prevent the clearing of markets. The auctioneer who, in the conventional equilibrium analysis, sets the prices in such a way that demand equals supply is a fiction; markets often do not clear because individuals do not have adequate information, and they have to decide in an uncertain environment. The theoretical challenge was to provide a model of disequilibrium process that was consistent with maximizing behavior and neo-Keynesian results. Robert Solow, Joseph Stiglitz (Solow and Stiglitz, 1968), Robert Barro, and Herschel Grossman (Barro and Grossman, 1976) were among those who began to try. They initiated a long series of explorations in disequilibrium economics.

The disequilibrium approach to macroeconomics found strong opposition in the new classical equilibrium approach. If there is one issue that more than any other separates neo-Keynesian and new classical economics, it is probably that of disequilibrium versus equilibrium analysis.

NEW CLASSICAL ECONOMICS: THE TAKE-OFF

John Muth is generally recognized as the father of rational expectations. In 1961 he suggested that, in the context of a model, expectations of individuals are rational when they are identical with the predictions of that model. With the advantage of hindsight we can now observe that this idea should have been taken up by neoclassical economists right away. But it was not; it took nearly ten years before economists began to use Muth's idea. How Lucas unearthed it is not clear from his writings, but he gave a decisive impetus to a research of the implications of rational expectations and thus to the new classical approach to macroeconomics.

A hint of the new approach was contained in an article that Lucas wrote with Leonard Rapping in 1969. The article did not use the rational expectations hypothesis, but its model of the labor market would later constitute the foundation of new classical models. The conclusions supported the monetarist claim of a natural rate of unemployment. Rapping abandoned the project after this article. His later work indicates a rejection of neoclassical economics in favor of a post-Keynesian approach. For Lucas, the article was a stepping stone toward his pioneering work in new classical economics.

The first important paper in which Lucas used rational expectations deals with investment behavior and was written jointly with Edward Prescott (Lucas and Prescott, 1971). In two other articles, he explored the consequences of rational expectations for the type of model that he and Rapping had developed (Lucas, 1972b, 1973). Both articles established classical results, such as the neutrality of money and ineffectiveness of government policy. This association with classical economics accounts for the term "new classical economics"; it also made a confrontation with neo-Keynesian economists inevitable. Lucas did not try to avoid such a confrontation. In "Econometric Testing of the Natural Rate Hypothesis" (1972a) and "Econometric Policy Evaluation: A Critique" (1976), Lucas spelled out dramatic implications of rational expectations for macroeconomic analysis. These include irreparable flaws in Keynesian and monetarist economics. His "Equilibrium Model of the Business Cycle" (1975) challenged the conventional wisdom that the notion of equilibrium is inconsonant with business cycles which, after all, reflect fluctuations in unemployment.

Lucas's criticisms spurred young economists to take up his ideas and elaborate on them. The first was Thomas Sargent, who demonstrated, with Neil Wallace, the ineffectiveness of active fiscal and monetary fiscal policy in a standard Keynesian model with rational expectations (Sargent and Wallace, 1975). Another major contribution of his is the development of econometric procedures which allow the test of new classical postulates. Other prominent new classical economists are Bennett McCallum, Robert Barro, who abandoned the disequilibrium approach to become a fervent protagonist of new classical equilibrium analysis, and Robert Townsend who is responsible for various theoretical innovations in the new classical argument.

The challenge is to find the common elements in the work of all these economists. Doing so may help us determine what new classical economics is all about and why economists are divided in their opinion of its merits.

ADAPTIVE EXPECTATIONS BECOME RATIONAL

The rational expectations hypothesis is undoubtedly the most salient characteristic of new classical economics. Rational expectations and new classical economics are commonly taken as synonyms, but this interpretation is probably incorrect. Rational expectations does not necessarily separate new classical economists from others. The policy ineffectiveness proposition and the issue of equilibrium modeling have turned out to be more controversial. Nevertheless, rational expectations is a crucial assumption in new classical models.

Expectations are a major obstacle in macroeconomic analysis. No one will deny their influence on economic decisions, but the question is how to incorporate them into a model. A straight forward way would be to *observe* actual expectations by asking people. Objections to this procedure are that the measurements are likely to be inaccurate (why would we trust the responses?), and that it does not help us to understand how expectations are formed. A good explanation or theory for expectations is difficult to formulate, however, and for that reason neo-Keynesian economists usually left them out in their models.

Milton Friedman, the monetarist, changed this practice of evading the problem. He reintroduced the hypothesis of *adaptive* expectations, holding that people adjust their current expectations to correct expectational errors made in previous periods. The hypothesis can be formalized as follows:

$$(1) \quad p_t^* = p_{t-1} + \varphi(p_{t-1} - p_{t-1}^*)$$

This equation tells that someone corrects an error of expection ($p_{t-1} - p_{t-1}^*$) for only a fraction. This equation can be transformed into

$$(2) \quad p_t^* = \varphi(1 - \varphi)p_{t-1} + \varphi(1 - \varphi)^2 p_{t-2} + \ldots = \sum_{i=1}^{\infty} \varphi(1 - \varphi)^i p_{t-i}$$

which tells us that adaptive expectations of p_t are determined by past observations of the price level only. Accordingly, if φ can be calculated and p_{t-1} observed, p_t^* can be determined.

Lucas and Rapping adopted the adaptive expectations hypothesis in their model, but they acknowledged some problems (Lucas and Rapping, 1969). In particular, price expectations could be left unaffected by changes in government policies when people know that those changes influence the price level. Adaptive expectations did not seem rational. Lucas found a more promising alternative in the hypothesis of rational expectations.

The formal representation of Muth's rational expectations hypothesis is as follows:

$$p_t{}^* = E_{t-1}(p \mid I_{t-1})$$

which reads: $p_t{}^*$ equals the optimal expectations of p_t at time $t-1$ (E_{t-1}) given all available information at $t-1$ (I_{t-1}). The commonsense interpretation of this expression is that people use all available information and their knowledge of the way the economy works to determine their expectations. For example, if people have the information that the money supply will increase and know that this will result in higher prices, then they will increase their price expectations and alter their behavior. The idea is obvious but difficult to realize in a model.

A major problem is to solve a model with rational expectations. In contrast to adaptive expectations, rational expectations requires a simultaneous solution for the actual and expected variables (p_t and $p_t{}^*$). In case of adaptive expectation, the expected price ($p_t{}^*$) can be determined first with equation 2. The outcome can be fed into the actual model, and the actual p can be calculated. This does not work with rational expectations because the actual and expected variables are mutually dependent. When p_t changes, $p_t{}^*$ is affected, and vice versa. Consequently, they have to be determined at the same time. This is not always easy to do.

THE POSTULATES OF RATIONAL BEHAVIOR

Although the rational expectations hypothesis has surprised and disturbed many economists, it is consistent with the attempt to derive macroeconomics relationships from neoclassical microeconomics. To adopt rational expectations is an extension of the new classical idea of optimality; it is assumed that individuals do not leave any opportunity unused to improve their decisions. It will not come as a surprise that post-Keynesian and Marxist economists have little use for rational expectations. However, it is not clear why neo-Keynesians and monetarists, who support the search for microfoundations, resist its inclusion in macro models. The conversations give an opportunity to talk about this.

The postulate of rational behavior is fundamental to new classical economics. In its models consumers and workers not only form optimal expectations, they also maximize utility; similarly, firms maximize profits. The models can be very precise as to the conditions under which individual agents reach optimal decisions.

These intentions are already clear in the paper that Lucas and Rapping wrote together. They model a situation in which workers make intertemporal decisions; they decide on current and future consumption. In this way expectations (of the future price of consumption goods) enter their model in an explicit way. Assuming, further, that workers maximize their utility under well specified constraints, they derive a labor supply function that includes the current and expected price levels. A straightforward analysis of the individual optimizing firm produces a labor demand function. The combination of both functions results in an aggregate supply (AS) function which specifies a relationship between the price level and the output supplied.

Theoretical research in new classical economics would later elaborate on the ideas that are contained in the Lucas-Rapping model. Throughout, the emphasis in the new classical theory was on the supply side (the labor market) rather than on the demand side (IS/LM); the unifying theme, as we shall see, is a strict application of the rationality postulate.

THE POSTULATE OF MARKET CLEARING PRICES

Another feature of the Lucas-Rapping model that reoccurs in later new classical models is the assumption of market-clearing or equilibrium prices. In a macro model, market clearing is obtained when the general price is determined at the intersection of AS and aggregate demand (AD). The conventional view is that such an equilibrium price marks a long-run position to which the actual price is moving. According to this interpretation, the economy is in a continuous disequilibrium. New classical economists defy the conventions and interpret the equilibrium price as the actual price. Their models, therefore, are equilibrium models.

The assumption of equilibrium provoked the predictable reaction. Neo-Keynesians see in it a contradiction of phenomena, such as unemployment and business cycles, which indicate the persistence of disequilibrium, and contend that new classical economists cannot explain the high unemployment rates of the early 1980s with an equilibrium model. Equilibrium and high unemployment do not match up well in their thinking. The challenge they see is the development of more adequate disequilibrium models.

Even monetarists, supposed kinsmen of new classical economists, object to the assumption of equilibrium. It takes time, they argue, to adapt expectations of a variable to its actual value, and during that time the economy is in disequilibrium. As we have seen, their account of the Phillips curve is a disequilibrium story. Marxist and post-Keynesian economists consider the assumption absurd in light of what they take to be the fundamental instability of markets and the recurrence of crises.

New classical economists brush aside these criticisms. They continue their experiments with equilibrium models of the business cycle. Neo-Keynesians may assert that new classical economists ignore the persistence of unemployment and the existence of business cycles, yet Lucas calls a collection of his papers *Studies in Business Cycle Theory*. Townsend turns out one highly elaborate model after another, all of which assume market-clearing prices and are consistent with alleged disequilibrium phenomena. One may well wonder how either side of this dispute justifies its chosen strategy in this situation. A partial answer can be found when we look more closely at the theoretical strategy of new classical economics.

THE CONDITIONAL VARIABLES

The rational expectations hypothesis imputes to individual agents a startling poise; they watch government actions, know the values of all kinds of variables, and even solve complicated econometric models to calculate optimal predictions. Such poise appears incompatible with the observations of, for instance, a trade-off between inflation and unemployment. If individuals know everything, it is unclear how they can get unemployed and generate a total output that is different from its natural or long run equilibrium level. And if rational expectations implies that no policy matters, this would fly in the face of overwhelming evidence that policy does affect real output. Thus, new classical economists have a problem.

This problem can be illuminated by comparing four distinctive situations in an AD/AS diagram.

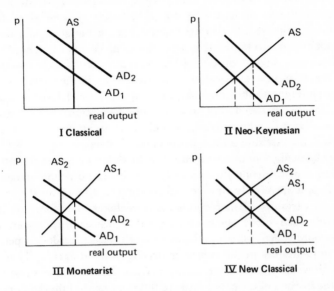

The *classical case* states the neutrality of nominal changes: the same amount of workers produces the same amount of real output, regardless of price level. Keynes's classical predecessors focus on the real wage in their explanation. According to them, workers consider *real* wages when they sell their labor and employers look at *real* wages when they hire labor. In the situation as drawn in the diagram (I), the AD shifts outward, possibly due to a higher money supply which generates more demand. The higher prices that follow from an increase in demand are an incentive for producers to produce more and therefore to hire more workers. The latter, however, understand that higher prices imply a *lower* real wage, and they will demand higher nominal wages. Higher wages are an incentive to produce less and the denouement is that the old levels of real wage, real output, and employment do not change; the AS curve is vertical. The change in AD has been neutral, as it affected only the price level and not real variables.

We have seen the neo-Keynesian and monetarist variations on the classical story. *Neo-Keynesian* economists refer to rigidities to account for the upward slope of the AS. In their model (II) a shift in AD has a lasting real effect. In the *monetarist* case (III) the real effect is temporarily due to adaptive expectations. The moral of their story is that workers can be fooled only temporarily.

The *new classical case,* model (IV), compresses the short run and the long run in the monetarist story and reinstates the classical neutrality proposition. The AS adjusts immediately after a change in AD; workers are rational and will know right away how a perceived change in AD affects their real wage. Consequently, the real effect of such a change is nonexistent, and the classical result applies even in the short run. This conclusion suggests that real output is at its natural level (y*) at all times, but that is clearly not so in reality. Deviations occur, and new classical economists have to adjust their story to allow for those deviations (which constitute a business cycle).

New classical economists account for the deviations in real output by imposing constraints on the conditions under which people make decisions. People have only limited information and often must guess the value of a variable. Misperceptions and mistakes, therefore, are inevitable even when the decisions are rational. These errors account for the upward-sloping AS curve and the fact that the AS curve does not always adjust immediately in the way it is drawn in the diagram. These two factors allow deviations of real output from the natural level. Accordingly, the burden of the proof shifts to the story behind the AS curve. So let us see how new classical economists achieve their results.

As in previous sections the Lucas-Rapping model is the point of departure. It shows that expectational errors on the part of workers are mainly reponsible for fluctuations in real output. Lucas used this idea to derive what has become known as the Lucas supply function:

$$(3) \quad y_t = k_t + \gamma(p_t - p_t{}^*) + \lambda y_{t-1}$$

where y is real output, k_t is a growth term, p_t the price level, $p_t{}^*$ the expected price level, and γ and λ are parameters. (All variables are in logarithm for sake of convenience.) This equation says that output supplied is determined by a growth term that accounts for technological advances and population increases, output in the previous period and, most important, the error in expectations of the price level. Whereas Lucas and Rapping had used adaptive expectations to motivate those errors, Lucas chose to stress *imperfect information* and *uncertainty* in the economy. Lucas illustrates these choices with a story, the so-called island story.

According to this story, firms and workers operate on a series of islands between which communication is less than perfect. The scenario starts with an increase in AD, which pushes up the price level. Agents perceive only the price increase for the product that is produced on their island and not the increase in the general price level. In this story, workers form expectations of the *current* price level based on the currently available information (i.e., $p_t^* = E_t(p_t | I_t)$). They need to know the current price level to determine their real wage. In neoclassical terms we say that they are constrained in making rational decisions by limited information. The firms are absolved from the problem of expectations because they need to know only the price of their own products and the wages they pay to make their decision.

The limitation on the information that workers have would still not be a problem if they knew the relationship between the local and general price level (i.e., if they had an economic model). Here *stochastic* variables, or variables subject to a probability distribution, enter the new classical story. Stochastic disturbances which result from unpredictable movements in variables, such as the money supply, render uncertain the conditions under which workers make their decisions. They must make guesses and may end up working for a lower real wage than they had planned.

So the combination of imperfect information and stochastic variables explains the continuous discrepancies of actual and expected prices and, hence, deviations of real output from its natural level. The addition of the lagged output term in the AS — equation (3) — accounts for some persistency in those deviations. Its justification is not immediately clear, but new classical economists have given various motivations that are consistent with neoclassical principles. One is that the information for workers is limited to the extent that they cannot perceive past expectations errors; another refers to costs that employers incur when they change employment. In both cases, adjustments are not immediate.

The story agrees with all the elements of new classical economics. Expectations are rational, and agents make rational decisions. Constraints on the available information and uncertainty due to stochastic disturbances suffice to account for the Phillips curve and business cycles. References to disequilibrium factors, such as rigid wages and adaptive expectations, are absent; actual prices are purported to be market clearing and are therefore given by the equilibrium solution of the model (that is, where AD equals AS).

A story is easy to tell; its transformation into a precise theoretical model is difficult. A string of articles attests to theoretical hurdles that new classical economists have to take in order to render their story theoretically plausible. Neo-Keynesians, however, are little impressed. They give various reasons why the new classical story is unrealistic. Benjamin Friedman, for example, asserts that workers need time to learn about new conditions. Expectations, therefore, are rational only in the long run. Others, such as Stanley Fischer and John Taylor, see in the existence of contracts a good reason for the persistence of disequilibrium. Contracts prevent a quick adjustment of nominal wages, so that workers may often work for an actual real wage that differs from its equilibrium value. This argument affirming price rigidities is probably the most important in the neo-Keynesian defense. Additional arguments point at high costs of information, costs of adjusting the work force in a firm, heterogeneity of expectations, and nonrational behavior.

There are good reasons for the neo-Keynesians to resist the new classical story. The most conspicuous reason is, of course, the radical policy conclusions that the story produces.

POLICY CONCLUSIONS

All the new classical arguments tend toward the conclusion that the government should abstain from an active stabilization policy. The basic claim is that systematic changes in policy variables have no effect on real variables. The Lucas supply function—equation (3)—and the accompanying story tell why. When workers know what the government is doing, they anticipate the effects; their price expectations will correspond with the actual price level ($p_t = p_t^*$) and real output will be unaffected by the policy. Only when workers are surprised and make mistakes ($p_t > p_t^*$) will there be a change in real output. Some may take this latter result as an encouragement for economic policy that sets out to surprise. But new classical economists counter that even if such a policy were effective, it is undesirable because of the additional uncertainty that it generates. Thus, they counter the neo-Keynesian policy advice to which students and policy makers had grown accustomed during the 1960s. And since their theoretical argument is rigorous and consistent with the rules of neoclassical economists, neo-Keynesian economists have a hard nut to crack.

POLICY EVALUATION AND ECONOMETRIC T

Conventional wisdom has it that a controversy as exists b Keynesian and new classical economists has to be settled wit. ~~al tests. The construction of empirical tests, however, is a complicated and controversial matter. From the outset, Lucas made it clear that he was unimpressed with the empirical tests of neo-Keynesian economists. Rational expectations according to him, render established econometric practice obsolete. In particular, the policy stimulations give misleading results. This point is clarified by a simple illustration (*).

Let us assume that output is determined by errors in expectations on the money supply (mt – m_t^*), a constant (a_0) and its own lagged term (y_{t-1}).

$$(4) \quad y_t = a_0 + a_1(m_t - m_t{}^*) + a_2 y_{t-1}$$

(a_0, a_1 and a_2 are parameters). Let us also assume that the monetary authorities set the money supply in accordance to the following rule:

$$(5) \quad m_t = g_0 + g_1 y_{t-1} + u_t$$

where u_t is a stochastic term and g_0 and g_1 are parameters. This rule states that the monetary authorities adjust the money supply whenever real output changes; the stochastic term tells us that they are not always perfectly successful in getting it right.

If expectations are adaptive, $m_t{}^*$ in (4) can be replaced by $\sum_{i=1}^{\infty} \varphi(1 - \varphi)^i m_{t-i}$. The parameters in equation (4) can subsequently be estimated. The effect of alternative policies can now be calculated by simply substituting alternative values for m_t in the estimated equation.

This procedure does not work when expectations are rational. In that case, the policy rule becomes relevant; rational expectations imply that $m_t{}^*$ equals the prediction of m_t according to the policy rule:

$$(6) \quad m_t{}^* = E_{t-1}(m_t | I_{t-1}) = E_{t-1}$$

$$(g_0 + g_1 y_{t-1} + u_t) = g_0 + g_1 y_{t-1} \quad (E_{t-1} u_t = 0)$$

When we substitute this result into (4) we get:

$$(7) \quad y_t = (a_0 - a_1 g_0) + a_1 m_t + (a_2 - a_1 g_1) y_{t-1} + u_t$$

---

*The reader can skip the illustration without losing the continuity of the discussion.

A change in monetary policy entails a change in g_0 or g_1 or both. Simulation of the change in monetary policy through substituting a different value for m_t is now inadequate, since it ignores the changes on the parameters in the reduced form equation (7). If the government changes g_1, for example, the constant in equation (7), $(a_2 - a_1g_1)$, changes. Since conventional econometric tests ignore this effect to a change in the policy rule, their results are deemed unreliable. To say this in new classical terms, this equation is not *invariant* with respect to changes in the policy rule.

Criticism alone is relatively easy and the new classical economists faced the challenge to come up with alternative test procedures. To support their claim that monetary policy is ineffective, they have to show that an observed *correlation* between money and real income does not imply *causation*. More precisely, they have to test their proposition that only the unanticipated or surprise component in the money stock *causes* changes in real income. Accordingly, they were compelled to deal with the issue of causality that has troubled economists for a long time.

New classical economists have experimented with a variety of tests throughout the 1970s, none of which has been especially convincing. The phase of experimenting appears to be over, and the empirical research has consolidated in what some people call the "new econometrics." This approach, which is beginning to have a profound influence on empirical work in macroeconomics, has two basic components, one of which is the development and testing of an elaborate model, the other the exploration of time series with advanced econometric techniques and with a minimum of economic theory. Let me elaborate.

The first component of the new econometrics can be seen in Lucas's "Output-Inflation Trade-Offs" article (1973). He presents a reasonably elaborate new classical model and shows how the rational expectations hypothesis imposes constraints on the parameters in the reduced form equation (or the solution of the model). The principle is very much the same in the example above, where the constraints in equation (6) are the corollary of the assumption of rational expectations. The neutrality proposition can be tested by testing the validity of the constraints. In case of equation (6) the new classical claims are confirmed if the parameters for y_{t-1} $(a_2 - a_1g_1)$ is inversely related with the sensitivity of monetary policy to changes in real output (g_1).

Sargent elaborated on this principle in subsequent work. His models are more sophisticated than Lucas's, but the idea remains the same. A good example is found in his article "Estimation of Dynamic Labor Demand Schedules under Rational Expectations" (1978). The model of the labor market that he develops embodies all characteristically new classical elements: agents optimize over time under well-specified constraints and form rational expectations, and the labor market clears. As in Lucas's initial model, the theoretical assumptions lead to restrictions on the parameters in the reduced form equation. The proposed test of the new classical theory is to compare the estimates of the model *with* restrictions with those *without* the restrictions. Sargent's results support the new classical theory.

The same article also contains the second element of the new econometrics, namely the exploration of time series without much a priori theory. Sargent applies the so-called *innovation technique* to determine the exogeneity of wages with respect to employment. An innovation in a variable is its anticipated component; it is the difference between its actual and predicted value where the predicted value is calculated through an estimated equation. Sargent specifies two equations for the real wage rate and employment in which only the current and lagged values of both variables enter as the dependent variables. The objective is to determine which variable of the two is exogenous. As neoclassical theory suggests that prices determine quantities, Sargent hopes that the real wage rate is the exogenous variable. The idea of the innovation technique is to investigate the way in which the innovation in one variable influences the time series of the other variable. The real wage rate is defined to be exogenous with respect to employment (or causes employment) when the impact of its innovation on the time series of employment is significant and the impact of the innovation in employment on its time series insignificant. Sargent finds that the real wage rate is exogenous indeed and uses this information on the construction of his elaborate model.

The innovation technique follows recent developments in econometric time-series analysis, such as the causality tests of Granger and Sims. We may also note the Box-Jenkins techniques which allow the prediction of a variable on the basis of its own time series without intervention of economic theory. The purpose of Sargent's purely statistical techniques, however, is not prediction, but the acquisition of information useful in the construction of the elaborate model. Accordingly, econometric findings motivate theoretical assumptions, an explicit use of econometrics that is quite uncommon in macroeconomic discourse.

Barro (1977, 1978) applies the innovation technique in a somewhat different form to test the neutrality proposition. He computes innovations in the money stock with a regression equation for money, and subsequently estimates the effects of the innovations and the predicted values on real variables. His findings confirm the new classical claim that only the innovations have real effects. His tests, however, are not free from theoretical assumptions; the results are sensitive to the specification of the equations for money and real output.

New classical economists are generally cautious in their empirical conclusions. McCallum, after reviewing the "evidence" up until 1979, concludes: "For the most part, the formal econometric evidence developed to date is not inconsistent with the neutrality proposition" (McCallum, 1979, p. 244). In various other conclusions the evidence is said to be "not obscenely at variance with the date" (Sargent 1976); and there is "A Little Bit of Evidence on the Natural Rate Hypothesis" (Sargent and Neftci, 1978).

This caution notwithstanding, new classical economists see ample support for their position in the empirical results. Neo-Keynesians remain sceptical. Blinder (1980) and Robert J. Gordon (1980), among others, severely criticize Barro's test by questioning his assumptions and techniques. The reaction to the new econometrics, however, is not yet clear. John Taylor, for one, seems to be committed to the new techniques plus major aspects of new classical theory. But where do the others stand? I shall ask them.

CONCLUDING REMARKS

The preceding sketch of the debate between the new classical economists and their critics suggests a variety of questions which will be raised in the following conversations.

As far as the new classical economists are concerned, we are first of all interested in the initial stage. How did Lucas come to adopt Muth's notion of rational expectations, and how did he and Sargent view the initial hostile reaction? We also would like to know more about their theoretical intentions. The concept of equilibrium, in particular, needs more clarification. And what are the properties that they require of a good new classical model? Is it true that the neutrality proposition underlies their theoretical and empirical work? And how do they use their theory to interpret current economic events and assess current policies?

From the neo-Keynesians, we would like to learn more about their opposition to the new classical arguments. How do they deal with the new classical criticism that their models are ad hoc as they are not well grounded in neoclassical postulates? Don't they endorse the striving for microfoundations of macroeconomics? What do they now think of the importance of rational expectations or of the notion of equilibrium? And how do they respond to the empirical arguments of new classical economists? Or to their new econometric techniques?

Talking with Taylor may help us to understand how a neo-Keynesian (is he one?) who is sympathetic to the new classical innovations maintains some kind of middle ground. Brunner will clarify why monetarists are reluctant to embrace the new classical approach altogether. The conversation with David Gordon will give us a Marxist perspective of the controversy. Finally, Rapping may add to our insight into both the initial stage of new classical economics and the present post-Keynesian reactions; we shall also ask him about his conversion from neoclassical to post-Keynesian economics.

In what follows we want to improve our understanding of the world of economists. We want to find out why economists disagree and how they communicate with each other. What is their basic vision of the world, and how relevant is that for their economics? And what is their vision of economics as a science? What makes an effective economic argument? Finally, this focus on communication creates a legitimate interest in social and personal details. How do they relate with other economists? What happens when they try to discuss their disagreements? We shall get to know these people as individuals with attitudes, values, and qualities of character, not just as economists with formal models.

Questions and more questions. Let us try to get some answers.

PART ONE

Conversations with New Classical Economists

2

ROBERT E. LUCAS JR.

If anyone is responsible for the current debates in macroeconomics, it is Lucas. He is generally credited with the introduction of the rational expectations hypothesis into macro models; his articles are widely read and discussed. He is, by acknowledgment of friend and foe alike, the central figure in the world of new classical economics. George Stigler, after receiving his Nobel prize, suggested that the same prize is in store for Lucas.

In 1964, Lucas received his Ph.D. from the University of Chicago, where he returned to teach after an 11-year stay at Carnegie-Mellon University. In 1969 Lucas coauthored with Leonard Rapping the famous article "Real Wages, Employment, and Inflation," which has played an important role in new classical discourse. In "Econometric Testing of the Natural Rate Hypothesis" (1972), Lucas suggested dramatic implications of rational expectations for accepted economic theory and econometrics. The conversation touches on these articles as well as upon his "Expectations and the Neutrality of Money" (1972) and "An Equilibrium Model of Business Cycles" (1975).

We talked in his office at the University of Chicago, a remarkably well-ordered place where papers are neatly piled and books carefully arranged on shelves. The desk is empty but for a note pad. It is May 1982.

BACKGROUND

Do you enjoy economics?

Oh, sure.

Why did you choose it?

I have always liked to think about social problems. It may have something to do with my family. We always argued about politics and social issues. I studied history at the University of Chicago and even started graduate school in history at Berkeley. But I came around to the view that economic forces are the central forces in history, and started trying some economics. It was a big shock to me to find books in English that were incomprehensible to me. Anything in English is accessible to a history student, so the only barrier to getting at something would be foreign languages. In economics, you could get a book out written in English like Haberler's *Prosperity and Depression* without being able to read it. Or Keynes's *General Theory*. I still can't read Keynes [laughter]. I realized I couldn't pick it up an an amateur. So I got into economics in a professional way and got my Ph.D. at Chicago.

Who were important teachers for you?

Well, Friedman was the big influence here. He taught our first Ph.D.-level price theory courses, just basic economic theory. Friedman is a really gifted teacher plus a superb economist. He spent almost all his time on applying economics. He would start with some real world situation, some quote from the newspaper, some *Wall Street Journal* editorial, some sentence. And then he would try and get into a class discussion. He would draw a diagram, and then try and get at the statement to see whether it was true or not true and under what conditions it would be true. Of course, he wasn't good for teaching tools, but I was picking up those on my own anyway, through my readings.

Another big influence was Samuelson's *Foundations,* which I read when I started here at Chicago. It's a "how-to-do-it" book, a great book for first-year graduate students. It says, "Here's the way you do it." It lets you in on the secret of how you play the game, as opposed to cutting you off with big words. I think the combination of Samuelson's book plus Friedman's class was what got me going.

Who taught you macroeconomics?

Well, as I say, Friedman taught price theory, not money. He had one lecture on his views in business cycles or monetary economics at the very end. We were all waiting for it, but you can't say that much in one lecture. When I was at Chicago the main teachers of macroeconomics were Al Harberger and Martin Bailey. They're the ones who influenced me the most. I should also mention Carl Christ, who is now at Johns Hopkins. They all used the Keynesian model, so my background was pretty much conventional Keynesian training.

My thesis was an econometric study on capital/labor substitution. Harberger was my thesis chairman. He was getting quantitative estimates of various tax distortions (in "welfare triangles"), and he had some ideas about certain parameters for which he needed estimates. He farmed out pieces of his project to students, so I took elasticities of substitution in production as my piece.

Did Gregg Lewis have any part in this?

Lewis was on my committee and helped me a lot. He gives detailed feedback. That's why students went to him, and that's why I wanted him on my committee.

ABOUT OTHER ECONOMISTS

How important was your collaboration with Rapping?

It was very important to me. I came to Carnegie in '63; he came in '62. We've talked about a lot of stuff. We were good friends right from the beginning, with our wives, as couples and so on. Rapping at that time was very conservative, a libertarian. He was also a very good arguer; he was the ideal person to have at a dinner party. He could get people away from talking about the weather to talking about anything.

I try to picture for myself two people working very closely together. He told me that you had talks almost every afternoon about everything—including economics, of course, but also about politics [see conversation with Rapping]. You were very good friends. Then the '60's came along, and Rapping was deeply affected by what happened in Vietnam. He had the idea that something was wrong and that Chicago economics didn't help explain the current problems. You were close to him, but I don't see any effect of the occurrences on you.

Rapping was always much more interested than I am in being where the action is. He did a lot of work for the Defense Department in those days. He'd come back all excited about the billion-dollar decisions he said they were making. I was interested in anti-trust issues in those days, and he'd come in and say, "Look, Bob. If you finish this paper—

which you probably won't — and if anybody pays any attention to it — which they probably won't — and if it ever gets any influence in policy — which it probably won't — it's going to be a matter of a hundred million dollars. And I was at the Defense Department yesterday talking about twenty billion dollars" [laughter]. So you get the feeling you're just sort of scribbling in your office doing trivial things.

The '60s had a bigger effect on him because, as I said, he wanted to be where the action is, and he reacted not just to Chicago economics, but to his defense work.

Did you then understand his change?

No, not really. His change affected our personal relationship very much, and Rapping lost interest in conversations by rules that I like.

Did the turbulence of the '60s affect you at all?

Vietnam affected everybody. I eventually came around to the idea that the war was a lousy idea about the same time everyone else did [laughter]. It was, however, never at the center of my life. Because Carnegie was a conservative engineering school, it was an easy place to avoid the issue. Students were mainly interested in what kind of job they were going to get when they got out. We had a little bit of a revolution, not much.

Do you talk with Rapping now about what he is doing?

We talk a bit at the meetings.

You also worked with Prescott. Can you tell me about that collaboration?

Working with Prescott was different from working with Rapping. Rapping was my senior and at times served as a kind of father to me. Prescott was younger. Of course I was just starting to teach, so in age we weren't that far apart. But still, I was faculty and he was a student. That makes a difference. I got him involved when I ran into technical trouble while working on some investment problems. I remembered that he had some experience in his thesis with methods that I thought would be helpful. He knew them a lot better than I did, so when he was at Penn I got him interested in this project. We did a hell of a lot of work on this paper "Investment under Uncertainty" [1971]. We thought it was a pretty straightforward applied problem, but then we got in way over our heads technically. We didn't want to quit, so we read tons of difficult mathematical economics and mathematics, even though none of us had any prior familiarity with it. It was a lot of fun; we both learned a lot.

Why do you think doing economics is a lot of fun if you run into all of these problems?

At the time it's not so much fun — you do want to get the paper out and get it finished. All the trouble on Ed's and my investment paper came when we were 99.9 percent done, and there was one step that wouldn't fall into place. That's where all the work was so it was frustrating to have this nearly completed paper here and then to have to do all of this work. But it *was* fun. I like learning new mathematics, and what I like about working with Ed is that he and I can very quickly get to the point on very difficult technical issues without a lot of set-up costs.

How did you get to know Sargent?

Tom was at Carnegie for a while. That was his first job when he got out of Harvard. I didn't know him too well then. I'll tell you what happened in those days — it's ridiculous in retrospect. There was a kind of Chicago faction and a non-Chicago faction at Carnegie. Meltzer was the Chicago leader, and Mike Lovell, a Harvard guy who had been at Yale, was the non-Chicago leader. Mike got very touchy about this whole thing and he eventually left. Even though Mike and I had been quite good friends, the relationship got very strained for a while. We stayed friends, but there was a bad period.

When Tom came, I associated him with the anti-Chicago group. I thought he didn't show interest in me. We didn't talk very much during the two years he was there.

I understand that he was also a very quiet person, and that he didn't talk very easily.

Yeah, I guess he's shy. But I never had a hard time talking with Tom [pause]. Tom needs to make some technical set-up costs before he wants to talk about something. Look at that paper we wrote together on Keynesian economics. There's quite a lot of notation there, more than there would have been had I written the paper myself. Tom likes to do that before he can talk. It's kind of hard to get people to sit still at coffee and lunch while you write out equations.

I remember a seminar here while Tom was visiting in Chicago. Everybody was talking; it was a very chaotic seminar. In the middle of the seminar, Tom made some point and the speaker didn't seem to understand it. Tom dropped it and didn't say anything for the rest of the seminar. At the end, he just handed the speaker a piece of paper with a bunch of equations on it and said, "Here's what I was trying to say." I thought it was a very friendly, constructive thing to do, but the speaker said, "This is Sargent's idea of a conversation" and laughed. I think it's just that Tom thinks he can get things settled on a more technical level. Tom and I talk quite a bit. I think that we influence each other a lot.

Who are the other economists you like to talk with?

I'm sort of a gregarious economist. I like to talk with a lot of people.

But what about the neo-Keynesians? Do you ever communicate with them?

Yeah [pause]. We're all friends. We go to the same conferences. There's no split of a sociological sort.

I guess when we first got going it was kind of exciting because the people who were interested in this rational expectations model were a tiny minority at first. We were pretty confident of what we were doing, but we were regarded as very far out by other people. I had a lot of fun going to Yale and other places to talk in these chaotic seminars where I stand up and people throw darts at me [laughter]. It was a lot of fun. But now the stuff is much more widely accepted. A whole new generation of people has gotten into these models, so they're not quite as exotic.

Tobin asked me to come and talk at Yale in 1977, and I was there for a couple of days. He was really nice in a personal way. He made it clear that he respected my work as a professional, so I didn't feel my professional standing was at risk. When I got there he gave me a nice introduction. It wasn't a question of whether I was a competent economist or not; there was nothing personal involved. These guys, however, had lots of disagreements and criticisms. I'd been thinking along these lines for many years, so I thought I did a pretty good job of taking care of the questions, but I don't know how it looked from the other side. It left me with a feeling of being way ahead of the game. It was an exciting feeling.

But you use very strong terms, certainly in that paper with Sargent [1978], to indicate that something is wrong with Keynesian economics. You talk about failures, about the breakdown of consensus, and about the fact that you get disillusioned with Keynesian macroeconomics. That's quite strong.

Well, sure. Those are serious criticisms of econometric models. They imply that the simulations coming out of those models are worthless, useless.

But then you go up against many of these reputations. You tell Solow and Tobin and all these people that they are wrong.

But they were wrong [laughter]. I don't think that Solow, in particular, has ever tried to come to grips with any of these issues except by making jokes.

Did you read any radical economics? Marx or Sweezy?

I've read some at various times, and I tried to talk with Leonard about some of the stuff, but he wasn't too interested in discussing it with me. I really haven't read much.

It is surprising to discover that people with good minds have such an incredible difficulty in settling down to talk sensibly about one particular issue. It seems that you are a good communicator; you like to talk. Nevertheless, you very often hint at the problem of talking with other economists.

A lot of these problems get solved by age. Sargent and I have had a lot more influence on younger economists. Everybody likes the idea of rational expectations. It's hardly controversial.

But if you talk with post-Keynesian economists they think it's a lot of nonsense.

Young people are actually doing the research. Post-Keynesian economists, well, I don't know whether to take them seriously [laughter].

ABOUT HIS WORK

How did Rapping and you get to work on your joint paper? [Lucas and Rapping, 1969]

I can't really remember. Both of us, at one time or another, taught master's level macroeconomics courses. The labor part of macroeconomic models, in those days, was pretty disgraceful. If you look at an old text you can't make heads or tales of it. There's no connection with ordinary labor economics. Rapping and I knew some labor economics, and it's hard to get up in front of a class and talk nonsense deliberately. So we were trying to cook up simple supply and demand models which would fit what you see happening over business cycles. We got interested enough in that so that we thought we'd pursue it as a research topic.

*It's quite remarkable that you had the courage to think in terms of demand and sup-
    ply models.*

In the tradition of Friedman and Lewis it is hard to think about labor
markets without supply and demand. You have to tell how wages and
employment arise from certain shifts in supply and demand curves.
That was the rule we imposed on ourselves.

But then the problem is unemployment.

We were really developing a supply and demand model for employment and wages. Unemployment gets tacked on as a side story. We introduced a Phillips curve to make contact with macroeconomic stuff.
We wanted to make sure that the labor supply piece didn't assume away
business fluctuations.

Would you characterize the model as a Chicago model?

I wouldn't think of that paper as a Chicago paper. That paper could
have been written almost anywhere, I would think. We were modeling
it after the work of people like Modigliani and Jorgenson, who weren't
Chicago people. If you think about labor markets in our way it might
have been thought about as a Chicago type, but I don't know why it
should have been. You notice in that paper we have a lot of defensive
comments and millions of footnotes. I think that Rapping made us put
in all those footnotes because we didn't want it to be thought of as an especially Chicago paper.

See, this business of microeconomic foundations has been kicking
around for years. Rapping's and my paper is pretty conventional; that's
what everyone was doing. You take a sector, you get some kind of maximum problem for a household or a firm, you work it out, and then you
hope that it suggests some kind of a fairly simple regression equation.
The idea was that if you do this for enough sectors, you can put them all
together and you have a model of the whole. That was really what
Jorgenson, for example, was trying to do with investment. Friedman
wasn't trying to do it because he really didn't care about these models.
But everyone who was involved in econometric model building of the
consumption sector was influenced by Friedman's work. Modigliani was
explicitly interested as he went from his work in consumption to actually building econometric models. That was a very common enterprise.

Was the econometrics important in that paper?

I think we overdid it. That was my fault; I was pretty much an econometrician in those days. Everything novel in the paper has to do with the supply of labor. The demand is entirely routine; it was even for those days. It would have been a better paper if we had called it a theory of labor supply and had just presented the theory of the household and then tested that. Of course we started with Ordinary Least Squares estimates of labor supply curves; be we somehow thought that wouldn't be respectable, so we added a demand side to take into account possible simultaneity. But in some sense the formality of the econometrics is excessive.

Rapping says that in his understanding the econometrics was essential in order to make connections with what had been done before.

I agree with that statement. One thing all of us admired about Friedman's book on consumption was the way Friedman integrated the aggregate time-series evidence and cross-sectional survey evidence. He gave a unified explanation of very different samples in a single theoretical model. If you ever look at my thesis, you'll see that I'm trying to reconcile time-series and cross-sectional evidence on factor substitution. Rapping and I try to do that in our paper. That was another reason it was essential to work with Rapping, because he knew all the cross-sectional evidence and I didn't. I think we did a pretty good job with it.

You also wrote a paper together that got published in the American Economic Review [1970].

I never liked the paper. It doesn't have any results in it. I didn't want to publish it, but Rapping insisted we do it. I remember he took an issue of the *AER* off the shelf and flipped it open to some paper — you know in any issue of any journal there's a lot of crap — and he said, "Look at this. Are you going to say our paper is worse than that? And he'd start going through the whole journal [laughter]. So he talked me into publishing it. When you do joint work you always argue about stuff like that. But I didn't want to reprint it in the collection of papers [Lucas, 1980]. Shortly after that I learned why tests of the sort we ran in that paper don't settle anything and aren't interesting. It didn't have much interest for me in the first place, and once I understood the econometric questions it had no interest whatsoever. The only economics in that paper is done better in Rapping's and my original paper, and that concerns the way the business cycle looks from the household's point of view.

In the papers with Rapping you used adaptive expectations. Did you know about rational expectations at that time?

Sure. Of course we knew about it. Muth was a colleague of ours at that time. We just didn't think it was important. The hypothesis was more or less buried during the '60s. Arrow used it in his paper on learning-by-doing in the '60s. Prescott and I used it in that paper of ours on investment. People were aware of it, but I didn't understand then how fundamental a difference it made econometrically. I didn't realize that if you took it seriously you had to rethink the whole question of testing and estimation. I guess no one else did either, except for Muth.

But he didn't do much with it later, did he?

No, but in the volume of Sargent's and mine we had a second paper of Muth's on the econometric implications of the rational expectations hypothesis. Maybe he just got discouraged because no one paid any attention. It must be quite an experience to write papers that radical and have people just pat you on the head and say "That's interesting," and nothing happens.

The models you are working on are obviously more than just rational expectations models. How would you characterize them?

The term I use is equilibrium models. The decision problems faced by individual agents in the model are clear, and the rules by which they interact are clear. You've got to spell out individual preferences and technology and you've got to spell out the rules of the game. In practice, in macroeconomics right now, that leads to competitive equilibrium models.

But then you exclude monopolistic behavior . . .

I don't think that that is crucial to business cycles. I'll give you an example: In a competitive model, prices are never a decision variable; they're always parameters in people's decision problems. When you're informally telling these rational expectations stories, though, it's much more natural to think of prices being a decision variable. So somebody sets a price, and then inventories or sales give them the signal as to what's happening to demand. You put some goods on the shelf at a particular price, and if demand is high you learn about that because you sell a lot more at that price than you expected to. So it would be nice to write down formal models in which price is a decision variable. The only barrier to doing that is that, at the present time, I don't know how to write down equilibrium games which have that feature. The features could look a lot like the competitive models, but some of the feaures would obviously be different. For example, it's a big thing in that paper on "Expectations and Neutrality of Money" [1972] that people get information from price movements. That really complicates the paper tremendously; that's the feature that makes the paper hard technically. Now, if I choose what price I set, I obviously can't learn anything from it. You can't get information from something you choose. So the informational structure of those models would change a lot.

And did that make the analysis much more complicated?

I don't know. You never know until you do it. I'm not much good even at writing down noncompetitive models. I spend a lot of time trying, though.

Your equilibrium modeling strategy seems to be essential. It also seems to have elicited quite a few comments. The question that always comes up is how can you explain depression, how do you explain a 9.4 percent unemployment. Can you explain it all by referring to mistakes or to information problems?

Well, what's the alternative?

People talk about learning problems; people talk about wage contracts and about the resulting rigidity of wages. About uncertainty . . .

Learning, uncertainty . . . These things have a lot to do with information. Learning, for example, is a red herring. According to the way I look at things, this is just a question of how you like to think about probabilities. Things that we model which have probability distributions I call "random variables" and things that don't, "parameters." Some people like to use Bayesian language in which some things that have distributions are called "random variables," and some other things that have distributions are, for some unexplained reason, called "parameters." From that point of view, there seems to be a distinction between learning and information. Name them all "random variables," and then you name everything that is "learned," "information." Just two points of view. Nothing operational is at stake here.

A Bayesian would describe somebody as having a certain prior distribution on a particular parameter. I'll describe that guy as "knowing" that this thing is drawn from a distribution with a particular shape. We're using different words, but the formalism is identical. I like to talk about distributions being known, and parameters being known, so that what one "learns" about is the realizations of paticular random variables. That's purely a question of language. But I know my language puts some people off.

Like whom?

Milton Friedman, for example. He's very influenced by Savage and by this Bayesian way of thinking about probabilities. So when I talk about people "knowing" a probability, he just can't reach that language.

But I'm evading your question about 9.4 percent unemployment. You have difficulty with our thinking that this is a mistake.

Or an information problem. I say that this is the reaction you get. And I'm just wondering how you react to that. My taxi driver here is driving a taxi, even though he is an accountant, because he can't find a job. He is obviously frustrated. It seems a lot of people are running around in that position.

I would describe him as a taxi driver [laughing], if what he is doing is driving a taxi.

But a frustrated taxi driver.

Well, we draw these things out of urns, and sometimes we get good draws, sometimes we get bad draws.

How do you account for the Depression. What is your story?

A possible way of looking at economic time series is as a competitive system's response to outside shocks. If you just think of an economy in competitive equilibrium you wouldn't expect its output series to be completely smooth; you would expect it to oscillate a bit. In such a set-up the usual connections between equilibrium and optimality would hold. There wouldn't be any policy problems raised by these fluctuations. That would be one point of view. And I should think it would be a point of view that would be embarrassed by your question, although it's hard to explain why. By calling the 1929 to 1933 episode a "mistake," I'm trying to treat these events not as serving a social purpose.

If intelligent actors pursuing their own self-interest are going through the same mistake over and over again, which is what seems to happen, we are led to think of informational difficulties. How else do you get someone, acting in his own self-interest, to do something that injures himself in the same way over and over again?

To put it another way, we know that monetary changes ought to be irrelevant, because units don't matter. Accepting the Friedman-Schwartz evidence that monetary changes are not only relevant, but the major cause of all these events, it is difficult to talk about a system responding in a very sharp way to something to which it "ought" not to have responded at all. These considerations lead into questions about information of some kind or another. That's a very old view. The particular mistake that people get led into by monetary changes is hard to determine, and the specific examples I've cooked up are dictated a lot by what's technically doable by me, given the methods I've got.

But you can attribute those events to "mistakes"?

If you look back at the 1929 to 1933 episode, there were a lot of decisions made that, after the fact, people wished they had not made; there were a lot of jobs people quit that they wished they had hung on to; there were job offers that people turned down because they thought the wage offer was crappy. Then three months later they wished they had grabbed. Accountants who lost their accounting jobs passed over a cabdriver job, and now they're sitting on the street while their pal's driving a cab. So they wish they'd taken the cab-driver job. People are making this kind of mistake all the time. Anybody can look back over the '30s and think of decisions which would have made millions — purchasing particular stocks, all kinds of things. I don't see what's *hard* about this question of people making mistakes in the business cycle. From the individual point of view, it's obvious.

The biggest puzzle is the changes in the average, the natural rate. Nine point four percent is a recession rate, and it's not that high above the natural rate. It's about as far above the natural rate as recession rates were in the '50s and '60s. The big difference is that the natural rate has gone way up, and no one seems to know why that's true. The unemployment rates at recent business cycle peaks are as much of a puzzle as the unemployment rates at business cycle troughs. I've heard a lot of stories, but I don't know if that problem has been nailed down. Some of it has to do with demographics, some of it has to do with secondary workers.

So, in this Keynesian work, you haven't found any reasonable explanation as to why the Great Depression occurred?

As I say, I find the Friedman and Schwartz story combined with Rapping's and mine to be very good for '29–'33. Afterward, I really don't know. There are many aspects of what happened after that I can't figure at all. But I don't think that unemployment is at the center of the story. For those who do think it is the center, I can see why they don't look to me for enlightenment.

How important is the neutrality proposition in your research program?

It's an ancient proposition. There's going to be a neutrality theorem in any well-formulated model of money. There's always a "units don't matter" feature somewhere in the model. A pretty severe criticism of old-fashioned Keynesian models is that they simply neglected that.

How important, then, are the policy conclusions you draw in your research program? It seems you are committed to the idea that economic policy cannot be effective, at least as long as it is systematic. And if any people show that economic policy is feasible, you say that it is not desirable because of the uncertainty it generates. In your 1975 paper on business cycles, for example, you argue that policy may be effective in case of an accelerator effect, but is undesirable.

All I said in that paper was that there is no reason to think that amplitude-reducing and welfare-increasing are the same thing. In that paper this is well enough spelled out. You can't gauge welfare effects with a model like that. I didn't mean to say I knew there wouldn't be welfare increases; I just don't know why you would assume there would be. That's a difficulty of macroeconomics generally. Economics' only criterion really is efficiency, but if you write down one of these standard macro models you can't say *anything* about efficiency.

Might I say that you believe markets do work more or less, and that government intervention is in general destabilizing, rather than stabilizing, and that it is undesirable?

I'm not very friendly toward government intervention in a lot of cases. If I were to focus on business cycles, and this is very much influenced by Friedman and Mitchell, it's a substantive question whether, in fact, fluctuations in monetary aggregate cause major depressions, and all government needs to do is simply stop that from happening. And that's it.

Rules, predictable government behavior: you follow the line of Friedman.

Yes. But both Friedman's line and my line have a hell of a lot to do with what we think is strong evidence that money is in some sense the villain in business cycles. It is in fact responsible for these depressions.

If all we had was the postwar data set we wouldn't know a lot, because there hasn't been enough action in this period. The '70s are an exception, as they give us a lot of information on inflation, but there haven't been any big depressions in the postwar period. In the old days, however — the pre-World War II period — the typical depression would imply a decrease in real output by 10 percent in a year. That's a different order of magnitude from anything we've seen in the postwar period. What Friedman and Schwartz do in their monograph is try to link up these big episodes with large-scale monetary collapses. The idea is that all you have to do is stop the large-scale monetary collapse. The collapses aren't *caused* by the government — they're all private system bank failures. Friedman's policy isn't exactly laissez-faire, since he's calling for government intervention in the banking sector to override events in the private sector. I don't think of the Friedman countercyclical policies as stemming from a general dislike for government as much as calling for a very specific, well-defined form of government intervention. That's all it takes. You don't need all of this fine-tuning; it's beside the point and dangerous as well.

I talked with several neo-Keynesian economists about your equilibrium modeling strategies. They usually said, "I've never understood that. I've never understood what they mean." Benjamin Friedman clarified this with a story about people who get into a rainshower without an umbrella — for him, a disequilibrium situation. They couldn't anticipate the rain, so they walk around in the rain without an umbrella. It takes some time, some learning, before they will carry around umbrellas.

What does he think about the question whether people have the same number of umbrellas in Phoenix, in Alaska, in London, in Rome? Surely the frequencies of people carrying umbrellas have something to do with the objective amount of rainfall in these places. People who live in the desert don't have any umbrellas. If you were seriously studying the demand for umbrellas as an economist, you'd get rainfall data by cities, and you wouldn't hesitate for two seconds to assume that everyone living in London knows how much it rains there. That would be assumption number one. And no one would argue with you either. In macroeconomics, people argue about things like that. But if you were presenting that in an ordinary econometrics seminar, everyone would say, "Of course. That's obvious." So we're not very interested in the dynamics of how someone comes to know whether he's in a rainy situation or not.

Other people say that there are periods with fundamental uncertainty. They refer to the Keynesian concept of uncertainty. As a matter of fact, Rapping tells this story, too.

It's Knight, not Keynes.

Keynes also has that in his Treatise on Probability *and in his 1936 journal article. He refers, for example, to the Napoleonic Wars as events that we can never anticipate, just like we cannot anticipate scientific predictions or innovations because, if we could, we would have invented what scientists will invent. Uncertainty is prevalent in some periods. Like now. People really don't know what's going on; there is uncertainty as to what the government is doing, uncertainty as to the future of nuclear power and so on. It's very unlike the '60s, when there was a general optimism. Post-Keynesians say that in some periods the uncertainty is so prevalent that talking in terms of probability distribution doesn't make sense, and that people have to go by rules of thumb. Different people go by different rules because in that environment there is no clear basis for rational decisions. What do you think of that?*

I think there is something to that. I don't know how you could really disagree with it. It just seems to me something that has to be handled question by question. I don't see talking about rules of thumb as being helpful. I certainly agree that people behave by rules of thumb, but if people want to know about where they are and how they got there and how they're going to change the circumstances, you have to talk about probabilities, too. That is why I try to view the business cycle as much as possible as a recurring event, because if it isn't you have a hard time thinking about how people are going to respond to it rationally. (Maybe I overstress that, because no two business cycles are exactly alike and no two years are exactly alike.) But a lot of it depends on your imagination.

A lot of behavior appears inappropriate or irrational. The example I use in class is that of little children on the first day of school. You see them doing things that you know don't suit the situation. They'll start crying when there's nothing to cry about. They'll kick another little kid when there's nothing at stake. They start doing all kinds of things that, to an adult or someone who knows what school really is, are crazy and irrational. They're in a new situation and they're trying to match it with their experience, but it's not at all clear how to do it because it's so different. So their reactions look crazy to an outsider. An hypothesis like rational behavior, in the sense of a rational response to an objective situation, just isn't helpful in understanding that. You've got to find out what these kids think is happening to them.

There are a lot of similar issues. For me, life-cycle issues are the ones that are easiest to think about as nonrecurrent, because you have these events that you only go through once. On the other hand, the thing we're all trying to do is to look at other people a few years older with the idea that we're pretty much like they are. I try to turn it into a recurrent event by viewing myself as a drawing from some probability distribution on which I have some information from observing others.

What do you think of the disequilibrium economics that is still done?

Look. You and I have been talking about human behavior. Those guys aren't talking about human behavior. These psychologists are. They're closely observing actual people doing something, and they're asking what are they doing and why are they doing it? What's going through their heads? What situation do they think they're in? I just don't think this disequilibrium economics is . . . I won't make pronouncements about it. You never know whether a line that you may not sympathize with will turn up something interesting or not. But I just don't get the sense that their theory is being driven by an attempt to get at, or model, some specific kind of human behavior. They're trying to explain other economists' words, but they're not thinking about human decision-making. That's why the key actors are always some external force in their models, like a price that just won't change. *Why* won't it change? In whose interest is it to keep it where it is? None of these questions is ever addressed. So in that sense I'm very unsympathetic with the way they're doing things.

But I've been in this business long enough to know that there are a lot of guys you don't have to be sympathetic with to benefit from what they do. People who seem to have the craziest motivations turn up really interesting economics. Often I dislike the introductory paragraph of a paper and dislike the conclusion, but think that the midddle is extremely interesting.

You seem to have abandoned econometrics.

I'm not a very good econometrician any more.

Would you be able to use these new innovation techniques?

Well, you can do anything if you just take the time to learn it. But it's not stuff I'm very familiar with. Part of it is that I started with some empirical work a few years ago in which I was interested and to which I was going to put a fair amount of time. Then, I learned that Sargent and Sims were starting on the same line. That was very discouraging. First of all, I don't like races. Second, those guys know a lot more time-series econometrics than I do. Somehow the idea that they were working on the same thing, and probably doing it better up in Minneapolis, just completely dampened my enthusiasm for my own work. And insofar as I had any ideas, I just tried to tell them, tried to influence them and not carry on some parallel investigation. I have regrets now because they lost interest in the line, too, so now no one is doing it.

ON THE REALISM OF ASSUMPTIONS

Your story on the labor market emphasizes information problems and ignores phenomena such as wage rigidity. Doesn't that story sound highly implausible to you? I know that my father, for example, who is rather suspicious of economists' talk, would find the story unbelievable. I am sure many people think the same. Do you think, then, that your story has any correspondence with the way in which the labor market actually works?

Did you ever look at Steinbeck's book *The Grapes of Wrath*? It's kind of a protest pamphlet from the '30s about migrant farmers in California. There's one passage in there that is a better anecdote than I could have written for the kind of models I like. It illustrates the auction characteristic of the labor market for migrant farm workers. He writes about a hundred guys who show up at a farm where there are only ten jobs available. The farmer will let the wage fall until ten people are willing to work for that wage and ninety people say "the hell with it," and just go on down the road. Steinbeck thinks the cure would be government-enforced wage rigidity [laughing], so he's not trying to support laissez-faire economics. He's describing what he thinks went on in the '30s.

There is nothing about wage rigidity. Nominal wages and prices came down by half between 1929 and 1933. Why would anyone look at a period like that and say that the difficult problem would be to explain rigid wages? I don't understand it. But I can see how someone trying to explain 1934 to 1939 could be puzzled about rigid wages. I have been puzzled about that, too.

When I suggest to students the idea that people form their expectations such that they are consistent with the predictions of a rather complicated model, I usually get a roaring protest. People think that it is absolutely absurd that people can know something that must be beyond their comprehension. How do you convince your students of that? Or your wife?

My wife isn't interested in economics. And Ph.D. students are pretty passive; they'll take anything [laughter].

I try to turn it around. People in business usually like to get into conversations about what they do all day and how they make their decisions. I'm always impressed with how sophisticated their thinking and their information-processing is. What puzzles me is the number of economists who seem to believe the reverse. It would be a *miracle* if I could write down a model for the demand for shoes and the supply of shoes, cook up a little difference equation, solve it, and the solution would reveal profits available to me from the shoe business that weren't obvious to people who have been working in the shoe business for 20, 30, 40 years. It seems ludicrous to imagine that we could discover sizable rents with our simple equations without knowing anything about shoes. But some economists think we can get an insight into someone else's business without knowing anything about the substance of his business.

Have you read Simon's *The Sciences of the Artificial*? He's got examples like "Why is it that Arctic animals have white fur?" You know it is handy if you're trying to escape predators to be able to blend into the snow, but that doesn't explain anything about how it came about. [Simon] says its outcome would be useful for animals trying to survive in the Arctic.

A lot of our theorizing is about outcomes and is very weak on the process, so I'm not surprised it doesn't look like the way businessmen think. But this is nothing new for economics. When you present a demand curve, you suggest that people solve some nonlinear program or find a tangency point. It's fairly complicated to write an algorithm for actually doing that. It wouldn't have any resemblance to the way a household makes decisions about anything. When I get the objection on the expectations point, which I often do, I say, "Why didn't you say that when I was talking about demand?" There's nothing descriptive in demand theory in terms of the process by which human people, families, and whole business firms make decisions. Economists have lived with that for years.

Do you like the rigorous way in which Gary Becker tries to model household decisions?

Yes. But again, I think Gary's work is focused on outcomes. Sometimes people react to it because they don't like it as a description of the process. They think about marriage; they think about what they went through when you got married, and they say it didn't resemble Gary's model. One doesn't think, "Was I calculating what my wife could get or could produce?" No one thinks about getting married in these terms explicitly. But the idea is that somehow those considerations are sufficiently important that they must be incorporated into the process. Moreover, you can test the model; so that if the theory is off, the data will let you know about it.

Herbert Simon, whom you just mentioned, is highly critical of such a neoclassical analysis of decison-making. He argues that we have to pay attention to the process. How did he react to your approach when you were both at Carnegie-Mellon?

He used to give us a hard time. He likes to take on the devil's advocate role. In his *Sciences of the Artificial* he's pretty balanced. The point of the Arctic-fur example is that for some questions, a superficial view of the process is safe enough. There's a sense in which that's a perfectly valid explanation. For other purposes it's inadequate.

In my house we don't use words like "marginal" every day. I don't find the language of economics to be useful to think about individual decision problems. I also don't use economic principles at home. I never pay my children to do their jobs. I try to use family loyalty or an exchange system; you help me, I'll help you.

I remember that Rapping used to tell his wife years ago, if she told him that the faucet was leaking and he should fix it, "Call a plumber. My consulting rate is so much per day: that's my opportunity cost. A plumber only costs half as much, so it's ridiculous to have me fixing faucets." He would go upstairs and watch a football game on the television [laughter]. At some point she just lost patience and said, "To hell with you, you're not making a hundred dollars a day watching a football game." I think a lot of this opportunity cost stuff is just to push people around who haven't caught up with the jargon yet.

ON DOING ECONOMICS

Are you after truth?

Yeah. But I don't know what we mean by truth in our business. I don't see economics as pushing that deeply in some respects. We're programming robot imitations of people, and there are real limits on what you can get out of that.

So far, we have discussed your ideas. However, it seems to me that the ways in which those ideas are expressed are just as important as the ideas themselves. In our case, your preference for mathematical expression is striking.

I'm not really a mathematician, so . . .

But do you like the language?

The only way I feel I understand something is if I can write it down in a model and make it work. I felt that from the beginning. That's why I liked Samuelson's book. He'll take these incomprehensible verbal debates that go on and on and never end and just *end* them; formulate the issue in such a way that the question is answerable, and then get the answer.

Economists seem to have different styles of argument; they use different languages. Might differences in language be responsible for problems of communication between, say, the Chicago and Harvard or M.I.T. people?

Tom and I have a very self-serving way of arguing. Look, for example, at my paper "Methods and Problems in Business Cycle Theory" [1980]. We want to claim ourselves to be right in the mainstream of the language that is shared by the best economic theorists and econometricians.

We think we're using the language of modern economics that, sooner or later, everyone will be using. I recall the responses to a paper that I presented in Washington on the methods and problems of business cycles; they strictly had to do with age. The older people like Phil Cagan, who's a Chicago student of Friedman, said "overkill" and "you don't need all this mathematics." He was very negative about the paper. I don't know whether he thought it was a bad paper, or whether he was just sorry that this was the way things were going. Sargent and I had a much easier time talking to younger theorists than more-traditional macroeconomists. When I was at Yale once, a young guy, an assistant professor, came up to me and looked like he thought it was probably not a good idea to be seen talking with me. He said he'd been trying to get interested in monetary economics. He'd read my paper "Expectations and Neutrality of Money," and it had been the only paper on monetary economics he could understand. I do think that we're using the language that everybody uses, or will be in a few years.

The M.I.T. people have great problems with what you are doing.

I think they're just missing the boat, mainly for political reasons. When new techniques come in, they get combined in accidental ways with particular positions and substantive presumptions. Sargent, Wallace, Barro, and I think that money is very important in business cycles. When we started working on our rational expectations models, the key variable was monetary shocks. And that's just chance. There's no necessary connection between rational expectations as an idea and the importance of money in business cycles. The latter is an empirical question: it's either true or it's not. But since Sargent and I were the guys that did it, it all got tied up with money. That's just transient. It's perfectly simple to have models in which fiscal policy plays a central role and have rational expectations. It's just a matter of time until people do that. Some people are talking the same language that I talk; but they've got substantively different ideas about what's important in business cycles. They think there are crucial difficulties with my models and are trying to write down other models that don't have the same difficulties. So, I think a lot of these connections are going to pass. Don't forget that a lot of macroeconomists are not well-trained economic theorists. They don't know modern mathematical economics. I think a lot of these differences have to do with that.

You told me that reading Keynes is impossible for you. Has that anything to do with language?

I was just kidding. But I *don't* like that book. It's not a very congenial book to read.

Some people find it the best economic book ever written.

I really find that amazing. I find it carelessly written, not especially gracefully written, sometimes dishonestly written. I don't like the bullying tone. I don't like the sort of British aristocratic stuff. He's got this great idea for solving index number problems — we'll measure everything in units of workers. Workers are obviously homogeneous: that solves the index number problem [laughter]. It would be impossible

for an American to come up with the idea that workers are homogeneous. It's a ridiculous idea. What the hell was he thinking about? But it's
written loosely enough that if I liked the book, I probably would find
enough quotes in there that I could use to motivate arguments. But
there's so much arbitrariness in that book.

*I noticed from reading your recent work that you have become reflective on what you
have been doing.*

A lot of it has to do with writing papers for a conference. I am influenced a lot by who's going to be at a conference, where they are coming
from, what their point of view is, what they understand, what they don't
understand, and what the common background is. You mostly can tell
that it is a group of people thinking about economic policy in a particular way, and you just try to get at them. You wonder what's wrong with
their way of thinking and why we are missing each other's point. This
happened also at a conference of the Boston Federal Reserve Bank for
which Tom and I wrote a paper. We knew we were going to be outsiders, and we wanted to come on strong. We don't write papers like that
for the *Journal of Political Economy.* They are very much specific to conferences. This really is very helpful, I find.

The first paper I ever wrote for a conference was "Econometric
Testing of the Natural Rate Hypothesis." I knew Tobin was going to be
there. And I knew that he was an honest guy and if I couldn't get
through to him, it was my fault and not his fault. That really helped me
in writing the paper; I tried to think about what he was going to see. I
knew he and Friedman could never talk. Tobin and I haven't gotten
that good at it either, but I figured that I could say what I wanted to say
in a way that would get through to him, and I did.

Are you conservative?

I don't know. I thought I was at Carnegie, but around here I don't
know. This place has a pretty wide spread of political opinions, and I'm
never going to be anywhere near the far-right end of the spectrum for
Chicago. But I'm not too close to the far-left end either. It's hard to be a
conservative with the Reagan administration turning to fine-tuning,
which seems insane to me. So, if being conservative means liking their
economics, I guess I'm not.

But do you, more or less, agree with Friedman's ideas in Free to Choose *or* Capitalism and Freedom?

I like *Capitalism and Freedom* a lot. It's really written for economists in a way that *Free to Choose* isn't. *Free to Choose* gets careless about a lot of points that *Capitalism and Freedom* is very careful about.

Do you think that there are ethical problems in a capitalistic system? Do you think there is something like social injustice?

Well, sure. Governments involve social injustice.

But doesn't government try to resolve social injustice?

That wouldn't be anything like my view. I can't think of explaining the pharaohs as being in existence to resolve social injustice in Egypt. I think they perpetrated most of the injustice in Egypt.

Are you an optimist as far as the economy is concerned?

Yes, I guess so. I think most economists are. I think this economy is going to grow at 3 percent a year, no matter what happens. Forever [laughter]. One administration, like the current one, can mess things up, but that's all transient. There's an incredible amount of stability in the last 100 years of U.S. economic history. I don't know why it's there and, of course, it could disappear at any minute. So I don't know why I think it's going to go on forever.

You don't share the ideas of radicals on an imminent crisis.

They have to talk about an imminent crisis; that's their job. I don't see it.

Do you think that the distinction between the positive and the normative side of economics is useful?

Yeah. It's an essential distinction [pause]. We've been arguing about that around here a lot lately. There's a feeling, and I guess I've helped encourage it, among a lot of younger people that the politics and the political role that economists play has had a very bad effect on macroeconomics. A lot of older economists seem to me to be solely concerned with politics, as opposed to scientific matters. People are asking the wrong questions; they are taking questions from Washington, rather than thinking about what's puzzling them or taking more scientific points of view.

Macroeconomics really got itself devoted to the question "What would I do if I were on the Council?," which may or may not be an interesting question for social scientists to study. It has some good effects, as it makes you think operationally. I'll often think of hypothetical policy questions, when I'm doing some theoretical work, just to force myself to be clear on what question I'm asking and what it would mean to have an answer to it. But it is certainly not the only question.

But politicians must make decisions. What can the role of economists be in this decision-making process when they can't agree?

Some people think that the most useful thing to think about is how to make things work better within the set of institutions under which our economy is operating. Others think that there are basic flaws in these institutions and that sooner or later we're going to have to reform them in some fundamental way. I can't imagine how one could prove, given the state of knowledge now, that one of those positions is correct and the other is not. Our experience is too indecisive.

I don't find it very useful to think through in very much detail how intellectuals influence things, but they do. When trouble comes in a set of institutions there's no time to think up new ones, so people take something off the shelf and do it. In the 1929 to 1932 period they went back to World War I and looked at how the economy was run then. They didn't have a good enough inventory of ideas. It was too quick. They couldn't cook up fundamental new ways of dealing with things on such short notice, so they grabbed something that was handy. And that's what societies always do in difficult situations.

A lot depends on what's around. I think Friedman's work has really proved this, in a way. A lot of the things he was writing about twenty years ago seemed almost utopian and silly for a serious person even to be thinking about, such as criticizing public housing, for which all of us had so much hope. And now twenty years later with the failure of the system, you can't find anyone who will endorse the public housing we have in Chicago. These projects are horrible places. And so you look back to the people who were explaining to you why this wasn't going to work and pay them a little more attention. The consensus of the '60s was artificial and unhealthy. Look at the way Friedman's work was criticized during that period. I think it's just a disgrace to the profession that he was treated as though he were some kind of nut. I'm glad that's changed; he was one of the most eminent scientists around.

Economic policy is not a matter for a few economists to settle. There's too much else involved in it.

But what do you say when journalists ask for your opinion on economic policy issues?

Journalists are fine-tuners. One reporter once asked me what I'd do if I were on the Council. I told him that I would resign. I guess he thought I was making fun of him. But I thought that if he was personalizing the question, it was alright if I personalized the answer. These just aren't questions that have much interest for me.

So you advocate a modest role for economists?

Again, the consensus of the '60s was a very artificial period and not at all a model for how you can expect economics normally to interact with the rest of society. At that time it looked like economics was taking over the world. You had the Kennedy Council, the tax cut (which I thought then was a good idea), and Kennedy's eloquent speech at Yale, in which he used good economic reasoning, without a lot of political nonsense. This way of thinking subsequently spread to other branches of government. It looked like rationality was settling in, but it all unraveled.

Do you oppose government activity altogether?

I don't like talking about how big government should be. I like talking about costs and benefits of particular projects. That seems to be the right way to talk about it.

As far as I see, the criticism of your approach is sometimes quite severe. People make jokes of it. Does it ever bother you that people argue that way?

We've been going through this for years, so it doesn't surprise me. If anything, I've been surprised at how generous people have been. The criticism pisses me off sometimes, and I guess it showed in that review of Tobin's book [Tobin, 1980; Lucas, 1981]. I don't think that this is an ideal way to carry on these arguments, but people are always going to make jokes. I make jokes, too, when I can think of them.

But do you have the experience that you don't know it anymore, that you wonder "Am I right?"

Yes. Sometimes I get so deep into a problem that I just lose the ability to hang on to all the pieces, and start being afraid that I'm thinking about everything in the wrong way. I read criticisms of my work that seem to me to be important, pointing up serious deficiencies in these models. But I just don't feel like working on all those problems. I don't have any good ideas on most of them, but I've got a general confidence that they are not fundamental, although I don't know why. I don't feel personally responsible for fixing it up, so I try to encourage other people to get interested in them.

What are the problems that intrigue you right now?

I've been thinking about monetary and fiscal policy from a public finance point of view. This question of time-inconsistency. A lot of these models have the property that an optimum policy, calculated from time zero on, wouldn't, if you recalculated it from time one, be optimal to continue from time one on. In which case, unless a policy-maker could bind himself to a whole infinite sequence of future policies, you could call it optimum, but there's no way the thing could be implemented. These are just interesting problems in game theory. In the work Nancy Stokey and I are doing on this, we're abstracting from business cycles.

Have you ever considered being more serious about the theory of economic policy? Why would policy-makers not anticipate the anticipations of the private sector?

That's the nature of the game I'm talking about. The private sector is one player, the government is another, and both of them correctly take account of the other player's actions. Kydland and Prescott are the guys who started along that line in macroeconomics.

Do you find that promising?

I think it's the only way to think about these problems in some sense [pause], but it's discouraging since we're short on good solution methods and it's easy to write down interesting definitions of equilibria that you can't do anything with. You can't prove there exist any equilibria, you can't characterize them. We're technically frustrated. In my work I always have the feeling that I can only think of one way to go: I never think of myself choosing between six different explanations for something. A typical situation is having no decent explanations for something, or one sort of half-way decent explantion. That is why econometric horse races don't interest me. You've got to get some horses first [laughter].

Do you think that what you have done is a revolution in economics?

No, I don't see that. I don't like the term. I do not consider the term "Keynesian revolution" appropriate, either. It seemed to be a more political event than a scientific event. The Depression discredited the whole profession; people were alarmed about it. The *General Theory* is a political response to the Depression and to the discrediting of conventional economics that resulted from it.

But I should acknowledge that Keynes left an opening for younger econometricians and mathematical economists to take over and to write down models. When their senior colleagues criticized their models, they could say, "Well, these are Keynesian models." And since the older people still hadn't caught up with Keynes, that shut them up. So people like Klein and Tinbergen took over because they had the exciting new methods.

Do you see that what you have started is comparable to what Keynes has done?

Well, I suppose everyone thinks his work is important. The sort of things I do are a return to a traditional research program, a pre-Keynesian research program, with the difference being that I, and people such as Sargent, are not hostile to mathematical methods. We love them [laughter]. The ideas of Hayek or Mitchell are interesting — worth building on — but their methods are not.

A lot of traditional economists were hostile to mathematical economics. I think it's an accident of timing that the early econometric, mathematical models of aggregate economies were called Keynesian.

In a way your timing was also kind of an accident, since there was a general discontent with Keynesian economics. Does that explain why your theories have gotten so much attention?

Yeah, very much so. But it's really not my theories, but those of Friedman or Phelps. They went way out on a limb in the late '60s, saying that high inflation wasn't going to give us anything by way of lower unemployment. So Friedman and Phelps have really pushed things away from the macroeconomics of the '60s, because they jumped to a general equilibrium level of thinking about these problems. You could see right away that what they were getting was a lot different from what you were getting from any of the conventional econometric models. If you look at the Phelps volume [1970] you can see where it all started. The question was how to get that down in modern mathematical theory.

But it was not easy for Friedman and Phelps in those times. Go back and look at the *Brookings Economic Papers* and you see that they were treated like crackpots. But they got lucky, I would say; it was just dumb luck. Most samples cannot tell you which of these stories about the Phillips curve is the best one. If you just get data from the 1950s and '60s, you can never answer that question. There just wasn't enough of an experiment, there wasn't enough inflation to tell. From that point of view we got lucky [laughing] with the more recent samples. From a social point of view, however, it is not quite so lucky.

3

THOMAS J. SARGENT

The prominence of Sargent among new classical economists is unmistakable. In fact, new classical economics is often referred to as the economics of Lucas and Sargent. By 1971, Sargent was discussing, independently of Lucas, the notion of rational expectations (Sargent, 1971). Since then he has had a profound influence on theoretical and empirical discourse in new classical economics. One article he coauthored with Neil Wallace has become a major target for criticism. Entitled "Rational Expectations, the Optimal Monetary Instrument and the Optimal Money Supply" (1973), it supports the proposition, now known as the Sargent-Wallace proposition, that only unanticipated monetary shocks can have real effects. Sargent also laid the basis for innovative econometric procedures that allow testing of new classical conclusions. The principles of the New Econometrics are contained in his "Estimation of Dynamic Labor Demand Schedules under Rational Expectations" (1978).

Sargent earned a Harvard Ph.D. in 1968. After a year at Carnegie-Mellon University, he moved on to the University of Minnesota and the Federal Reserve Bank of Minneapolis. We talked in Cambridge, Massachusetts, where he spent a sabbatical at Harvard and the National Bureau of Economic Research. It is July 1982.

BACKGROUND

How did you come to study economics?

[Long pause and hesitation.] I liked it when we studied it in college. But also I was truly curious, ever since I was a kid, about what causes depressions. The Great Depression had a big effect on me: a lot of people in my family got wiped out. My grandfather ran a quarry in the construction business, and he got wiped out. My other grandfather was in the radio business, and he got wiped out. It was the common story.

So I was interested in what caused the Depression and why we didn't have something similar later. When I started studying economics they said something about that. Also, economics is a nice mix of subjects: it is about people, it relates to political issues but it also uses technical things, mathematics. It's a way of saying analytical things about virtually every issue in politics.

At Berkeley where I was an undergraduate, I had a very good professor and a very good teaching assistant, Jerry Kenley, in Economics 1. The professor, Benjamin Ward, was really good; he gave beautiful lectures. We read things like Charles Beard's *The Economic Interpretation of the Constitution* and started putting economics to work right away. I recall that he was critical about our society in class.

Were you political in those days?

The students at Berkeley had a critical tone at least since the '30s. It was always a place that attracted critical and radical students. I was one in a quiet way. I read a lot of philosophy and political philosophy, largely in courses, and I thought a lot about it when we discussed it. I was certainly very liberal, but I wasn't a political activist. I studied hard.

Then you came to Harvard?

Yes. That was an interesting experience. It was different from my experience at Berkeley. At Berkeley I was close to a lot of teachers but at Harvard you're much more on your own. I wrote my thesis with John Meyer, an all-around economist who is also a very good econometrician. I'm glad I went to Harvard because of the intellectual freedom. In those days the students were free to inquire about things; they weren't given a good set story about, for example, macro in class. They had to figure it out for themselves. And in those days the set stories weren't very good anyway. There were big problems in both Keynesian and monetarist stories that needed to be challenged. But I wasn't aware of that then.

Did anything in particular inspire you, give you the intellectual stimulus, or was it more a matter of getting a diploma?

No. I was interested in things, but I didn't really start learning things until I got out of graduate school. Then I started thinking about time series very seriously. I read lots of books on time series. I tried to figure out the relationship between time-series and economic models. At the time I started, the links weren't formal. You would write down static models, models that weren't even stated in probabilistic or dynamic terms, and then apply time-series procedures. But these models weren't really in any shape to confront the time series.

My research into interest rates was one example. My dissertation, also on interest rates, was not very good because I didn't know how to solve that particular problem. I didn't know enough about time series and I didn't know enough about theory to do things satisfactorily, but I did recognize that the link between them wasn't satisfactory.

I started to learn more about the relationship between theory and observations in the late '60s. I was really influenced by a number of colleagues such as Neil Wallace and Chris Sims at the University of Minnesota. I was learning from Sims, even before I went to Minnesota, by reading his papers. Neil Wallace really taught me macroeconomic theories; he also taught me a lot about the relationship between theories and data, or at least posed a lot of good questions.

How about Lucas?

At first, I learned from Lucas mostly by reading his stuff. I first met Lucas at Carnegie-Mellon, but I was way behind him. I didn't really know what he was up to; I didn't completely understand it. The thing that's attractive about his work with Prescott is the message about how to go from theories to time series in a clean way. It indicates how a lot of the problems can be resolved and creates the foundations for a new econometrics. Only details have to be worked out.

How was the year that you spent at Carnegie?

It was great. And that was not necessarily just because of Lucas. I talked to a lot of people; I talked to Leonard Rapping a lot, to Mike Lovell, to Allen Meltzer, and to some younger guys like Peter Frost, Richard Roll, and Lester Lave.

Rapping told me that you were a shy person then.

I was. I still am. Leonard was really nice to me. I knew he was struggling with neoclassical economics.

Did you experience the tension that Rapping and Lucas noticed, Mike Lovell at one side and the Chicago faction at the other?

No. I knew there were things like that going on, but for me it was great. I came right out of Harvard, and those guys were a little older. I learned a lot from the people from Chicago. It was my first contact with them, and I was really influenced by them. I may mention that the one who put me onto rational expectations wasn't Bob Lucas; it was Mike Lovell. Mike was doing a study on expectations. He'd also done some work on inventories, and I was looking at his work on inventories very closely; we had many conversations. He then put me onto the Muth article. That was in '67. I read that and we talked about it some. I didn't understand fully what Muth was up to. I didn't even pursue his idea at the time, but I set it at the back of my mind. I never talked to Lucas about it then; I didn't talk to Lucas very much that year.

At the end of the '60s, Lucas and Rapping were doing important work together. In 1969, they published a now very famous article. Were you aware of all that at that time?

I remember when Lucas and Rapping were writing their paper. I used to talk to Leonard about it, not Bob. I didn't completely understand what they were up to, I don't think they completely understood fully what it meant either. All of us were essentially in between rational and adaptive expectations.

I'll tell you what I thought: I thought that rational expectations was a more elegant way to do it, was the right way to do it; but we didn't really understand how to do it. We didn't know the right techniques. What we didn't see was that it would give completely different ways of looking at things. Bob and Ed Prescott may have seen that, but I sure didn't.

When did you begin to focus on these new ideas?

I really started struggling with these things when I got in touch with Neil Wallace. I met him while I was in the Army. John Meyer arranged for me to go to the National Bureau of Economic Research when I took leaves from the Army. You get 30 days to a year leave, so I went up to New York and spent some time at the Bureau. It was very nice of Meyer; it helped me. I met Neil there and we started talking about macro. For me, he was a good match. I think it's because of what both of us knew and what both of us didn't know. When I think back to how we were struggling with this rational expectations stuff, lots of it is pretty funny because we didn't do things in the cleanest way. For example, if we had known more math, we would have done things in a completely different way; we would have solved problems right away; we would have seen things right away, which we didn't. It took a long time but it was a lot of fun.

Did you go to Vietnam?

I went through ROTC, was commissioned, and then worked in the systems analysis office of the Pentagon. It changed me in some ways, made me more conservative. I came to understand more clearly the limitations of government actions. It was a learning experience. My conclusions came from seeing the whole decision-making process by which the US got into the war: how we evaluated the situation, how we processed the data from the war, how we understood our options, what we saw as the resources and costs in Southeast Asia, and what we thought was the likely outcome. We didn't do a very good job. There was an incredible volume of inefficient and bad decisions, which one must take into account when devising institutions for making policy.

My impression is that you were a kind of withdrawn person who reflected on these things to himself, who got into Berkeley and Harvard in a very quiet way. Were you indeed the quiet intellectual observer?

I don't have much to say about that.

When did you start working with Lucas?

I don't really work much with Lucas. I spent a year at Chicago. I took two courses from him. He's a very good teacher. I learn from him, I read his papers. He's been a big influence on me. We have done some work together: we wrote a couple of articles. [pause] I work with a lot of other people. I work with Neil Wallace but also with students. Things are really advancing. The young people who are ten or twelve years younger than I am are really doing extremely exciting work now.

Which other economists have been important for you?

Milton Friedman has been an important person in terms of educating me. I've never taken a class from him, but I've read his stuff. His work and Tobin's work are important to me. Trying to figure out what those guys have done has been a continuing souce of education to me.

Friedman is not very technical . . .

There's some wonderful macroeconomics in what he's done. For example, his program for monetary stability is something I've read and reread and plan to continue to. There are some extremely good insights. It's clear that thare are models that underlie his thinking . . . He was at Chicago the first quarter when I visited. I've talked with him, but I've learned more from him by reading. As far as Tobin is concerned, I've read his stuff. I've talked to him three or four times and that was pleasant. I think he knows what the basic issues are, and I really respect his judgment, but I don't agree with him on the way things are going.

Have you ever met Muth?

I don't really know him. I have met him two times. I've heard him give papers.

You and Lucas give him a lot of credit in the introduction to your book [Lucas and Sargent, 1981].

That was appropriate. Bob wrote those lines, but I certainly concurred. The papers that he wrote are really marvelous.

ON ECONOMICS, HIS OWN WORK, AND
RATIONAL EXPECTATIONS

When you came to Harvard you were somewhat aware that there was something not right with Keynesian economics. What started your thinking about time series?

When I was a second- or third-year graduate student, I did not understand the connection between theories and statistical tests. I assumed it was because I didn't have a firm enough grasp of the subject. But as I learned more and more, I realized that the connection wasn't there. What I mean by the links not being clear is that often the models that we used had no randomness in them. They analyze individual behavior in a context in which there is no uncertainty, but they treated the data probabilistically, thus adding randomness. That procedure is not a tight one, not even an understandable one. The statistical model you're using implies that there is an environment in which there's uncertainty, whereas the economic model that you're using assumes that away. The hunch is, and it's a hunch that turned out to be right, that it's not just a matter of adding a random term. If there really is uncertainty, it ought to change the way you think about individual behavior.

But it's not only the uncertainty, it's also the dynamics. Lots of times economic theories would be not dynamic, but static. When one would get the data, one would make various assumptions, not part of the theory, in order to capture the dynamics in the data. I thought a lot about how the dynamics come out of individual behavior and equilibrium and how one could build models which were in good shape to go to the data, which captured both the dynamics and the randomness. That was the agenda.

Were you aware of the agenda?

This question about the relationship between theories and time series has guided my studies. I try to learn both about theories and time-series econometrics with a purpose. I get particularly excited when I see possibilities of merging the two.

Do you consider this development revolutionary?

You can characterize something as revolutionary or as a continuous development at your pleasure. I could construct an argument that rational expectations macroeconomics is the logical, continuous consequence of what people like Koopmans and Hurwicz and other people, who founded the econometric techniques underlying Keynesian models, had in mind. The same philosophical desiderata for a model that those guys had in mind are what we have in mind. Koopmans and Hurwicz, very early on, said that you want to build models based on optimizing behavior. Koopmans complained that macroeconomic models weren't satisfactory because they didn't handle randomness. He talked about building models in continuous time, which is something we're trying to do now. Hurwicz talked in 1949 about the need to model strategic behavior. He said that Keynesian models were ignoring the fact that individuals aren't just stupid players who responded passively to what the government did, but that they had the option to change their strategy when the government changed its strategy. That's the rational expectations program. He was ignored for 20 years or more.

What are the crucial elements of the language that you are talking about?

The language is probably new to macroeconomics, but not completely new in other areas of economics or in other areas of statistics and probability theory. What we're doing I'd say is natural and inevitable as an intellectual development. It's one route that was going to be developed. The basic idea of thinking about the agents as living in dynamic and uncertain environment and being concerned about strategic considerations is something that's come up in other areas, such as industrial organization, the exhaustable resource area, the dynamic duopoly and oligopoly area. Individuals choose strategies that they're going to be using repeatedly over time. They are not just making one-shot decisions, but they're choosing decision rules. That's a new language to macro, which, as you said, only some people speak. That accounts for some discussions in the '70s which were at cross-purposes. But I think it's too bold to say that we invented it.

Benjamin Friedman, Modigliani, and others argue that there is nothing new in your approach. They refer to the neo-Keynesian portfolio, consumption, and investment theories which incorporate that approach.

There's a sense in which those statements of Modigliani and Ben Friedman are right, and there's a sense in which they completely miss the point. The sense in which they're right is that the recent developments are really an inevitable consequence of the logical development of Keynesian economics. When you go back and look at the history of macroeconomics since the '30s, there's an underlying effort to build more and more optimizing theory underneath the decision rules of Keynesian economics, such as in the consumption function, the portfolio schedule, and the investment schedule. Various people, and in particular Modigliani, Tobin, and Milton Friedman, resorted to optimizing theory to explain paradoxes in the theory of the consumption function. They went back to the theory of choice of Fisher. Jorgenson, Lucas, and others tried to use optimizing theory to get the investment schedule. As of about 1969, the trend in Keynesian models was to use more and more optimizing theory, and that's when Lucas and Wallace and I came in.

The next natural step was to use rational expectations, because why not optimize over expectations too? The only reason why it hadn't been done then was technical. We didn't know the right techniques, such as filtering procedures to construct models with rational expectations. So the valid part of Friedman and Modigliani's statements is that this very much was an enterprise that other people were involved in.

The invalid part is this: Once we understood how to build in rational expectations and to go all the way to an optimizing setup, there were some real surprises. The earlier literature proceeded as if you could build an optimizing consumption function, an optimizing investment schedule, an optimizing portfolio schedule, in isolation from one another. They're essentially partial equilibrium exercises which were then put together at the end. The Brookings model, built in '65, is a good example of this practice. They handed out these various schedules to different people and put them together at the end. The force of rational expectations is that it imposes a general equilibrium discipline. In order to figure out people's expectations you had to assume consistency. The literature that Friedman and Modigliani were referring to derived one decision rule at a time. Then the strategy was to hold those decision rules fixed as you varied government policies. The key assumption of those models is that the decision rules would be fixed in the face of alterations in govenment policy, and that you would pick an optimal government policy as the one that gave you the best performance in the economy, holding private decision rules fixed. The key insight of rational expectations is that private agents change their decision rules when the govenment changes its policy. This is an implication of optimizing theory, and a new insight of rational expectations.

It is no coincidence that Lucas, Prescott, Wallace, and myself were all Keynesian economists. But we experienced a discontinuity, a very radical change in our conception. The fact that private agents' decision rules change when the government changed its policy really opened an entirely new vista of issues. For example, the main way the Fed.-M.I.T. and the Wharton models assign a role to activist monetary policies is by imputing to people systematic errors of expectations, which could be exploited by monetary and fiscal policy to influence the state of employment. When you impose rational expectations, you do not accept that systematically manipulating forecast errors is feasible. It is not a matter of which variables go into the expectations function. Rather, any expectations theory that has any element of rationality will predict that private agents' decision rules, and ways of forming expectations will change systematically when there is a change in the government's policy strategy. Decision rules are outcomes of optimizing problems, and those outcomes are going to change.

The proof of my claim that Modigliani and Friedman are misstating things is that these new theories amount to the assertion that standard ways of simulating with the Fed.-M.I.T. model or the DRI model contradict optimizing theory. We're asserting that the way that these people are simulating their models and the answers that they were producing to questions about policy are wrong. You can't have it both ways. You can't continue to simulate that way and say that there's nothing new in what we are saying. You either have to say that we're wrong or that what we're saying has operational significance.

Isn't is possible to alter the large-scale models to meet your objections?

The big models can't be revised; it's not a matter of adding variables. It's a matter of fundamentally changing those models. They must be grounded in optimizing behavior. It's a whole new ball game. What we do is actually a child of the enterprise in which the Cowles Commission was involved, both in terms of its econometric challenge and in terms of its theoretical challenge.

Modigliani made tremendous contributions and we learned from them; there's no question about that. He's a great economist. I just don't happen to agree with him on this particular issue.

One of the main criticisms of rational expectations macro models is that they proclaim to be equilibrium interpretations of what has always been conceived of as disequilibrium phenomena. People have a hard time understanding how you can do that and how these claims of equilibrium are consistent with what they observe. What's your reaction to that?

Again, it's a language problem. We're not talking about static, nonrandom equilibria. The notion of equilibrium in some of our models is a lot fancier than that. Some models include roles for queues and unmatched agents. There are versions of models in which agents get thrown out of work and don't get matched right away.

There's a lot of misplaced criticism of equilibrium models. For explaining 1950-, 1960-, 1970-type business cycles, they're a lot more robust than some people give them credit for. The failure of wages and prices to adjust is no problem because there's a lot of reasons, many of them coming from contract theory and models of enduring relationships, that would lead one not to expect the current real wage/price to adjust to clear the current labor market. I am thinking of models of job matching, some of Hall's work, and Townsend's work. Radner's work on contracts, for example, makes you think in terms of repeated, enduring relationships. All this will be quite different from what you get from just a static demand and supply curve for labor. One has to think

in terms of statistical dynamic equilibria, which are a lot more complicated. Agents who are thrown out of work are in some sense not happy
about being unemployed, and yet cope optimally.

What we mean by equilibrium is esssentially two things. First, we set
out to explain data on prices and quantities as resulting from the interaction of individual decisions; that's the key thing together with the notion that markets clear in some sense. That doesn't mean everybody has
a job every period. The notion of clearing may be much more complicated and may involve lotteries. There are various responses why workers are unemployed. In some sense workers choose professions knowing
that. An example would be construction, an industry in which the probability of being thrown out of work for a certain fraction of the year is
higher than it is in many other industries. Instead of saying that that's
disequilibrium in the construction industry, we would seek reasons why
the industry is organized that way, and why individuals choose to put
themselves in that kind of situation. So the models seek to permit the
theory of choice to explain things. Another thing is that these environments are sufficiently complicated so that it's not automatic that
equilibria are optimal. If they're not, we try to analyze institutions and
government interventions that will correct the non-optimality. That's
the real goal in doing rational expectations policy analysis.

Do you mean that there is not something like a disequilibrium situation?

That's neither what I said nor meant. The first part of my answer was to
respond to the claim the economy's obviously in disequilibrium. It's not
so obvious with the cycles that we observed over the last 20 or 30 years.
We see unemployed workers, but that doesn't tell you whether you want
to use an equilibrium or disequilibrium model. The question is which
model fits the facts best and gives you the best explanations and predictions about interventions. The first part of my answer to your question
is that it's not obvious, with these fancy new kinds of equilibrium models, that the observations don't fit.

The second part is that it should be recognized that it's very hard to
do disequilibrium work. Some modern people who are interested in
modeling optimizing behavior are also interested in disequilibrium
models. It turns out to be very hard, the reason being that the possibility of disequilibrium complicates agents' decision problems. One reason in favor of the equilibrium models is that it solves lots of technical
problems.

What kind of disequilbrium device would you introduce?

In place of something that operates as a Walrasian auctioneer, you would have another mechanism. Such a workable mechanism is now not known, but perhaps is on equal footing with a Walrasian auctioneer in terms of a device that can be interpreted as a way of organizing the economy. In other words, one could imagine a non-Walrasian equilibrium of a game that agents are playing that looks like a disequilibrium. There are pheomena, a lot of them connected with the '30s, which one might want to explain with something that looks like a disequilibrium model or a model in which there are multiple equilibria.

Could you characterize it as a disequilibrium in which plans don't match and adjustments don't occur instantaneously?

I wouldn't characterize it that way. In our equilibrium models, dynamic ones, adjustments don't occur instantaneously. There are lags, but the adjustments occur at about the right rate. I don't work on disequilibrium things right now.

Whose work are you thinking of?

I don't want to mention anyone in particular. There's not a lot of it because it is very hard.

High unemployment rates are plaguing us these days. You mentioned before that you have some personal interests in the Depression years, but you do not deal with that directly in your work because you are more concerned with money in the context of business cycles. Isn't that odd?

There are two separate issues. I do not have a theory, nor do I know somebody else's theory that constitutes a satisfactory explanation of the Great Depression. It's really a very important, unexplained event and process, which I would be very interested in and would like to see explained.

How do you explain the current high unemployment rate?

I think, as of now, the kinds of models of rational expectations Phillips curves that we have work pretty well to explain it.

A core claim that is associated with new classical economics is the neutrality proposition. Is that association right according to you?

I think the key thing about the new classical economics is a commitment to some notion of general equilibrium and some notion of
optimizing behavior, strategic behavior. Those two things are very
broad and sufficient to accommodate all sorts of models which don't
have neutrality. However, I think the natural rate hypothesis is important. It certainly limits what we think can be achieved by countercyclical policy, but it doesn't totally eliminate interesting issues about
how to conduct tax and monetary policy.

The neutrality proposition was an important element in my work six
or seven years ago, but not recently. As a matter of fact, most of my recent work wouldn't have any reason for existing if I took the neutrality
proposition seriously. Same thing with Lucas's work. The whole point
of the work that Wallace and I did on neutrality was to produce a
counterexample to Friedman and Modigliani's statement that there was
nothing new. We took a model that was essentially a version of the
Fed.-M.I.T. model, and we showed that if you put rational expectations
into it, you got extreme neutrality. That doesn't mean that we thought
that that model was the best. Both Neil and I have talked about building other kinds of models. Some people, however, took that model seriously. They, therefore, took the neutrality proposition more seriously
than we did.

Are you committed to the idea that active stabilization policy is ineffective and that a
change in demand variables initiated by government institutions cannot affect real
variables?

We showed in those articles that if you are going to use those kinds of
models and impose rational expectations, you get such and such results.
My current view is that those models aren't satisfactory.

I'd like to distinguish sharply between statements that Neil and I
made about particular models, and statements that we make about policy and the world right now. I certainly wouldn't endorse the proposition that any policy doesn't matter and is ineffective. For example, I
think that huge mistakes in policy have been made in the last year and a
half. Reaganomics really hurts, and not only the US. Neil and I have
written about this in a paper called "Unpleasant Monetarist Arithmetic" which is in the Federal Reserve Bank of Minneapolis quarterly review, Fall '81. We argue that the idea of coupling a very loose fiscal
policy with a very tight monetary policy is a big mistake. It has brought
very high unemployment, not only to the US, but also to our trading
partners. It's not going to bring inflation down; it'll probably make it

worse eventually. We still have Phillips curves in our models. Policy
actions that are incredible, that cause a lot of second-guessing, a lot of
uncertainty, can induce recessions. We say that is not the kind of thing
that you want to do. Both Lucas and Wallace and I wrote things early
on, that were very critical of this policy . . .

*Some of these government people refer to you for a justification of what they were
doing.*

They never asked. I've had some contact with some of them, but not
anyone very high. The kind of work Lucas, Wallace, and I do would
imply a very different policy.

[Pause] I could tell you the policy Neil and I would have. It is essentially just the opposite. There are two questions — what would you do
now, and what would you do in January 1981. The first is the harder
one. If you were committed to Reagan's objectives, and that's a big if,
which are roughly to decrease the size of the government and try to
stimulate private investment, you try to leave taxes unaltered and un-
dertake measures to reduce the size of the government and run a very
loose monetary policy, a low-interest-rate policy. Supposing that he did
get his tax cut and has these big deficits, his second-best policy is still to
run a low-interest-rate policy, even if you have the big deficits. You'd
have a high inflation, but you're probably going to have that anyway
because of the big deficits.

That sounds very Keynesian . . .

These are very different arguments. These are rational expectations arguments that have to do with the best way of financing the government
deficit, coupled with a view of the rational expectations Phillips curve.

The theoretical backing isn't completely tight, and it's based on some
models which haven't been entirely worked out . . . I'm not really
working on those much more than what Neil and I wrote in that "Unpleasant Arithmetic" paper, although it's basically a hunch on how
things would work out if you extended that. But the basic ideas stem
from reflecting on what the consequences are of different ways of
financing the government deficit, and what the best way to do that is
from the point of view of effects on subsequent inflation, meshed with
some speculations about how credible alternative announced plans are.
It's very clear that the administration's fiscal plan together with the
tight monetary policy is something that generated a hell of a lot of uncertainty, not about economic things but about political things. The

kind of uncertainty that's injected into the system is totally avoidable; it could be avoided by proper fiscal and monetary rules . . .

So, then, is it correct to believe that the policy proposal that you advocate is that the government should be anything to reduce uncertainty?

That's not quite true. That comes from some models, but as a general proposition it is probably not true. There are plenty of models in which there are situations in which the government wants to induce some uncertainty. For instance, when it regulates, it wants the people who are regulated to be uncertain about some aspects of the regulator's behavior, like when he is going to come and inspect the books. But the hunch is that in monetary and fiscal policy it's probably not good to be uncertain. I'm not sure what's there in terms of a general proposition. According to some models uncertainty should be reduced, but you can certainly construct other models in which that is not optimal. My hunch in the matters we're discussing is that uncertainty is to be avoided. You should follow certain rules and stick to them, but the rules have to be coherent and credible. They can't be inconsistent, or else it's impossible to stick to them.

Like they are now?

I think so. As far as the high-interest-rate policy and inflation are concerned, the unemployment trade-off comes from the uncertain part. Somehow the net effect of this policy is that it's surprisingly contractionary. These high interest rates are unprecedented and are really clobbering the hell out of the economy. So there is some kind of temporary trade-off. There's something else going on, too, that makes me very uneasy. These unprecedented high interest rates are jeopardizing lots of institutions that we have. There's a debt structure throughout the world that was contracted on the assumption that interest rates were going to be a lot lower. The shift to a much higher interest rate regime is making bad a lot of debts that were good under the old regime. Something similar to that happened in the '30s and in the late '20s. The reminiscences of that are not comfortable. I think you have to be very sensitive to the jeopardy that a lot of corporations are in and the high bankruptcies which are essentially induced by this tight monetary policy.

Can your models deal with these institutional breakdowns?

Not the models that are in the literature, but there's some work being done. Some theoretical work that people are doing now carries promise for a lot of insight into these things. Neil Wallace and Townsend have described some work to me. It may help in describing what happened after '34 because of institutional breakdowns. I think that's the key.

Milton Friedman wouldn't like very much the conclusions you draw with Neil Wallace.

Ask him.

Do economists pay too little attention to the theory of policy behavior?

Yes, but some macroeconomists are paying attention. It's all right to proceed on the assumption that the government behaves optimally or to seek techniques for figuring out how the govenment could behave optimally. In determining the optimal governmental policy, one gets into what is called a dynamic or differential game. That's one area that's being developed to determine optimal governmental policy in light of the fact that individuals are going to choose their strategies to react. It's a direction in which rational expectations will go.

How do you deal with learning? Do you think that it will be an important issue?

It's an important issue, but I don't think anyone's going to get very far. There are some really hard technical problems. My prediction is that in terms of models for explaining time series, the models of learning aren't going to be a big help because of the technical problems in the structure of learning. You can get rich theories of learning. But in the context of individual agents facing dynamic types of problems, you have the choice of either making the technologies dynamic or making them static in order to focus on the learning. Right now you can't do both. It is a hard choice imposed by technical consideratons.

I think Robert Townsend has done some really interesting work on learning. His work is continually rubbing up against these technical constraints that I'm talking about. His is the most promising in terms of econometric implications, but even that is very difficult to apply.

ON ECONOMETRICS

You concern for theoretical as well as empirical issues is unusual. Economists usually specialize. Is your dual specialization a problem?

Yes, it is a problem. Fortunately, people who are a lot more capable than I am are doing both of these things now — young people. They are doing really exciting things. They share the vision that it's a fruitful enterprise to link dynamic theories with econometrics.

Your own econometrics has become progressively more difficult.

My published work is just a record of my learning. I'm sharing it with people so they won't make the same mistakes that I did. It's been a painful and slow process. My work is like a journey, a journey of discovery. Lots of this stuff may have been known to other people, but it was news to me.

One of the important moments of discovery was learning how to construct a rational expectations equilibrium. Neil and I very clumsily learned how to do that using homemade techniques. It wasn't till later that we discovered that Lucas was doing it in a more general, elegant way. Understanding the relationship between what Lucas was doing and these clumsy things that Neil and I were doing was a lot of fun. Learning from Chris Sims about time series and about Granger-Sims causality and how that fits in was fun, too. Very early on I had a hunch that Chris's stuff would fit in with rational expectations, maybe because Granger's criterion was about prediction. It turned out that there's an intimate connection between Granger causality and rational expectations in a whole number of directions, so intimate that if Granger and Sims hadn't talked about that, someone else would have had to invent it. It was increasingly fun to see how these things get merged.

The article that you wrote on the estimation of the dynamic labor demand schedules is instrumental in setting out the heuristics of this econometrics . . .

That paper is full of mistakes. Everything in that paper can be done much better and was in a later paper of Hansen's and mine. That paper is again a step along the way. I don't feel bad about that paper because it attracted interest from people who could do it better. That's basically the philosophy of doing it. When we do research, the idea is that you don't produce a finished product. You produce an input. You write the paper with the hope that it will be superseded. It's not a success unless it's superseded. Research is a living process involving other people.

Am I right in saying that the process of doing your type of econometrics is composed of two processes, one being econometrics without much a priori theory?

That's one line. Chris has taken that much further than I have, and I respect that line. The other line is the cross-equation stuff and doing econometrics with new dynamic theory.

That is very complicated and requires a lot of theoretical work. In a way, the econometrics without the a priori theory helps you in doing the theory.

That's the way I understand it. Bob would probably agree. You have to know what you're after when you're inventing theories. It's a sensible procedure but you can't prove that it's a good idea. There are all sorts of philosophical contradictions in that procedure. The procedure basically contradicts both classical statistics and Bayesian statistics. Classical statistical theory says that you have a hypothesis with which you come to the data in advance. You estimate some regression coefficients and do the tests. It's critical that you didn't look at the data before. Acquiring priors from the data and then going back and using the same data does not seem to be right. Such objections are important for me. I think about them all the time but I don't let them stop me. . . .

I understand that econometric results are uncertain. The models from which they are derived are uncertain. For example, in your paper on the dynamic labor demand function, you have to make all kinds of ad hoc assumptions to make things work.

And that's always going to be true. You can't eliminate arbitrary and particular ad hoc assumptions. You can make them specific and clear to the reader. I think econometrics has a hell of a lot of value in term of clarifying interpretations. I claim that rational expectations is terribly fruitful, even if it never provides a single reliable answer. The reason is that it changes the way you think about policy.

Rational expectations econometrics drives you in the direction of thinking about government strategies and regimes and repetitive actions. You can say that easily, but when you actually grind through all these calculations and understand the analytics of building one of these models and live with it for a couple of years, it forces you to think about what's going on in Washington. It forces you to think not only what's going on today, but of the whole strategy. You look for different things in interpreting different actions. It changes the way you interpret regressions that you see other guys run. In terms of interpreting distributed lags, it gives you a whole arsenal of new ways to interpret. The way that those things used to be interpreted is very different from the way a modern person would interpret them. What's also interesting is the relationship across different equations. To learn how to read those things you have to go through these exercises . . .

ON NONCONVENTIONAL ECONOMICS

You talk a lot about uncertainty. Post-Keynesians do, too.

I don't know that well enough to comment. I read some of it, but not enough.

Is there a communication problem between people like Paul Davidson and you?

I think you can overdo these communication gaps. There's extensive communication with the theorists who are working on uncertainty.

But they reason in your terms, that is, in probabilistic terms. Some Keynesians say that it is impossible to capture uncertainty in those terms.

I don't have anything to say about that . . .

What about Marxists?

I read them a long time ago. I don't know enough about them.

ON DOING ECONOMICS

Math seems to be incredibly important to your work. When did you get interested in math, in college?

No, it didn't happen until I went to Carnegie. If you want to build models, not just talk about them, you have to pick up some tools. Many people told me so. But I have a tremendous aversion to math. I avoided math classes in college. I avoided math when I was a graduate student at Harvard. I didn't start taking formal math until after I went to Minnesota. Then I started taking classes again, essentially because the students knew more math than I did. I still take classes. I have a lot of difficulty with it, so I try to confront it.

Once I can apply math, I like it. I appreciate the beauty of various arguments. But it's a struggle. It's not like watching a movie. One thing that puts people off about this literature is that the mathematics is demanding. I can understand that.

You have the reputation that you prefer to express yourself in math, rather than just talking about things.

It depends on the context. I'm just learning how to talk about these things in nonmathematical ways. So I tried recently to write a couple of papers in economic history without any equations. It's hard.

Lucas says the equations in your joint work come in there because you want them; he gives in.

[Laughter] Bob's work is much more technical than mine; it is very demanding. He uses much harder mathematics than I do. My stuff is mainly a lot of algebra; his stuff is deep mathematics.

Lucas told me about chaotic seminars, for example, at Yale. He enjoyed the feeling of being ahead and stirring emotional reactions. How about you?

I had that experience at a few conferences. I didn't like it. At Minnesota I have a very supportive environment. It's kind of a sleepy environment, a very unpretentious place. It is really nice, very serious. We have discussions that are really dispassionate, very professional.

The controversy about these things is over, though. I recently went down to Yale to give two talks. The atmosphere was very cordial. Everyone was very courteous and kind. I think the revolution is over. The people at Harvard have been really nice to me during my recent stay. I don't have the same sense of controversy that I used to have.

When I'm saying that the revolution is over, I'm talking about what young people are working on. That's the tip-off. Look at what assistant professors are working on at the best places; the questions have changed. Schumpeter and other people have said that the revolutions in science are brought about by young men. They are opposed to the death by old men. Then the young men become middle-aged. The new young men take their pick and generally go with people who pulled off the revolution. That's what's happening this time. . . .

I want to tell you a story about Tobin. There was a conference at the Minnesota Fed in honor of Walter Heller, and all the old people, the heroes of my youth in economics, were there. It was a really nice occasion. Gardner Ackley was giving a talk; it was very negative about the direction of modern macro, saying that there was too much mathematics and that too many assumptions were unrealistic. He also was very critical of rational expectations and of all sorts of modern theorizing. It occurred after two days of really negative things being said about rational expectations. Everybody, including Samuelson, was taking shots at rational expectations. Nobody on our side said anything, in deference to Heller, I suppose. Then Tobin stood up and said that listening to

Ackley's talk reminded him of going to the AEA meetings, after the war in 1946, at which the most-prominent old members of the profession were criticizing the young Keynesians for being unrealistic and too mathematical. Tobin said: "We've had our chance, we haven't solved all the problems. There are a lot of problems left, there are unsatisfactory things about our models, and it's time to give these guys a chance." It was very gracious.

I remember Klein saying something about how uncomfortable he felt about being placed in the position of opposing the recent revolutionary developments in macroeconomics. Those guys pulled off the Keynesian revolution in the US. They were the young guys then. Samuelson and Tobin made it operational. The econometricians were very important; what they were doing was really exciting. I can understand the way Klein feels now.

I myself, however, like going to conferences and seeing these young people running circles around me. Some of the people are people I have taught. To see them surpass me is really a fantastic experience. That's the most rewarding experience I have had in this profession. A guy you remember, who first came to class and didn't know anything, is now inventing new stuff that you have a hard time even understanding, arguments in general that you couldn't have thought of. What's also nice is that some of them got the message, they are building on our shoulders. . . . They are smart. . . . I'm not as smart as some of these guys.

The view you have to have of research is that it is cooperative; you don't have to know everything. The thing is that you want to publish a paper that has an idea that somebody else can make use of and improve on.

What makes an article effective?

I don't think you can answer that question in isolation from a process. The research I'm involved in has this momentum, almost like a deterministic process. Even though there's a lot of uncertainty, you can see what the next step is. There are technical problems in taking it, but you see where you want to go. There are surprises in how it comes out. . . . I feel very much like a player on a team, and I find it very hard to identify anything that I've done by myself. Everything I've written is so heavily dependent on conversations with Neil, Chris, and Bob, and my students. . . . Lots of the credit I have received is not justified. A lot of it belongs to Neil and Chris and my students.

There's a lot to be done in the next 20 years. My prediction is that 15 years from now, macroeconomics is going to look a lot different than it looks now. The prospects for change are much greater now than they were in 1965.

People say that many of your assumptions are unrealistic.

It is true that these assumptions are unrealistic, but what is equally true is, if you take any macro model the assumptions are unrealistic. The Keynesian model is terribly unrealistic. It's equally as unrealistic as ours. These little models are abstractions. The test for whether they're realistic or not is in the econometrics. This is Milton Friedman's line and the line of just about anybody who handles data.

The basic conception of a rational expectations theorist or of an equilibrium theorist of any kind is that he wants to model the world as if there aren't large, unexploited profit potentials which he can spot easily because he's an economist. In some rough way these assumptions make sense to me, but not in every individual case.

They make sense to you as a way people act?

Yeah.

Do you feel comfortable with them?

Yes, about certain matters. I'm aware of all the problems with them. There are philosphical contradictions about using this methodology. Deep down I don't believe in them, but I don't have a better method of understanding what's going on out there. Do I think no one engages in irrational behavior? I don't believe that.

What do you think of Simon's criticism?

People who take that criticism seriously end up doing work like Radner's on the allocation of effort and putting out fires. They end up doing more difficult rational expectations. It remains to be seen whether Simon's criticism is constructive or useful in the sense that I defined earlier, namely that someone builds on it. No one has yet, with the exception of Radner. Radner's work amounts to being a very difficult exercise in rational expectations. The general principle here is that the less information and the harder the choice problem of agents, the more learning you load in, the more difficult is the problem to analyze and to solve. The art is in keeping a model that captures some elements of these things, but is still tractable.

Are you after truth?

Yes. One has a more and more sophisticated notion of what truth is. You find a way of making a model better and better, a model that holds over a wide range of interventions. . . . The notion of truth is a tricky one . . . a continuous process.

Are the political aspects an important motivation?

I'm not really interested in politics. This rational expectations stuff is clearly not politically motivated. People from all sorts of different political perspectives contribute to it. It's more a technical revolution. One of the early lines of criticism was that this was just a new version of right-wing economics. The trouble with that criticism is that most of the guys were voting for McGovern; they were liberal democrats. More than half of the guys anyway. That's not the issue. These are technical issues about staring at models. Actually, the way I got into all this was by staring at Keynesian models. If you look at the Keynesian models, if you stare at them hard, you get to the same point that Lucas was at. That means you're on to something.

No, it's certainly not politically motivated. It is technically motivated. . . . I don't dislike government intervention per se. When I came out of Berkeley and Harvard I had a really naive view of what the government could accomplish. It was my own fault, but I was very pro-intervention: the government should intervene in all sorts of things. I distanced myself from that, but I'm certainly not anti-government. Clearly, you need governments to do things; the question is how are you going to optimally devise institutions for those things. . . . That's the thing we're trying to learn.

4

ROBERT M. TOWNSEND

Sargent urged me to talk with some of the young economists who are "running circles" around him. Townsend is one of these economists. His work is highly theoretical and, consequently, inaccessible to all but a few macro economists.

Townsend received his Ph.D. from the University of Minnesota in 1975. This suggests a direct connection with Sargent and Wallace, who teach at the same university. Currently, he is a full professor at Carnegie-Mellon University. The date of our conversation is December 1982.

BACKGROUND

Why did you get into economics?

My father is an economist. I resisted going into economics for that reason, but I was probably influenced to be interested in the social sciences. When I started to take courses in other social sciences as an undergraduate, I decided that economics had more content and was more satisfying to me.

Do you know why that is?

One other course I had was a course in political science. That was more descriptive and encyclopedic, rather than offering an explanation of things.

What did you like in economics then?

I think it was the contrast. I am not sure; I may be filtering from my current beliefs. As far as those current beliefs are concerned, I like economics because it helps me to understand what I think I see out there. It is a search for explanations. We search for abstractions that shed light on existing arrangements.

Who influenced you in your studies?

I was deeply influenced by the professors I had as a graduate student at the University of Minnesota. I think in particular of Neil Wallace. His influence is general. He taught me how to attack problems: What are the observations? Is there a puzzle? Can we resolve the puzzle? Can we write down a model that is explicit about preferences, endowments, and technology so that we can apply contemporary welfare economics?

I also think of Tom Sargent. We did not interact as much when I was a graduate student as we have done since I left. As of late Tom has had a big influence on my thinking about the relationship of theory to observations, and in particular about time-series analysis. Talking with him always has big rewards for me. Sargent is an important person for many economists these days, through his writing as well as through personal contact. He very much believes in economics and gets excited about it. That is important for me. It helps in getting a little bit of enthusiasm about what we are doing.

Were you good at math when you were studying economics?

I always wish that I had taken more math. As an undergraduate I had enough to read standard-level material in economics; but when I was a graduate student I took a course in real analysis, which was very helpful to me, and for the remaining years I would sit in on math courses. I have continued to build that capital here at Carnegie. There is always a temptation to settle on a fixed capital stock in terms of mathematical tools. That is a mistake. First of all, you have to keep moving forward. Better techniques are needed for that. A second reason for the importance of developing mathematical tools is that somehow you begin to think about a problem differently. I have often been surprised that after you have learned something of interest in mathematics, you discover there is a neat way to use it.

Who do you consider to be the major figures in contemporary macroeconomics for you?

In addition to Sargent and Wallace, I was fortunate to have spent a number of years with Ed Prescott, while he was at Carnegie-Mellon. Ed is an excellent colleague; he has taught me a lot, including dynamic programming and Bayesian analysis.

If you move away from geographical proximity, Bob Lucas has had a tremendous influence on a number of people, directly but also indirectly. When I was at Minnesota the faculty was getting very excited about some of Lucas's work. We studied some of the working papers which are now very important, and often cited pieces in the literature such as "Expectations and the Neutrality of Money," "Equilibrium Search and Unemployment" with Ed Prescott, and a little later his paper on business cycles.

Would you describe him as one of the leaders of the new macroeconomics?

Lucas? Sure.

What do you consider the main events in macroeconomics in the last 10 to 15 years?

Age catches up with me on this one, as I finished my Ph.D. only in 1975. My feeling is that what has happened is a combination of development of techniques and observations of the economy directly. The '70s have been a challenge to the macroeconomic theory of the '50s and '60s, in the sense that the economy seems to grow slower with higher inflation rates. You can try to explain those things with some of the macroeconomic models that I was taught in graduate school, but an alternative seemed to be needed, namely, developing dynamic models in which you are very explicit about the uncertainty. These models can be solved now because we know so much more about dynamic programming and we know a lot about statistical decision theory. So one can think about writing down highly stylized, general equilibrium models of the economy and actually hope to generate time series that fit the observations — if not quantitatively, then qualitatively.

So the development has been mainly technical?

Yes, in large part. I have been going back recently to some older literature and have been surprised by how much is there. For example, I have hit upon a book by Pigou, *Industrial Fluctuations* of 1929, in which there is a great deal. He talks about forecast errors, about waves of optimism and pessimism, and about people getting confused in the sense that they see what other people are doing but are not sure what it means. A lot of that literature is very suggestive. Our standards about what we regard as a good model have changed, but it is possible to read Pigou with great profit.

Why Pigou?

I have been doing some work on dynamic equilibrium models in which decision makers have different information sets. So they are uncertain abou what other people are doing. It was my father who suggested that I read Pigou for this research. A lot of these things are in Keynes as well, such as the emphasis on the dynamics and expectations. I found their books difficult to read as a graduate student and perhaps still do. But I seem now to be able to go back to some of the classics and get a lot more out of them. I am not sure why, but I suppose it is because I now have a larger number of formal models in my head and I am better able to interpret what Pigou had in mind. That is why one wants better techniques. One can now do things that Pigou suggested. He didn't use systems of nonlinear equations.

Lucas also went back to the classics. He didn't like Keynes, though. How about you?

I haven't read enough to say much on that. I tend to think that Pigou dominates Keynes. As I said, I like certain things in Keynes such as his emphasis on expectations, but I have a hard time reading his monetary theory. I have a hard time mapping what Keynes is saying on neoclassical economics into concepts with which I am familiar.

Some people point at new classical economics as the major occurrence in macroeconomics. How would you characterize that type of economics?

What do you mean by new classical economics? I don't use the term.

That is interesting in itself. People use the term to refer to the work of people like Lucas and Sargent. New classical economics, in this use of the term, involves the claim that systematic government policy is ineffective.

I can comment on that. The ineffectiveness proposition is unfortunately still plaguing the profession. It is not right, for example, that rational expectations imply that any policy is ineffective. What people have in mind, I think, is a paper of Sargent and Wallace which shows that, in a traditional macro model, the foreseen parts of monetary policy do not have an effect on real variables. More generally, it is not right that money does not matter. One can write down explicit dynamic models that allow for uncertainty and include rational expectations, but produce the result that money matters.

Lucas and Sargent still maintain, this possibility notwithstanding, that the government should not conduct an active stabilization policy because it increases the uncertainty.

There may be a reluctance to adopt an active policy for that reason. But I should not attempt to speak for others.

I try to make the following distinction. New classical economics, if I can use the term, does not go hand in hand with policy ineffectiveness. New classical economics means a modeling strategy which allows for a variety of results.

How could we characterize that modeling strategy?

There is probably a continuum, from one model to another. It is hard to come up with a tight definition. To me it is, ideally, writing down the model at the level of the tastes or preferences of the decision-makers, the technology available, whatever initial wealth or endowment decison-makers have, and then imposing some additional structure. One can have long discussions on the fruitful way of doing the latter. One way is to put limits on the ability of decision-makers to communicate with one another or, more directly, to impose costs of exchange on the agents, or to impose constraints on the information available to the decision-makers.

Is the specification of the available information important in your work?

Oh yes. There are some explicit restrictions on communication in some of that work as well but, it is right, in general, that differences in information are quite important.

Anyway, you take these models, specified at some level, and try to confront them with some observations, at least if that was the initial motivation. That is the message of the neutrality paper of Lucas [1972] where the observation was the Phillips curve. That is also what Lucas was up to in his business cycle paper [1975].

But people like Tobin and Modigliani say that there is not much new in that modeling strategy. They too have been trying to ground macro relationships in neoclassical maximization postulates.

I am sometimes surprised by the extent to which there seems to be disagreement among these people. We should talk about a specific model to say what was new and what was not.

Well, let us take Lucas's neutrality paper [1972].

In that paper he made use of statistical decision theory or the idea that people try to use all available information. But information is limited. When you see prices moving, you are not sure whether that is because money has moved or whether it is a local, real movement. The point is that it was done precisely and explicitly, that is, worked out in a formal model.

Should I add the introduction of stochastic elements?

That goes hand in hand with statistical decision theory. But yes, that was new too. In this model people understand that stochastic processes generate the data that they see. They just do not have enough data to figure out the underlying movement in the shocks. So it is a formalization of ideas that have been around for some time. Again one can go back. For example, the idea that prices convey information, some but not all, is in Friedrich Von Hayek.

A lot of people are confused by the notion of equilibrium which seems to be crucial in the modeling strategy about which you are talking. James Tobin, Alan Blinder, and John Taylor, for example, do not see how you can model business cycles as equilibrium phenomena. What is that controversy according to you?

I think that if you would sit down with people who seem to disagree, you might find less disagreement than is apparent. The term "equilibrium" has often implied different things to different people. By way of example, in the physical sciences people have thought of *equilibrium* to mean at rest, static, or something to which a system tends if it is stable. In applied economics that language can be very misleading. It is certainly possible to write down an economic model in which decision-makers face intertemporal problems and generate time series which may or may not tend to something. But you can do it in a way that you can, in the end, refer to the model as an equilibrium model, even though it is not at all at rest. In fact, you can have uncertainty as well, not just the time element, and have decision-makers hit by well-defined shocks and still call it an equilibrium model.

I haven't yet told you, though, what I mean by an equilibrium model. There are two ideas in any concept of equilibrium as I use it. One is the idea that decision-makers try to do as best they can; that is, they not only try to make optimal choices, but also make the best use of the available information. The second idea is that there is consistency between outcomes that are generated by the model and the outcomes that the decision-makers anticipate. An extreme form of that is perfect foresight. Less extreme forms of that have uncertainty, and require the specification of the distribution of prices generated by the model. Here we get into rational expectations. It is possible that decision-makers have different information or anticipate different distributions that are all consistent with the time series generated by the model.

I guess that what a lot of people have in mind when they speak of equilibrium is market clearing. It is certainly true that in a particular instance, if we are thinking about a Walrasian world, we get an equilibrium where the prices that are anticipated are the ones that are generated under market clearing. But one can also define a broader class of games, that is, write down the strategies agents employ. They may set the prices themselves.

John Taylor, among others, appears to disagree with the idea that you can formulate realistic models with market-clearing prices.

The issue is how you write down the frictions. John says, "Look, contracts seem to be limited; they specify a nominal wage over the duration of the contract." Let us take as given that is the way the world is and model it that way. Let us then proceed with the usual postulates of what you call new classical economics. In terms that I have been using, the issue is on what level you impose the frictions. John is not really modeling the underlying circumstances that generate contracts of fixed duration. Attempts to model the underlying rigidities quickly reveal that there is no magic. We always impose structure somewhere. But in my view it will prove fruitful to push the structure further back. In that way we may hope to actually explain observed contractual arrangements and limited price movements, and, in addition, find a basis for economic policy from contemporary welfare economics. But, of coure, we shouldn't try to do everything in a given model. John Taylor's work provides us with valuable insights.

John Taylor also suggests that the new classical equilibrium models presume perfectly flexible prices. Others have asserted the same.

A lot of the well-known equilibrium models do postulate market clearing and therefore flexible prices. We do not have a lot of models in which decision-makers actually set prices. I can imagine that in a world with costly communication there might be some reason for not changing prices all the time.

Frictions are important in your models. How do you decide on a particular form of friction? For example, why do you assume costs of verification and problems of communication?

I should be candid and say that I have been exploring lots of alternatives. You may have in mind some observations. To go back to the example of contracts, you could ask which type of contracts we see. Your observations may suggest a certain type of model. I don't think there are general rules. Sometimes it works; sometimes it doesn't.

When does it work?

If we take contract theory again, the observation is that there is a lot of simple, noncontingent debt. If that is the stylized fact, you are successful when you get it out, that is, if the model generates a contract that has that property.

I should quickly add that things are often not what they seem. Debt is often contingent, even though we act as if it weren't. That suggests a number of things. First of all, you may not have correctly characterized the world; your stylized facts may be wrong. Sometimes you are not done because you imposed some structure in the model when you didn't want to. For example, in the contract theory I am referring to, you get a form of apparent arrangements if you do not allow for random auditing. If you allow random audit, however, then there may be better contracts than the ones I have described. That means I haven't succeeded in modeling observed arrangements. And we do see some auditing. One direction to go is to find out more about audits and try to match up the model with the findings.

In some work that I have been doing on monetary economics, the restrictions are much less obvious. I have been experimenting with a number of alternatives, and I am certainly open to new directions on that. We know relatively little about these models yet. For example, the popularity of the overlapping generations model as a model of money is that it is an explicit model and you can get results out of it. I have moved away from that toward spatial models. But we are still learning about these models.

One problem is that the restrictions imposed by spatial separation leave the equilibria nonoptimal. That is troublesome. It suggests that you failed to model the limitations on exchange.

Do I sense another criteria, namely that your models should be Pareto optimal?

I am talking about modeling strategies, not about the way the world is. There is a danger that if one insists that the outcome be Pareto optimal, it is easily translated into the statement that we live in the best of all possible worlds. That has all kinds of implications for policy. My thinking about policy is still very early on. So I don't want to say that my models should produce a Pareto optimal outcome, but I do think that as a check on the model, it is very useful to ask whether the outcome is Pareto optimal and if not, why not. If you can't figure out where the structure is imposed, that is to say, why the outcome is suboptimal, then it leaves something up in the air.

That means that you are discontent with the model?

I am quite happy with many aspects of the spatial models. Many of the results are often quite intuitive. I am less happy that these models are associated with Pareto-nonoptimal outcomes. But, as I said, we are still learning about the spatial models. It may well be that there is a way to write down the limitations that you impose explicitly so that the equilibrium is optimal in some sense.

It is suggested that the notion of a stochastic equilibrium, as introduced by Lucas, and as you describe it, is novel. Is that right?

I believe that it is.

How does it connect with the tradition of Kenneth Arrow and Gerard Debreu?

It is very much in that tradition. The contribution of Arrow and Debreu, for example, has been to write down formally the decision problems of households and firms and not only to define competitive equilibrium, but also formally prove that an equilibrium exists.

Some people say that learning is a major problem that you should deal with. You have dealt with it somewhat by using Bayesian techniques. Lucas and Sargent are quite skeptical as to the possibilities of this direction of research. [See Lucas and Sargent, 1977.] How do you look at it now?

I am not sure that they are skeptical. One has to be careful with Bayesian techniques. If one writes down a model with arbitrary a priori beliefs, then indeed you may not have much content. Lots of time series can be generated: it is only a matter of finding the right prior. But you can do Bayesian analysis and can get rid of the effect of arbitrary priors. One way to do that is to imagine that although priors are arbitrary at some initial data, decision-makers are forming posteriors over time as they see more and more observations. If you are explicit about the information structure, that is to say, how the exogenous information sets are generated and therefore how the endogenous variables are generated and what decision-makers see, then it may well be that in some limiting sense the priors don't matter.

What I am thinking of is a dynamic model where indeed there may be some initial conditions that correspond to the parameters, but in which nothing remains the same and stochastic processes move the parameters around. We try to learn about the initial parameters, but we also try to learn about the new shocks and the history of shocks. This system settles down, not to a situation in which everyone is sure about everything, but to one in which there is more or less a constant degree of uncertainty; the variances of beliefs are constant, but means of beliefs move around with current information sets. So you can generate a lot of movement in time series and match the theory with observations.

ON DOING ECONOMICS AND ABOUT ECONOMIC POLICY

You suggest that there is not really a controversy and that disagreements are not fundamental. Other economists, such as the neo-Keynesians, seem to disagree with that.

There are various kinds of disagreements, I suppose. There can be disagreements over methods and disagreements over the plausibility of existing models.

How about disagreements on policy?

Certainly that. I guess that such disagreements have generated much of the differences. It is certainly right that not everyone agrees on monetary policy.

How is that possible with all the rigor and precision of economic models?

We can be rigorous and precise and still write down different models. It depends on what you put in.

But we should be able to check which theory is best.

That is the hope [pause]. It is harder in economics, perhaps, than in physical sciences. It is harder to check theories against observations (although I am still learning about this). You don't get sharp rejections of a model.

Why do you think you are right?

I am more convinced that there be a big pay-off to some of the research strategies that I have been describing than I am that the current models give all the answers. Perhaps that is why I think that there can be less disagreement than there seems to be. Take, for example, the idea that there ought to be an activist monetary policy. That is true in Keynesian models in which one a priori fixes something like a wage on the basis of the observation of contracts (I think of Taylor's models). But the issue is to explain the contracts. Well, people who work on contract theory have been able to generate contracts which are of a limited form. That leaves open the question of whether such contracts allow a role for monetary policy. It is possible. That is perhaps the bridge.

You have to be very careful. The tradition that argues against an active policy does so with a premise that the monetary authorities are not better informed than the individual decision makers are and that monetary policy creates more uncertainty than it resolves.

Do you find that argument reasonable?

I am still thinking about these ideas. It is clear that we can write down explicit formal models which imply an active monetary policy. And I believe we are close to writing down models with explicit frictions in which monetary policy emerges naturally as an essential part of an efficient social arrangement. My guess is that policy rules in such models will be active in the sense that monetary choice variables will be nontrivial functions of the current state of the economy, or, better put, nontrivial functions of individual announcements or indications of privately observed states. But I suspect these optimal rules will not be time consistent, that there will be pressure to change the rules over time. In that sense we would still not want a discretionary policy, though the policy rules themselves are nontrivial.

I don't think it is clear to me, yet, why you, on the basis of your models, are reluctant to accept the discretionary policy for which neo-Keynesians argue.

It is hard to write down formal models which argue for a discretionary policy as distinct from active policy. I guess it is not clear to me what is meant by discretionary policy. The fundamental difficulty in all of this is modeling what we mean by unanticipated economic changes or, perhaps, uncertainty in the sense of Knight.

Do your models help you to understand current events, such as an unemployment rate of 10.8 percent?

Not completely. The unemployment has gotten worse in the last decade. I wonder why that is so.

What is your story? What do you tell your students?

When I give students a series of models, I tell them that the models miss something and that we have to keep working on them. I really think that we are missing something.

It seems to me from talking with you that you are more committed to your modeling strategies than to any ideas, say political ideas or ideology. Is that right?

I have been surprised a number of times by the results of my models. I like to think that we are writing down a version of reality. If those versions produce results contrary to my own earlier thinking, then I would take the results seriously.

So it is not that you are necessarily opposed to government intervention?

I am still very early on in thinking about what the government is. It is clear that we need rules and regulations; we don't want anarchy. But which rules . . . that is not quite clear.

I believe that the distinction between laissez-faire and government control is somewhat overdrawn. Again, it might be fruitful to think of searching for efficient social structures and to ask what form of collective agreements are implied by particular economic environments. Government, then, might be thought of as a collective agreement. The problem of this conception is that governments, as we know them, seem to become institutions in themselves, often resistant to change, though individuals or groups of individuals seek to innovate. Eventually, though, innovations from groups of individuals often become the basis for new forms of government. Again, the difficulty is modeling unanticipated economic change.

It is common to associate conservative ideology with your type of models. Is that association right according to you?

I don't know what the term conservative means. If it means no government intervention it is a nonsensical position. No one will agree with that. It seems clear to me that societies at various points in time have gotten stuck with bad regimes and that people did not live in the best of all possible worlds. The issue, then, is how to implement change.

Are you sympathetic of what Reagan is trying to do to the U.S. economy?

I favor the deregulation as I did with Carter, but in general I am disappointed. More often than not, Reagan seems to fall back on dogma.

Many people characterize your models as esoteric and question the realism of the assumptions. How do you react to criticisms like that?

I do believe that we have to get better and better in building these models. It is certainly a legitimate path. Some papers may seem to be technical and removed from actual observations, but I think most of what I do is relevant for explaining observations. It may appear to be abstract, but in some cases that is because it is unfamiliar. We all interpret what we see, that is to say, we all use abstractions. One might have in mind competitive markets or a Walrasian abstraction; but then you look and you do not see market clearing in the usual sense. Still, there might be an abstraction that is consistent with equilibrium and the observations.

What about Milton Friedman's argument that the realism of assumptions does not matter?

I essentially agree with that very much. One is looking for the key elements.

Let me give you an example. In the work on contracts with Prescott, where we try to do standard competitive analysis when there is private information, the commodity space that we need is essentially a space of contracts which have lots of contingencies in them, contingencies which are effected entirely by the individuals. So, that is what the theory predicts. And you see these things. For example, future contracts are not simple promises to buy a commodity at a certain time and location; they are loaded with all sorts of contingencies. The point is that the highly abstract theory, when believed in and used to filter observations, makes you see things that you did not see before. I always find that very satisfying.

Do you believe that people in the street are using optimizing strategies or that they strive for self interests?

I do think that people try the best they can.

What about Herbert Simon's criticism?

He was rightly complaining about some, if not a lot, of the economic literature at the time that he was moving away from economics. I have a couple of comments. I think a lot of the models that we have now, with the dynamics and the uncertainty, address a lot of the observations that were troubling Herb Simon. He is, by the way, a big proponent of positive economic methods.

Another thing that I want to say is that we still fall short of models that explain a lot of observations. I don't think that we know what a firm is yet and decision-making within a firm. So a lot of work still has to be done.

And you are optimistic that it can be done?

Yes, I sure am.

PART TWO

Conversations with Neo-Keynesian Economists: The "Older Generation"

5

JAMES TOBIN

The Nobel prize-winner in 1981, James Tobin hardly needs an introduction. He is a major figure in the effort to join neo-Keynesian macroeconomics and neoclassical microeconomics. The Nobel prize was awarded — according to the official citation — "for his analysis of financial markets and their relationship with spending and thereby with employment, production, and price movements." The citation also mentions his development of portfolio theory which he explained to the press at the time as the theory that rational people do not put all their eggs in one basket. He has also played a significant role in politics as a member of the Council of Economic Advisers in 1961–1962 and as a continuing adviser and commentator on economic policy.

It is told that a student who wrote a dissertation under Tobin once felt compelled to explain to Tobin an advanced econometric technique that he was using, presuming that Tobin would not know about it. Tobin listened and seemed interested, but did not say very much. The student told a fellow student about this, and to his surprise the latter burst out laughing and replied, "So you didn't know that that technique was Tobin's idea?" Apocryphal or not, the story tells us much about Tobin's character.

His Ph.D. degree was from Harvard (1947), and his main career commitment has been to Yale University. We talked in New York in October 1982.

SOME BACKGROUND

Why did you choose to study economics?

I went into economics for two reasons. One was that as a child of the Depression I was terribly concerned about the world. It seemed then that many of the problems were economic in origin. If you thought that the world should be saved, and I did, then economics looked like the decisive thing to study. The second thing was that you could have your cake and eat it too, because it was an intellectually fascinating subject.

How did you discover that?

I discovered that very simply. When I went to Harvard as an undergraduate, I took a course in economics. In those days you had a "tutor", as you have in Cambridge or Oxford, as a kind of fifth course. I was assigned to a young man, Spencer Pollard, an advanced graduate student (he was also my teacher in the introductory economics course), and he said, "There's this new book that's just come over from England and let's you and I read that this year." I was just a sophomore in college and I hadn't had any economics — I was just taking the introductory course. I didn't know enough to know that I should be scared, so I started out reading *The General Theory*.

That is a difficult book!

It was a difficult book, but when you are 19 you don't know what's difficult and what's not. You just plow into it.

You realized then that it was good?

Well, it had everything that appealed to a young politically conscious, socially conscious person with quantitative theoretical interest and aptitude.

The General Theory *is not that quantitative though.*

It's quantitative in the sense it's theory and there are functions, and simultaneous equations and all that.

So, that's what got me started.

Which people do you consider to have been your mentors during your education?

Spencer Pollard was important to me. But then there were important senior people who had a big influence on me. One, of course, was Alvin Hansen, who came to Harvard just about the same time I did. Another was Seymour Harris who took a generous interest in my career from freshman year on. So did Ed Mason. And Edward Chamberlin who was my tutor in senior year. Schumpeter was my teacher, friend, and my Ph.D. thesis adviser. He didn't sympathize with Keynes, but he was very helpful to all young students.

What did you learn from him?

You know, I don't think I learned anything particularly substantive from him. I just learned a kind of general style of being an economist.

I suppose those were the most important people to me. But there were many others around, brilliant younger faculty and graduate students like Lloyd Metzler, Richard Goodwin and Paul Samuelson. Paul Samuelson was an *enfant terrible*! He was a brash, young guy who was sort of a bull in the china shop, asking embarrassing questions of the senior people.

How were you in those days?

I was certainly not like that. I was a very, very shy, noncompetitive individual.

Did people think you were good?

Oh yes. They did. I wrote good papers. I wrote a senior paper as an undergraduate that also led to an article in the *Quarterly Journal of Economics*.

The war interrupted your studies . . .

Yes, I was away from economics for four and a half years. Completely away from it. After the war, I went back to Harvard and finished graduate work.

Was it hard to come back?

It was surprisingly easy. It's hard to tell you what a golden age it was. There was a confluence of several generations of people — veterans — coming back to graduate school. Very bright people, and very highly motivated and mature after being in the war. It was a very stimulating group. A whole battery of people who are the senior members of the profession now were there. Paul Samuelson, Bob Solow, Jim Duesenberry, Tom Schelling, Carl Caysen, John Lintner, and so on. Paul Sweezy was there at the time too. I had a course with him.

I understand that many of the teachers at that time did not want to have all that much to do with Keynes.

Yes, Alvin Hansen was an exception and Seymour Harris was too. Seymour Harris was very much a Keynesian and promoter of Keynes. I don't think I ever took a course with him.

There was this feeling that we were on the right path and had the right answers, or at least that we would find them.

You mean that you had the feeling that Keynes was it?

It was not just Keynes. Econometrics was just coming in, and that was intellectually exciting as well. I also attended as undergraduate a course on general equilibrium theory with Schumpeter as teacher and people such as Paul Samuelson, Lloyd Metzler, and R. G. D. Allen as students. As you know, Hicks, Allen and Samuelson basically imported general equilibrium theory from the Continent into Anglo-American economics.

Was there a sense that you were fighting the establishment in economics?

You had that sense more before than after the war. Before the war you were fighting the establishment, but there were many people at Harvard fighting, so you were not alone.

Did you believe that what happened then was something revolutionary?

Definitely. There wasn't any macroeconomics as a subject before Keynes. If you look back at the history of economics you can find things which you can say in retrospect are macroeconomics. But the idea of a theory of output as a whole—I guess that this was Mrs. Robinson's term—was new.

Then it was a general equilibrium system in that it was a closed system with simultaneous equations that determined all the variables, given the exogenous variables. In that sense, it was methodologically consonant with what Paul Samuelson was doing in the *Foundations* for microeconomics. The happy circumstance was that it became more operational because national income statistics were just becoming available. The methods of economic statistics of those days may not seem sophisticated now, but they did then. The most important thing, in the intellectual sense, was simply the realization that you had a model that fitted the obvious facts much better.

But not everyone agreed at that time.

That was true, but the debate was all in favor of the revolution [laughter].

And then you achieved a near consensus in the '60s.

That was building up during the '50s, in the so-called neoclassical synthesis, better called the neoclassical-neo-Keynesian synthesis, I think. The main thing was that classical economics didn't explain the Great Depression and didn't give you any hope of solving it. Keynesian economics did.

How important was the Council of Economic Advisers for the introduction of Keynesian economics into politics?

There was a very Keynesian council under the Harry Truman presidency which was chaired by Leon Keyserling. It was swept away in 1953 when Eisenhower came in, and Arthur Burns became the chairman. So when Heller, Kermit Gordon, and I came in in 1961, it was a bit of an exaggeration to speak of New Economics. It was't all that new, but it certainly had a heyday then.

Some people told me that there was an excitement within the council because politicians, and in particular Kennedy, really listened.

That is right. There was.

ABOUT KEYNESIAN ECONOMICS

Do you mind being called a Keynesian?

I don't mind that. I think that I am neoclassical also. In the view of people who call themselves post-Keynesians I am a reactionary.

What is a neo-Keynesian?

I think the basic issue there is the question of whether there are any dead weight losses or market failures of a macroeconomic nature in a market economy. Neo-Keynesians think there are and that the government can do something about them. They think that demand management policy can assist the economy to stay close to its equilibrium track.

Does a political or social sentiment underlie this position?

Logically there need not be any. But there is a correlation. A neo-Keynesian seems to be more concerned about employment, jobs, and producing goods than people who have a great faith in market processes.

We experience stagflation, or a combination of high unemployment and inflation rates. How would you account for this experience within a neo-Keynesian-neoclassical framework?

That gets us into the history of the economic world in the US since 1966. Probably there were some mistakes in demand management policy. I wouldn't deny that. In fact, it was a council of neo-Keynesian advisors that told Johnson that he should raise taxes for the Vietnam War. But, actually, I think the main source of the stagflation is to be found in the shocks from OPEC in the '70s. They are stagflationary shocks because they reduce aggregate demand and raise prices at the same time. The dilemma of economic policy in 1973–74 and again in 1979, the times of the two OPEC crises, was how much you accommodate and how much you don't. Most countries did a bit of each.

How about problems in the labor market?

There are problems in the labor market and there always have been. When I was a graduate student back in 1946 we had a common saying around the department at Harvard among the students that, of three objectives — price stability, full employment, and freedom from wage and price controls — a democratic capitalist country could not expect to have more than two. So we thought there was a basic structural problem, an inflationary bias, or something like that in the wage- and price-setting institutions. That kind of thing was magnified in unprecedented proportions by the OPEC shocks.

You believe in incomes policy.

That is for the reason I just gave. I don't think it is possible to combine the objectives, at least all the time.

Economists generally resist any form of incomes policy.

I know they do. I would say that you don't have easy choices, and you have to weigh the costs of alternative options.

How do you justify an incomes policy theoretically?

I have read about and thought about policies like TIP, the tax-based incomes policies, and satisfied myself that, although it won't be easy to do, it would be a less costly method of disinflation than what we are doing.

So why isn't it implemented?

It is politically difficult. It takes presidential leadership of a high order and the establishment of a consensus that would support that kind of a policy. I believe that the invisible hand theory is pretty powerful among politicians. So a policy like TIP gets dismissed. I would ask what costs are you worrying about and are they of the same magnitude as the costs of 10 percent plus unemployment. I don't think that they are in the same ball park as far as social costs are concerned. But that is not an argument to which most members of the profession would agree.

After trying for a long time to push for Keynesian policies to combat unemployment, isn't it frustrating to see an unemployment rate of more than 10 percent?

Yes, that is frustrating. It has a *déjà-vu* sense about it [laughter]. I don't know what you could do about it. The things that I have written on this subject in the last couple of years have been right.

Have you ever been wrong to the extent that you have reversed your position?

I was never under any illusion about the theoretical possibility that the Phillips curve is vertical. In fact, I could cite passages that precede Friedman and Phelps, which say that it could well be. But all the empirical findings before 1966 suggested that the feedback term from price inflation to wages was considerably less than one so I accepted a nonvertical Phillips curve. I was probably overoptimistic about the degree to which you could expand employment in the '60s. In fact, I have acknowledged that in print. We at the Council had stated 4 percent as what would now be called the natural rate of unemployment, I suppose, with a nonaccelerating rate of inflation. We did get the 4 percent before the Vietnam War, and we didn't have any accelerating rate of inflation. Maybe that was because we had an incomes policy. It was a rather weak one; it was sometimes called "open-mouth" policy. It was an informal guide-post policy, but in retrospect it looks like it made more difference than people credited it for. At any rate, the acceleration of inflation came when Johnson disobeyed his economic advisers. We went down to 3 percent unemployment which was probably well below the natural rate. So, I could admit to having been too optimistic.

But that doesn't imply that your theory has been wrong, does it?

I hope, well, I guess not.

Economists used to say that they change their theories if proven wrong. But that almost never happens, at least not as far as general theories are concerned. Economists do not change their perspective, it seems.

I know one who changed, Alvin Hansen. He changed at the age of 52. He had written a very negative review of the *General Theory* when it first came out. Later, he clearly reversed his position. But I agree with you that that is quite unusual.

In your work, you sometimes refer to factors such as confidence and the animal spirits. What do you mean by that?

This is another point on which I have changed my mind. In my work on growth theory, in particular the neoclassical part, I took investment to be a more mechanical function of the interest rate and some other factors. I don't think I really appreciated Keynes's point until more recently.

But that makes the theory less tight. Irregular events are now simply attributed to "animal spirits." That must make a theorist uncomfortable.

That is right. It's too bad.

What about expectations?

I think I was slow to use expectations in my work. It was a failure of understanding, I guess. It is interesting that there is a lot in Keynes about expectations of the marginal efficiency of capital but very little about expectations of inflation. So we all learned something from recent experiences.

ABOUT THE MONETARIST CHALLENGE TO NEO-KEYNESIAN ECONOMICS

You suggest in your writing that there is a crisis in macroeconomics. Not everyone appears to agree.

The crisis results from the problem that Keynesian macroeconomics has never been anchored in the normal paradigm of theoretical economics; that is, in a theory that is satisfying to microeconomists and general equilibrium theorists. That is one side of a crisis that has been smoldering for many years.

On the other side the paradigm of utility maximization, competitive markets, and profit maximization does not explain the facts. Not only does it fail to explain them by the standard of econometric tests, it fails to explain facts that everybody can see without doing any further testing.

When did you begin to realize that Milton Friedman's counterrevolution was something to reckon with?

I could go back to Clark Warburton, who was a very dedicated scholar in monetary economics and who wrote monetarist things in the '40s. I had a published controversy with him.

I think that people started to take Friedman seriously as soon as his stuff with Meiselman on the explanatory power of money came out. I also recall attending a conference on the Friedman-Schwartz volume when it was just coming out. That was in the early '60s.

Did you ever talk with Friedman about these things?

Yes, but not an awful lot. Friedman came to Yale once and gave a talk called "Yale versus Chicago in Monetary Theory" before a house of 500 people.

How was that?

[Laughter.] It was quite interesting. I didn't get much involved at all in public, but we had a small private session afterwards. The thing I remember most about the occasion was that there was a very earnest, well-meaning graduate student who stood up at the big meeting and asked Friedman politely: "In your model, money is the basic concept, and yet, you haven't ever told us exactly what money is conceptually. Could you help us understand it now?" Friedman cut the guy down in the withering way he can do by telling him that he didn't understand scientific methods. He said Newton didn't have to tell what gravity was; he only had to tell what it does. The same applied to money. That illustrates Friedman's methodology of positive economics which I think has done great damage.

Why?

You see that in Lucas, too. Their idea is the as-if methodology in which it is not a question whether the assumptions are realistic, but whether the results derived from the assumptions are consonant with the facts of observations. My reaction is that we are not so good at testing hypotheses so that we can give up any information we have at whatever stage of the argument. The realism of assumptions does matter. Any evidence you have on that, either casual or empirical, is relevant.

This issue played throughout the controversy that I had with Milton Friedman. The controversy began about the interest elasticity of the demand for money. Friedman always said that, in principle, the demand should be elastic but that empirically the elasticity is not large enough to matter. He used his pseudo reduced form expressions to show that money and nominal income are highly correlated, and he dismissed all the evidence acquired with structural equations. Eventually, he abandoned that tactic and concluded, in his famous remark, that no important proposition of theory or policy depends on the interest elasticity of the demand for money, at least as long as it is not infinite.

You are brilliant, but so is he. Still, it seems to be hard for the both of you to come to any form of agreement. Why is that?

In this case, one reason it didn't work is that Friedman always replied that he didn't say what I said he had said. And I was simply saying what everybody believed Friedman had been saying.

Do you think that such a problem of communication is typical among economists?

No, I don't think so. But I believe that Friedman had a crusade that he was pushing all over the world, not just in the profession. He saw the big picture, and the big picture was right for him. He didn't really want to be bothered by these little technical problems.

ABOUT NEW CLASSICAL ECONOMICS

The new classical revolution appears to have much in common with the monetarist revolution.

You could say that it is as much a revolution against old monetarism as it is against Keynesianism. The disagreement between monetarists and Keynesians was about the value of some parameters. It is not as fundamental a split as we experience now.

You were at the 1970 conference where Lucas presented his first paper, in which he combined the natural rate of unemployment hypothesis and the rational expectations hypothesis. You criticized him quite severely. Why?

I criticized him but also praised him. I really thought that it was a neat piece of theory and very interesting.

Was the concept of rational expectations new to you at that time?

I knew about it only casually. I had heard at second hand about John Muth. But I could see that Lucas had come up with a good argument, that observations that you have interpreted one way could have been generated another way. That is the basic argument, it was ingenious and it was new to me, at least at the time. So I took it seriously. But I don't think that I was conscious at that point that this was going to become as important to the profession and beyond the profession as it turned out to be.

Initially, the new classical position was highly controversial. Lucas and Sargent recall chaotic seminars at which they were severely attacked. Did you experience that?

I was friendly but critical of Lucas at the Washington conference. I met Lucas again at Yale when he presented his "Inflation-Output Trade-off" paper [1973]. Sargent gave a paper at Brookings in 1974 that I didn't understand very well. I though he made a mistake and we talked about that. But he didn't make his general stance very clear to me at that time.

What do you think are the contributions of new classical economists?

Rational expectations is an innovation in model building. It exposes the problem in other models, that actual behavior may be inconsistent with the behavior predicted by the model.

But isn't the assumption of rational expectations unrealistic?

That may be so, but other assumptions about how expectations are generated open models to all kinds of arbitrary implications or results.

But rational expectations cannot be all that new classical economists have contributed?

Once you assume rational expectations, there are all kinds of technical problems. I, personally, do not find them interesting. I might, if I took the time to go into them, but I have not tried to do that. It seems to be very difficult to me.

For example, Sargent makes the point that the way theory was linked with econometrics is arbitrary. One tacks on stochastic terms without any explanation.

That is true. It is a good point but a very difficult one to implement. It is not different from the spirit of the Cowles Commission econometrics

40 years ago. Koopmans, Habelman, and their colleagues, they too had the idea that you should use methods of econometrics which are consistent with the way in which you model the generation of the data and the error terms. The difference, as I understand it, lies in the question what you take as exogenous and what you take as endogenous. Lucas, Sargent, and so on will say that the structure, as written down by macroeconomists, changes when policy regimes change. A more general way to put it is that the structure changes when the environment changes, whether by policy or not. Think of supply shocks. It is a good point, but again very difficult to implement. I understand, though, why it is exciting for young people in the profession. It is challenging; it provides new mathematical problems.

Does it appeal to your own students?

Oh, yes. I think that they should be intrigued by it, but they should also realize the limitations of the application of these things to the world.

I think that you can separate new classical macroeconomics from rational expectations. New classical macroeconomics includes, in addition to the assumption of rational expectations, the assumption of market clearing by prices.

New classical economists stress the importance of policy rules. The effect of a government that adheres to rules would reduce uncertainty. What do you think of that?

I don't think that it is actually functional. I notice that rules usually come down to being very simple rules. You cannot imagine operating with complex feedback rules. You just cannot write the formula down in sufficient detail to cover all the things that might happen. Therefore, I think that the idea of rules versus discretion is an overdrawn dichotomy. If we incorporate new information for the determination of policy, and I think we should, the policy is bound to become discretionary. Most of what actually goes on in policy-making is vague, as to whether it falls within a particular regime or without. That makes the idea of policy regime rather difficult to apply.

New classical economists also stress the importance of grounding behavioral assumptions in neoclassical postulates of optimizing behavior. Do you agree with that?

I agree with that to a certain point. I think that they are overambitious in that respect, unrealistically so. In their view, paths of adjustment to

change, as well as basic choices, should be described as explicit outcomes of maximizing behavior. You should derive the times of adjustment, decisions, alterations of previous habits, and so on. I don't think
you can do that. I always thought that we have a lot of freedom to specify what happens in the adjustment from one situation to another. We
don't have the apparatus to deal with things like decision and transaction costs. The technologies are probably not convex, so they probably
do not correspond to the paradigm that we like to use. I don't think that
you can carry out that program.

*That is quite fundamental. They say that if you take their program seriously, then it
implies that you assume market clearing prices.*

Yes, but I haven't been able to understand that proposition at all.

Why is that?

Rational expectations by itself seems to me separable from the assumption of price-cleared markets. It could be used in a model in which
quantity adjustments were helping to equate supply and demand.
Lucas himself says that he adopts the market clearing assumption because it is convenient, not because it is realistic. We are back to the "as
if" methodology again. He says he doesn't know how to cope analytically with prices which are decision variables for businesses and other
economic agents.

The new classicals will also say that if you observe long-term contracts, which on the surface seem to depart from market clearing prices,
you can simply reinterpret what market clearing prices are. You
reinterpret the demand and supply functions under the constraint of the
contracts. But then, they are not able to maintain the strong propositions that they were able to derive from their other models, notably
about policy ineffectiveness.

Their point is also that you must understand why people make contracts.

I know that, but then you will no longer have policy ineffectiveness.
Contracts will change when the government changes its policy, but that
takes time. Most of the problems of stabilization policy, about which
we are actually worried, occur within the period of learning and adjusting that they say is insignificant or trivial.

I notice that in discussions on the content of contracts, new classical
macroeconomists tend to argue that rational agents will cover all contingencies. In short, they ask why rational agents don't make Arrow-

Debreu contracts. Of course, if we lived in an Arrow-Debreu world — or a world where people can buy and sell all commodities for delivery in all future periods and in all states of nature — there wouldn't be any need for money and there wouldn't be any macroeconomic problems. The fact that covering all contingencies is costly, indeed impossible, and that a full set of Arrow-Debreu markets doesn't begin to exist, is in a sense the source of macroeconomic difficulties and the reason that macro policies can make a difference.

But they reply that the possibility of an effective policy is still not an invitation for such a policy. Their point is that active policy adds only to the confusion.

I don't think that they have solidly examined the time scales that are involved in these adjustment and learning processes. They try to explain business cycles solely as problems of information, such as asymmetries and imperfections in the information agents have. Those assumptions are just as arbitrary as the institutional rigidities and inertia they find objectionable in other theories of business fluctuations. They are just as ad hoc as talking about habitual patterns or contracts or business confidence.

Lucas was clearly not pleased with your interpretation of his work in your Jahnsson lectures. Why do you think that was?

I don't think I misinterpreted him. It is not clear to me why he reacted the way he did. He didn't really discuss my interpretations and criticisms of new classical economics. Instead he took the opportunity of the review to say that Keynesian economics was discredited by the stagflation of the '70s, as he and Sargent had already argued in their polemical piece "After Keynesian Economics" at the Nantucket conference in 1978. The idea seems to be that we were very wrong about the 1970s and therefore had no standing to criticize the new classical macroeconomics. Of course, I do not agree with that interpretation of the events of the last 15 years. In that review article Lucas didn't explain anything new. He just restated his point of view.

Does that mean that there is a gap between his way of thinking and yours?

Of course there is a gap. I try to point out how incapable the new equilibrium business cycles models are of explaining the most obvious observed facts of cyclical fluctuations. Arthur Okun listed in detail 15 or 20 such facts that are inconsistent with those models. I don't think that models so far from realistic description should be taken seriously as guides to policy. Evidently, Lucas thinks otherwise.

Keynesian large-scale models are irreparable in the view of the insights that new classical models have given?

I don't take that point at all. I always thought that macroeconomic models are pretty pragmatic exercises. They are condensed general equilibrium models; they are, therefore, simple. The very fact that they are aggregate models makes that true. You like them to be as consistent with reasonable assumptions about the individual households and firms as you can. At the same time, since they are aggregate models, they also describe the behavior of lots of different agents. I don't think that there is a way to write down any model which at one hand respects the possible diversity of agents in taste, circumstances, and so on and at the other hand also grounds behavior rigorously in utility maximization and which has any substantive content to it.

The fact that you cannot derive a Keynesian consumption function by maximizing utility doesn't disturb me an awful lot. You see, new classical economists may emphasize utility maximization, but they avoid all problems of aggregation in practice by simply assuming, for example, that everybody is the same.

So, everyone calls the theory of the other ad hoc . . . Where are we, then?

Where are we? Well, in the end we have to look for models that explain what goes on and fits the data. I realize that this is very difficult. But economics is difficult.

New classical economists claim that their models fit the data reasonably well.

But they don't. They haven't fit the data very well at all. I am not convinced by their econometric work. Their results are outperformed by tests with traditional models all the time. Ray Fair [1978] showed that, for example.

Are you not impressed with the new econometrics by Sargent and Sims?

I am impressed by their doing it, but not by the results.

Listening to you, to Lucas, and to the others, and knowing that you all are among the best in the profession, I cannot help wondering what economic truth is?

[Laughter.] That is a deep question. . . . As far as macroeconomics is concerned, my objective has been to have models in which behavior is assumed to be rational, in which the gross facts of economic life are explained, and which may not give great forecasts in a technical sense but at least an understanding of what is happening and what is going to happen. I admit that that is an imprecise judgment, but we do have to explain certain economic facts.

Lucas and the others also realize the limitations of their techniques.

Lucas says: "You don't know anything," and in his more humble moments: "I don't know anything either, and therefore the government shouldn't do anything." Well, there is no well-defined criterion of the government's not doing anything. What he says the government should do and calls doing nothing is doing something very different from what the government has been doing for the last 40 years. Why is making a radical change of regime suddenly doing nothing? You see, we have had a regime that can be associated with the most successful period of capitalism in recorded history. Suddenly, he calls for a constant money growth rule. How, possibly, can one conclude that? I say, if he doesn't want "to do anything", then we should keep doing what we have been doing, for we haven't been doing that badly. To make a radical change in regime all of a sudden, gives us what we have now: a new depression. Right? We have a new regime now, or maybe we have if it is not overturned, partly because these guys come along saying that compensatory policy, that is Keynesian policy, got us in all kinds of trouble. But it didn't get us in all kinds of trouble. In effect, they say that if you don't know what you are doing, you should do something entirely different from what you have been doing. I don't understand why that is a conservative or risk-avoiding policy.

It is my understanding that much of the disagreement between neo-Keynesian and new classical economists can be reduced to a difference of opinion on the relative importance of rigor and relevance of an analysis. You have suggested several times before that the rigorous new classsical models lack relevance. This would mean that the disagreement boils down to a disagreement on the way economics should be done. Do you agree with this?

I would not disagree with that. I hinted at that by referring to the support of new classical economists for the methodology of positive economics.

As active participants in policy-making, economists assume certain responsibilities, even though they don't know, even though they know that other economists disagree.

My attitude toward that has never been very bashful. And the reason is that I had a chance to observe, while I was in Washington, the kinds of advice that would be taken if economists' advice was not. It is not that we are any good, but that the alternatives are much worse. Therefore, rather than thinking about how much I and my colleagues don't know, I prefer to think that we at least understand how to think logically and consistently about economic problems and how to use statistical information in a sophisticated way.

It is not really fair to blame economists for economic difficulties or the failure to find economically and politically viable solutions. Meteorologists, for example, are not able to correct the weather and not terribly good at forecasting it. I notice that the physical scientists, even though they may argue about basic science, generally disagree on practical policy applications, for example, nuclear risks. Economics has always flourished and acquired energy from controversies generated by practical policy questions of the day. That was true in the times of Smith, and Ricardo, and Keynes, and it is true today. These periods of division and revolution and counterrevolution are generally followed by periods of synthesis and consolidation from which the science emerges stronger. I am optimistic that this will happen again, and that the best of the insights of the new classicals will be absorbed in a mainstream, in which the essential insights of Keynesian economists also survive.

6

FRANCO MODIGLIANI

Modigliani was one of the few neo-Keynesians quick to point out the contributions of new classical economics. In his presidential address to the American Economic Association in 1976, Modigliani spoke of the "macro rational expectations revolution." In spite of this praise, he rejected the new classical conclusion that active policy is ineffective. This, however, was not Modigliani's first involvement with the new classical argument. In 1961, Muth acknowledged him in the first article in which the rational expectations hypothesis was formalized; and when the article was otherwise ignored in the literature throughout the '60s, Modigliani commented on its ideas in a couple of articles. The anticipation of the idea of rational expectations can even be found in an article that Modigliani wrote with Emile Grunberg in 1954.

Modigliani, born in Italy, came to the United States just before the start of World War II. He registered at the New School for Social Research, which was a popular place for intellectual refugees at that time, and received his Doctorate in Social Sciences in 1944. He taught at University of Illinois (1950–52) and the Carnegie Institute of Technology (1952–60); he is currently Institute Professor at M.I.T.

His sympathies are clear from a cartoon that is attached to his office door: "With your permission, gentlemen, I'd like to offer a kind word on behalf of John Maynard Keynes." Our conversation took place in August 1982.

BACKGROUND

How did you come to study economics?

[Laughter.] That's a good question. I'd say, by chance. I started my university years with the expectation that I would become a doctor, because my father was one. (He had died shortly before.) At the last moment I realized that I wasn't cut out for that profession; I cannot stand the sight of blood. So I went into law, which is in Italy very general.

Then there was a national competition among university students to write an essay about the effect of price controls. I decided to participate in this. I had talked about the subject with a cousin of mine, who lived with us and, as an officer of the trade association of wholesalers, he had given the matter some thought. I wrote my essay and won first prize. The judges said that I should pursue the subject of economics and so I began. I mainly studied on my own. Shortly thereafter I left Italy. . .

For political reasons?

Yeah, both for racial and political reasons. My family is Jewish and on top of that, I had gone into a very anti-fascist direction on my own. I left for France and then came to New York. There I attended the New School for Social Research, where I learned economics and also learned about Keynes.

Who was important for you at that place?

I had the fortune to meet Jacob Marschak. He took me in his hands. There were other good people there, but he was very instrumental in giving me a style.

What kind of style?

I would say the combination of theory, that is, modeling, with testing of empirical facts. The objective was to develop models that could be tested. Marschak also emphasized the importance of mathematics and econometrics, something that was quite unusual at that time. He was a wonderful teacher. He taught me macroeconomics. We discussed Keynes and Schumpeter. So he helped me to develop both in terms of tools and of ideas.

Marschak invited me to a very distinguished seminar, attended by prominent economists such as Oskar Lange, Tjalling Koopmans, and Abraham Wald. Abba Lerner would come now and then.

What did you discuss at that seminar?

I don't remember anymore. The topics were general; we would discuss econometrics, macroeconomics, and so on.

Your invitation to that seminar suggests that you were a promising student.

I guess that Marschak always had great expectations of me. From the very beginning he was very attached to me. He helped me a great deal. He got me, for example, my first job at the New Jersey College for Women. When he left the New School, he got me to take over his econometric courses.

So he was from the very beginning a great influence. I recognized him as my most important teacher. We were warm friends, and I loved him very dearly. So on the two occasions that I gave a presidential address, once for the Econometric Society and the other time for the American Economic Association, I asked Marschak to chair the session. I did this in spite of the fact that he had developed a different interest. He had lost somewhat his interest in macroeconomics.

You clearly were a good student. Was it because you were exceptionally intelligent or just eager?

[Laughter.] Well . . . I worked hard, undoubtedly. I also had to earn money. During the day I sold books, Italian books; I went to classes in the evening and studied at night. I probably was helped by a craving for clarity. I cannot rest until I really understand a problem, when I can formalize it so that I understand what goes on. That was important. I also had some passion for the subject. Once I was with Marschak I got very deeply involved in the subject.

Was there any particular reason?

I think that a major fact that got my interest in the subject was the experience of the Depression and the high unemployment rates of the '30s. It might be true that there was no unemployment in my immediate family, but the tragedy of the Depression was clearly visible. And then there was Keynes, who said that it should not have happened. His paradigm swept the profession because it provided a simple and unified explanation for the occurrence of the Depression. There was a great need at the time for an assurance that it would never happpen again. And that fascinated me.

You seem to like mathematics quite a bit. You taught mathematical economics in the beginning of your career, and you also make ample use of mathematical language in your articles. Does that mean that mathematics is one of your passions?

No, I don't think so. I don't have a great mathematical inclination. I have enjoyed the tool and I have been impressed by its power, by how it can help in solving problems. I have, however, never had a great deal of interest. I studied a certain amount of mathematics when I was young, but I would not say that I have a great passion for mathematics. I am probably reasonably good in it.

It is fair to say that in most cases mathematics has been a tool for confirming what my intuition told me. It is very seldom that I got some results out of mathematics. Mathematical analysis is a way to make sure. There are exceptions. In some occasions, going through the mathematics reveals a number of things that I had not even suspected would be there, a number of interesting propositions.

The amount of work you have done is awesome. I couldn't help wondering how you have done it all. Has there been life beyond economics for you?

Well, I have never felt that I was overworked. I must say that I don't write fast. Writing is very difficult for me. When I get going, I write at a considerable pace, but normally each article goes through many drafts. No, I am rather relying on working hard. I do work at night. A typical day starts not too early, but after dinner I am used to putting in three hours. I also had a light teaching load ever since I came to M.I.T. And I have had very good collaborators who have been very helpful, at times crucial. Well, I don't know. I have written a lot of articles but very few books. There is no book that is entirely mine — though there is the three volume collection of my shorter articles.

When I look back at my life, I do not see that I did nothing but work. I have a family life, I like to relax. I ski, I play tennis, and so on. My wife and I have common interests. We do not have a very active social life. We do not like going to cocktail parties, for example.

There must be something about you that enables you to work so well with other people. Can you tell me something about your collaborations?

Many of those people were students. It quite often is the case that I provide a student with some basic idea on which he works. After he has done that, we put that, and possibly some other work of mine, together. In some cases, the collaboration occurs by chance, such as the one with Jacques Dreze from Leuven. He came by to see about my work on the consumption theory. We got to talk and so it happened. Paul Samuelson and I once got an idea for an article while we were playing tennis. Of course, the man with whom I worked most is Albert Ando. We have not done a lot together during the last ten years, but before that . . .

In general I feel very comfortable working with other people. I have had no experience of conflicts. Working with other people also helps me in my thinking. It really helps when someone knows more about some part of the problem, or is familiar with the techniques that are necessary to formalize a problem. It often takes a considerable effort to acquire the necessary background to be sure. For example, once I had an idea in the field of international finance. There were, however, all kinds of technical aspects about which I did not know very much. So it was important to get the assurance from a person like Peter Kenen that those ideas could be worked out. Something similar happened in other cases of collaboration. The mathematics needed for an analysis can be very complex, and then it is useful to work with someone who is well trained in that stuff. I can do it, but it would take a very long time. So this is an efficient way.

You are Italian and you often return to Italy. Why is that?

It is a matter of attachment. My brother, for example, lives there and I like to visit him. I also like to be involved in economic events in Italy. Because of my detachment now, I can see things that Italians themselves cannot or frequently do not want to see. There have been occasions that I would speak out against measures which were foolish from an economic point of view, but about which other economists would keep quiet. I have been successful in it: people have paid attention to what I say and often invite me for lectures and so on. I just came from Italy and bought a *Corriera della Sera* [Italian newspaper] that carries a big title "Modigliani says that . . ." I also write in Italian, for example in the *Corriera della Sera*.

Some of my influence is probably due to the fact that quite a few Italian students came here under a variety of arrangements.

Has the Italian experience been important for your economics?

I had an opportunity to apply my economic knowledge. In certain occasions I was inspired by looking at Italian problems. I probably learned something about the structure of financial markets. The Italian situation helped me to understand some problems that, at that time, were not important in the United States, and since have become important.

I am thinking now in particular of the role of money. I had gotten convinced that money is what controls nominal income, but the situation in Italy pointed to a different conclusion. At that time there was in the United States a clear distinction between money and other types of deposits. Money was a means of payment and the other deposits were not. In Italy I found that the distinction between money and other type deposits was very blurred. Interest was paid on all deposits; the interest on demand deposits was frequently even higher than the interest rate on time deposits. This experience came as a shock to me; the consequences for policy were clear. Money is by no means unique as a device to control income. So when the erosion of the traditional concept of money started in this country with NOW accounts and other innovations such as the money market funds, I could see the parallels with the Italian situation.

ABOUT ECONOMISTS

When you worked at Carnegie-Mellon, did you discover any friction between the Chicago and other factions?

No, at my time Carnegie-Mellon was an ideal place for working together. I was there until 1960. That was before any of the people associated with Chicago were there, except Allan Meltzer. He was still very young then and was still quite flexible. Now I have a lot of problems with him.

How so?

I find him dogmatic and prone to pick a fight.

Do you still talk with him?

Well [laughter], of course I do when I run into him on various occasions. We are still personal friends.

The main figure was Herbert Simon, who is no longer in the department of economics (he is now with the psychology department). He was pushing ideas of his own that were against some of the things in which economists believed. But the interaction was always very friendly. I took his arguments seriously, but it is a question of what one wants to do. It is clear that the basic postulates of economic anaysis are only tools. Nobody believes that they are an exact description, that is, that every agent acts according to them. The question is whether Simon's hypothesis of satisficing behavior is more helpful than the neoclassical hypothesis of optimizing behavior.

Charlie Holt was there, too. We still think of him and his wife as the closest personal friends who we trust completely. The other central figure was Cooper, who was doing applications of linear programming. I could also mention Bronfenbrenner, who spent some years at Carnegie—first as a student, then as a colleague. Muth was there, too, but he is hard to classify. Of all our students he is no doubt the one that has had the deepest impact on the newer generation, as the father of rational expectations. He was not conservative. Undoubtedly a very original and talented man, but he always seemed to take pains to appear as an oddball.

Why did Muth leave Carnegie-Mellon?

That is a great question. I do not really know the details.

Did you realize the clash between the Chicago and, say, the M.I.T. people later?

I was very aware of the problems with the Chicago people. In some sense I have become more understanding of what Milton Friedman has been arguing. Friedman is driven by the idea that whatever the government does is bad. He has a mission and seems to be willing to sacrifice some intellectual honesty for that.

He is a good debater, but you are one of the few who dared to take him on in a direct confrontation at the Federal Reserve Bank of San Francisco in 1977.

[Laughter.] One must admit that Milton was very kind at that occasion. I was prepared to meet him, I knew that he is tough and very fast and dangerous. . . .

Dangerous?

Yes, in the sense that it can hurt your ego. But he didn't hurt mine. I think that I did fine. The best part was, I think, when I said that people do not look at the money supply and that, therefore, Milton's story does not make sense. Someone in the audience said: "Of course, they do." I asked him what people do with their knowledge of the money supply figures? He said: "Well, if I get a larger supply of money I spend more" [laughter]. He was, of course, confusing macro with micro.

Apart from that debate, do you communicate more often with Friedman?

Not really. Friedman doesn't come out that often. He might cosponsor a conference but does not come. As a result, I have not talked very much with him.

You seem to form a cohesive group at M.I.T.

Yes, that is probably true. We share similar values and have compatible approaches. The younger people, such as Peter Diamond, however, are probably a bit more conservative. But the senior people (Samuelson and Solow and I) have a lot in common. We talk a fair amount with each other. We are generally very compatible in our points of view. We have somewhat different interests, but we are all interested in macroeconomics.

ABOUT KEYNESIAN ECONOMICS

You suggested in earlier remarks that Keynes's paradigm revolutionized macroeconomics. When you make a remark like that, do you think of Kuhn's notion of revolution?

I think that Kuhn exaggerates when he says different scientific points of view cannot coexist. He gives this simple picture of somebody who comes along with a new way of looking at things, to the effect that everybody says, "Ah, of course, why didn't I see it before?" Subsequently, the old way of looking dies out. I think this is an exaggeration, even in science. In the social sciences there is extensive coexistence of different points of view. That is true in economics and, of course much more true in sociology.

Do you think that the effect of Keynes's ideas fits Kuhn's story well?

Yes, I think that Keynes was certainly a good example of a new paradigm. His work is possibly the best example of a case for which I think Kuhn's theory fits as well as it can in the domain of the social sciences. In a fairly short period of time, Keynes gave a new way of looking at the economy, a way which was widely accepted, at least by the younger generation.

What is a main component of his new way of looking, compared to the old way?

You have to distinguish between the scientific essence of what he did and the way he presented it. His permanent scientific contribution is the combination of wage rigidity and the theory of liquidity preference. The assumption of wage rigidity is to be understood broadly as that wages don't adjust permanently. I think he pushed it sometimes by saying that they don't adjust at all, but that is not essential to his argument.

His theory of liquidity preference per se may look like a technical refinement of the quantity theory of money, an innocuous amendment to which no one could object. But it turns out to have very strong implications, in particular in combination with the assumption of wage rigidity.

And that meant a new way of thinking?

He was able to package this into the effective demand theory, which in effect is the theory of absolutely rigid wages. It is an effective description of the short run, because in the short run wages are quite rigid. That was the new paradigm, that really led people to think in quite different ways. It was a scientific revolution in the sense that it combined some important ideas and a way of packaging them.

You haven't mentioned yet the policy conclusions that are connected with these ideas.

Oh, they are an immediate consequence of all this. The idea that wages do not readily adjust was so important because of its far-reaching policy implications. The important implication of these ideas was to shake the laissez-faire attitude which was accepted very broadly by mainstream economists, that is, excepting the Marxist or radical schools and others critical of the capitalistic system.

Keynes showed that the system was not rapidly self-equilibrating and that, therefore, there was a role for government intervention: that is, that there was room for monetary as well as fiscal stabilization policy. And, again, I think that Keynes shaped things in a sophisticated and very persuasive way.

His main ideas were actually very simple. A number of things that happened since then suggest that they are a little more complicated. Fiscal policy, for example, turned out to have consequences which he hadn't even seen. Of course, Keynes, being a very wise man, often had seen things; you can find references to almost anything in *The General Theory* [laughter]; almost anything that has been said later. If you're very careful you will find at least the seed in his writings. But I think the message that came across was a simple one. There's no doubt that an essential part of this new paradigm was the conclusion that stabilization policies were needed. Since the system will adjust, at best, slowly when left to itself, there is need for public policy to increase the efficiency of the system; and this entirely within the capitalistic framework.

ABOUT NEW CLASSICAL ECONOMICS

What is your opinion on new classical economists such as Lucas and Sargent?

I think Lucas is an extremely capable man, and an undisputed intellectual leader of the school. On top of that, I think he's a very interesting and impressive human being. But I disagree with him, and I think I also disagree with his interpretation of his results. I have many, many objections.

In what way do you react to their economics?

Fundamentally, my view is that rational expectations is a perfectly fine concept; it is a good starting point for the study of situations in which expectations are important. But I have great reservations about the application of this concept to macro. I believe that Lucas and Sargent are pushing the idea of rationality well beyond the range where it is useful.

Macro rational expectations, as I have labeled the hypothesis, seems to say that expectations in an economist's model must be perfectly consistent with his model that embodies these expectations. In other words, the agents of his model must all share his views of the relevant economic mechanisms, as well as his data. Why? Because if he holds them they must believe they are God's truth and, if so, rational people can have no other views (and of course we should never ask how they would come by these views and data, that not even other specialists may have heard of yet, let alone accepted). I submit that this view is pretty absurd—I would almost say offensive! I certainly believe that I know more about economics and the economy than (almost) everybody else, and I can even prove it: If everybody shared my views, then the economy could not be in today's troubles (though it might conceivably be in some different ones!).

The basic conclusion of these models, namely that there is no room for stabilization policies, is therefore entirely based on an absurd model of the world. They also assume that all adjustments are instantaneous. The economy evidently does not work that way. There are delays and there are various reasons for imperfect adjustments. The most conspicuous and formal representation is Stanley Fischer's notion of long-term contracts and the like.

Lucas gets quite annoyed with these criticisms. He wonders why one would reject rational expectations and still accept neoclassical utility analysis, when most agents have never heard of utility functions or know how to compute first- and second-order maximum conditions!

But there are profound differences. It is one thing to say people speak prose, even though they do not know what prose means, and quite a different matter to say they all believe that the quantity theory of money holds instantaneously (and, by the way, it does not). Yet they need that hypothesis to come to their very strong, sweeping conclusion. They don't say monetary policy does not make much difference; they are saying it is irrelevant. That is a very strong statement.

In addition to that, I am hesitant to accept those complicated calculations in maximization problems, except when they reflect a long, repetitive process. I believe people can solve complex problems eventually. By repeated trial and error they will get there; but they need a long time. At this point I agree with Herbert Simon. People do not learn immediately, as those rational expectations models seem to imply. I don't believe that.

The statement that assumptions do not matter is nonsense. It is funny. Yes, I assume people are consistent in their behavior. I assume that not because I believe everybody actually is, but because I believe, on the average, you do not get too far from it.

There is one thing I do not understand. You contend that a major objective in your research is the reconciliation of macroeconomic theory with the optimization postulates. Why then do you resist the introduction of the postulate in the modeling of expectations?

I agree completely with the intention. We need a sensible model for the formation of expectations. Rational expectations is one possibility, and there are circumstances in which I think the assumption is sensible. I think of situations in financial markets, where there is an immediate large pay-off to superior forecasts. For this reason I accept, by and large, the random walk hypothesis as a good approximation, but with the understanding that it is consistent with fairly long-lasting disequilibrium. In the short run you can get trapped into a situation in which no gain can be made, even though it is not one of fundamental equilibrium. The stock market is now way off, but I wouldn't advise anybody to rush in. I expect that some years from now it will be three times higher, but it can get a lot worse before it gets better.

We clearly need a model of expectations. I agree that people read newspapers and try to find what is going on. For example, in my view, interest rates now are high not because current short term rates are high, but because people expect that future short rates will be very high because of the large deficits.

So, how do you model that?

I haven't done it, because we are dealing with a unique event. Never before in peacetime has there been so much fanfare about such huge deficits. I do not exactly know how to do it, except that is what we mostly use dummy variables for!

You had a lot to do with the birth of rational expectations, it seems. You wrote, for example, an article with Grunberg in 1954 that contains the idea.

It is true, though I must confess that that article with Grunberg and my two articles with Miller on corporate finance are written with tongue in cheek, to really make fun of my colleagues. The article with Grunberg does not say people anticipate government policy and therefore render it ineffective. No. See, people had been saying that economists cannot forecast, because when they do, something different happens as people react to those forecasts. We say that economists can forecast, even if you take the reaction of people into account.

In a final footnote to the Grunberg article you express the rational expectations idea. Do you remember?

[Laughter.] No.

Well, you say there that people anticipate actions of the government.

Oh yes, absolutely. I agree with that. See, what bothers me about rational expectations is that these people are really pushing specific implications. If it is just a matter of saying you have to take reactions to policies into account, I would agree. Yes, policy measures can change the structure of the economy. Modeling this will be very hard, but there is no objection of principle. I recognize that Lucas has a sound point.

But my objection is not one of principles, but of applications. I am critical of the fact that these authors write technically beautiful articles using an extremely specialized model — such as the overlapping generations model with no durable physical events — to come to strong practical conclusions about the working of money, even though in such a model there is no demand for money as medium of exchange. I find particularly objectionable the postulate that all rational agents believe the quantity theory of money holds instantly, because there is no reason in the world that that should be true. I tend to believe very few people know what money means and what it does. For example, I could imagine people are much more responsive to the announcement of a tax reduction than to an announcement that tells them at what rate money is growing. It may be that that has an effect on unemployment, but I do not think it means anything to people. So the fundamental way to proceed in modeling, I think, is to take into account the role of expectations in whatever way seems best and most productive. I can think of situations where assuming that expectations are consistent with the model is a convenient way to start. But we cannot base all our conclusions on that assumption.

I should also say the new classical economists cannot explain the current unemployment. When the reply that unemployment can be explained within rational expectations models by referring to technological change and so on, I think they are wrong. They are confusing employment and unemployment. You can explain variations in employment that way, but not unemployment. You can explain why people want to work some of the time and why they don't want to work at other times. But these are changes in the labor force. There is no reason why unemployment can be explained that way. It takes time to clear markets; particularly in the area of employment, finding the market-clearing price is a highly complex and time-consuming process. When the market-clearing real wage declines as with an oil shock, it will take a long time before workers accept that. In the meantime you have unemployment and at least some inflation.

7

ROBERT M. SOLOW

"Why don't you talk with Solow?" people asked time and again. They usually referred to his impressive intellect and to his renowned wit, which apparently is funny to some but annoying to others.

Solow is a Harvard Ph.D. (1951) and spent all of his career at M.I.T., where he is now Institute Professor. He is generally well known because of his role in the economic growth debate (he emphasized the economist's point of view and called attention to the role of prices); in the world of economists his reputation is mainly based on his papers on growth and technological progress and his theoretical contributions to neo-Keynesian economics. An article that he wrote with Alan Blinder on fiscal policy in the early '70s, "Does Fiscal Policy Matter" (1973) has become a standard reference. In his presidential address to the American Economic Association (1978) he discussed "Theories of Unemployment."

We talked in his office at M.I.T. in February 1983.

BACKGROUND

Why did you study economics?

That goes back a long way. I came to Harvard College in 1940, not intending to study economics. If I thought of anything it was botany, biology, or genetics. I discovered very quickly that I was not good at those things, so I stopped. I was interested in social questions because the Depression was just over or not quite. I remembered from my childhood what an unpleasant time the Depression had been for my family and more so for others.

I began to study sociology, anthropology, and some economics. I had very good teachers in those subjects, such as Talcott Parsons, the sociologist, and Clyde Kluckhohn, with whom I became very close friends. I also had a course with Paul Sweezy, who was a favorite economics teacher of mine . . . . and I think I was a favorite student of his. I was fairly left wing at that time.

Then the war came and I decided that was more important than studying, so I left school and joined the army. When I came back in 1945 I had to decide what to do; I still had not finished my undergraduate degree. In the meanwhile my girlfriend, whom I married in 1945, had finished her economics degree at Radcliffe College. She said that economics was an interesting subject. I had to do something right away, so I decided that I might as well do that. I began, and I rather liked it. It was almost pure accident.

Did you ever seriously consider sociology as your major?

I found that I was dissatisfied with sociology. I presume from what happened to me afterward that I wanted to be able to understand things in a more systematic way. I found that whenever Talcott Parsons, whom I liked and knew 'til his death, talked about something concrete, like the way doctors deal with their patients, he was full of fascinating insights; but as soon as he began to generalize, even I, as an ignorant 18-year-old, found it too vague.

My acquaintance with sociology has been good for me, because it has left me more sociologically oriented than most economic theorists . . . assuming that's a good thing. I do take social institutions seriously as an important determinant of what happens in the economy.

You mentioned Sweezy as an important teacher for you. Who else was a mentor for you?

At first mostly Sweezy and Richard Goodwin. Afterward Wassily Leontief became the most important teacher I had.

When I came back after the war, Harvard still had the tutorial system: every undergraduate was assigned a tutor whom he would see for an hour each week. Wassily was my tutor; he taught me most of the economics that I learned. He was then the only mathematical or rigorous economist at Harvard. He got me to study mathematics. I was a very good mathematics student in high school, but I had no particular interest in it. Then Wassily would say, when we had to decide what I should read for the following week, "Why don't you read such and such . . . oh no, no you could not read that because you don't understand the mathematics." This went on for three weeks, and I decided that I had better learn some. So I did and I enjoyed it. But it has always been instrumental for me. I never really got fascinated by mathematical economics for its own sake.

In retrospect, I got a lot from Alvin Hansen, but I was less aware of him at the time because I was wound up in learning elementary economics a rigorous way.

At that time lots of things were happening at Harvard with people like Tobin and Samuelson around. They discovered Keynes and argued a lot about it, apparently. Were you aware of all that?

No, because at the time I was still an undergraduate. I also had the bad luck that the money and banking course that Alvin Hansen usually taught — there was not a macro course then, that came later — was taught that year by someone else who was not very enchanted with Keynes's economics. So I missed the introduction of Keynesian economics and the excitement that went with it.

Then you entered graduate school, again at Harvard. . .

Yes, in those days it did not occur to you to change universities, at least not if you were a student at Harvard.

By then, that is in 1947–48, Samuelson, Tobin, and Lloyd Metzler were gone. There was still some discussion about Keynesian economics, but it wasn't very exciting. The talk was mostly about whether savings is equal to investment or not, and about the relationship between the liquidity preference theory and the loanable funds theory of interest. It was interesting economics, but the sense of excitement was gone.

To which subjects were you attracted in those days?

I was not primarily interested in what you would now describe as macroeconomics. I was interested in economic theory, which meant general equilibrium theory; I was very interested in input-output analysis (I was a research assistant of Leontief). I also discovered probability and statistics, a subject that was not taught to economists at Harvard then. Well . . . the courses in statistics that were taught were really dreadful; it was a scandal. So I took courses in the mathematics department. I was very excited by that.

I wrote my dissertation on the distribution of income by size among families treated as a stochastic process. After that I came to M.I.T. as professor of statistics in the economics department.

I got the sense that there was a scientific optimism at that time; economists believed in their methods.

Yes, I think that the feeling was that serious econometrics was capable of making a science out of economics. I felt it too.

Is it right to characterize the '50s and '60s as the Keynesian era?

Yes, I don't know whether that is a complete description, but it was certainly a period in which Keynesian economics was the dominant way of thinking about macroeconomics. The Keynesians had won the debates that came in the late '30s after the hostile reviews of the *General Theory* by Viner, Leontief, and others. The first mathematical models of a Keynesian kind had appeared; Klein had started estimating econometric equations.

You said that you were a left winger as an undergraduate and that you liked Paul Sweezy. You must have changed quite a bit. . . .

Well . . . yes and no. I still think of myself as a left of center person. I still don't find it a particularly attractive notion that property rights should take precedence over all other rights.

Why?

That is a long evolution. As a student of Paul Sweezy's, I was excited by Marxian economics. As I studied economics I came more and more to the conclusion that there is really no good economics in Marxism; Marxian economics has been a failure as an economic theory. For a longer time I found soomething useful in the notion of historical materialism, that ideas tend in a large part to reflect interests — vulgar Marxism, so to speak. There is something to that, though it's far from the complete story.

My first intellectual influence was a high school teacher who had been anarchist. So I never felt the slightest attraction to Stalinism or Soviet communism.

I was once at Oxford and went to a seminar . . . it was in 1968 so the place was filled with radicals. They asked me what I thought of Marxism, and I said that Marxism made pseudo-science of one insight that

Proudhon had, namely that property is theft. Locke saw the institution of private property as a great thing because it was a way of protecting private citizens against the encroachments of aristocratic power. There is still a lot of value to that. The danger of socialism is the concentration of political and economic power in the same hands. Nevertheless, I still believe that the institution of private property has to keep proving itself. For that matter, capitalism still has to keep proving that it can be economically efficient without being destructive of reasonable equality.

I am not anti-socialist in any absolutist way but I am not a socialist either, because I do not think that socialism is a practical prospect for a good society. If there were an opportunity for democratic socialism somewhere, I would be willing to see it given a try. I am not pessimistic about the managed capitalism that you find in northern European countries. They have learned to combine activist economic policy with democracy. I don't see that the Dutch or the Norwegians have less liberty, all things considered, than we do.

ON KEYNESIAN ECONOMICS

You are a Keynesian economist.

That is true. I have no problem with that. Pretty clearly, I am also a neoclassical economist, but I am content with the Keynesian label.

What is Keynesian economics, according to you?

In the first place, what I believe about macroeconomics is not exactly what Keynes believed. I couldn't care less, and in any case, it would be a sad thing if nobody learned anything in all those years. I think that today Keynesian economists primarily distinguish themselves from other economists through their belief that you cannot understand the behavior of our economy on the assumption that it is always at or near a full, or Walrasian, equilibrium, and that you cannot account for the movements that you see in output and employment on the assumption that everything you see is at the intersection of traditional supply and demand curves, and that the movements are only accounted for by shifts in those curves.

People who think of themselves as Keynesian economists can be divided as to what they would put in place of Walrasian equilibrium. Some of them think that what we observe in the world is a disequilibrium. If the economy is moving toward Walrasian equilibrium, it is doing so very slowly. Another group of Keynesian economists, who are in some ways closer to Keynes, believe that the economy is characterized by multiple equilibria; a modern capitalist economy is capable perhaps of producing a good Walrasian equilibrium, but also a bad equilibrium, that is, a situation with bad welfare properties and without forces that move the economy away from such a situation.

I find myself halfway between those two schools of thought. I used to think that the correct analysis would emphasize disequilibrium. Now I have some doubts about that. Either of these approaches is a Keynesian alternative to the idea that the economy should be regarded as being in a Walrasian equilibrium.

How do you explain the current recession that we are experiencing?

My diagnosis of the current recession goes like this: As a response to the inflation that was set off by the inflationary financing of the war in Vietnam (that was a traditional demandside inflation) and was then reinforced and made worse by the adverse supply shocks in the period 1973–75 and again in 1979, and with due account — I am trying to be very careful — of the fact that a prolonged inflationary period must have had expectational effects, which are difficult to measure but it is hard to believe that they were not there, the economy found itself in a state of continuing inflation, which did not seem to be burning itself out fast enough to satisfy either people in power or most ordinary citizens. The consequence was a sharp deflationary effort, mostly by the monetary authorities, which is the main source of the recession that we have now.

I think that it can be analyzed with reasonable adequacy by the old apparatus of IS/LM curves and aggregate supply and demand curves. We suffer from all of the symptoms of excessively tight money. We see very high real interest rates and a shortfall in aggregate demand, which is concentrated in the interest-sensitive expenditures like housing, plant and equipment and durable consumer goods.

How do you tie all this in your disequilibrium or multiple equilibrium models?

I would not want to burn at the stake for what I am about to say, because it is not a set of ideas that I hold with firm confidence. You can imagine a situation (by the way, this is very similar to the Friedman-Schwartz diagnosis of the Depression of the 1930s or equally consistent with Leijonhufvud's notion of a corridor — I will say more about that in a minute) in which the economy is disturbed from a reasonable equilibrium. If the disturbance is small the economy would slowly, I might think too slowly, return to equilibrium. But if something happens, such as a prolonged period of tight monetary policy and a not very expansionary fiscal policy, and the economy stays away from full employment equilibrium for a long time, the expectational self-validation that probably underlies the kind of multiple equilibrium that I talked about could take over. Keynes described this as a collapse of the marginal efficiency of capital. That seems too dramatic to describe what has happened now, but it could be that the initial reaction to the deflationary policies was a departure from equilibrium that got so prolonged that now the economy, if left undisturbed, cannot find its way back to full employment.

The idea that I attributed to Leijonhufvud is in an article that he published a few years ago called "Effective Demand Failures." He proposed the hypothesis (it is rather vague) that there is an equilibrium path that is surrounded by what he calls a corridor, a range above and below the equilibrium path. If the economy is disturbed off the equilibrium path and remains within the corridor, normal market forces can bring the economy back; if the disturbance moves the economy outside the range, then inflationary and contractionary expectations and assumptions may become so strong that the normal market forces are unable to push the economy back to a satisfactory state. Physically, it would be like the cup on the desk. If you tilt it a little bit, it will go back to upright. But if you tilt it too much, it will fall. Tobin has written down analogous models, and so have I.

Do you expect the cup to fall in the current economy?

It is conceivable, but not much more.

It seems to me that your generation of neo-Keynesian economists is a very solid and coherent group with similar ideas and a similar language.

Yes, I think that is right, although you may get that impression from a very small fraction of Keynesian economists who all happen to know each other and have worked together. You would think of Tobin, Ackley, Okun, Paul Samuelson . . . this is a group tied together not only by intellectual similarities, but also by friendship. I am not sure, if you enlarged the group, you would find it quite as coherent.

That group has been a very important force in macroeconomics.

It has certainly been important for us, for me. I think that in the early '60s this group was the dominant set of voices in macroeconomic policy discussions..

Is it true that you believed, at that time, that economists had the knowledge to effectively fine-tune the economy?

I often balk at that, in particular at the phrase "fine-tuning." I wonder where that phrase comes from. Walter Heller may have been the inventor, although I think he says he's not. I am not sure how much fine-tuning I ever thought was possible. You can say for sure that we believed in the '50s and early '60s that it was possible, with the available tools, to avoid prolonged recessions and inflation.

I am not so sure that we were wrong. Had policy been more sensible, perhaps we could have avoided the bad years.

The point at which policy went wrong was with the financing of the Vietnam War about 1968. I regard the economic profession as blameless for that; records will show that Okun and Ackley, who were Johnson's economic advisors, warned him of the inflationary consequences of his policies. You most likely will find similar warnings in Paul Samuelson's columns in *Newsweek*.

Although we could not be blamed in that case, in another case our analysis showed a weakness, which was after the oil shocks in 1974. My part of the Keynesian wing was not instantly ready with a clear analysis of the macroeconomic implications and the policy choices. The reason, I suppose, is that for years most Keynesian macroeconomics had been conducted on the implicit assumption that disturbances were aggregate demand disturbances, not supply shocks. It is clear that Keynesian economics is perfectly capable of dealing with supply disturbances; even the *General Theory* has a supply analysis, though not what one would accept now. But there was a period of a few months when not only Keynesians, but everybody was at a loss. We had simply lost the knack of dealing with supply disturbances, because there had not been any major ones for some time. But it took only a short time for the profession to come up with a perfectly reasonable analysis of the supply shocks, which can already be found in textbooks.

CRITICISMS OF NEO-KEYNESIAN ECONOMICS

Around 1970, you were challenged. Many people did not agree with you anymore. The first criticism that comes to mind is Milton Friedman's.

Yes that is right.

There are two aspects of the monetarist version of macroeconomics that have to be separated. One was Milton's initial line, which was that "money matters." He asserted, as a matter of fact, that movements in the money supply are the main forces moving nominal income. That version of monetarism was a useful corrective to what one might describe as English Keynesian economics, the economics of Richard Kahn and Nicholas Kaldor. They perhaps needed to be told that money matters and that shifts in the LM curve can affect real output. They probably still don't recognize that. The English Radcliffe Commission in the '50s represents this point of view. Their version of macroeconomics was that the velocity of money is infinitely malleable; there is no structure to velocity.

I don't think that this version of monetarism had a lot to teach me, because I had learned about the monetary side of Keynesian economics from Tobin and Modigliani. I don't think that they ever thought that money doesn't matter. I never thought that either, but I am, of course, always open to arguments about how elastic the LM and IS curves are.

As far as Friedman's arguments are concerned, I always thought that he sang two tunes. In the economic profession, he was absolutely reasonable. I could find no distinction between his modern quantity theory of money and eclectic Keynesian economics. But in writing for *Newsweek*, he argued a hard monetarism, as against the soft monetarism of the "modern quantity theory." In hard monetarism, velocity is constant and *nothing* but the money supply matters for nominal GNP. I thought that was just factually wrong.

Anyway, that aspect of monetarism did not bother me much. The part that became a much stronger intellectual challenge was Milton's presidential address [for the American Economic Association in 1968]. It does not have much to do with the importance of the money supply or the elasticity of the LM curve, as with the stability of the Phillips curve and the speed with which the Phillips curve becomes vertical—the notion of a natural rate of unemployment, which implies that it takes an accelerating inflation, or an accelerating deflation, to keep the economy away from that natural rate.

I had a complicated attitude to that. I once wrote that the vertical long-run Phillips curve could hardly help but be true in the very long run. So everything turned on the real calendar dimensions of the long run. If you look at Milton's presidential address, he actually says at one point that the time it takes the Phillips curve to become vertical is measured in decades. If this is so, accepting the natural rate notion requires no fundamental change in the way we look at the economy.

I am still dubious about the long-run vertical Phillips curve. I may be the only one who still is. Although I had no trouble visualizing a Phillips curve that becomes vertical without too much lapse of time for very low unemployment rates, I can't imagine that if you are *above* that *same* unemployment rate, a modern economy would begin to have its price level falling and falling at an increasing rate.

I want to get on the record that I think that the belief that I have had before — in a very stable Phillips curve — was very badly damaged by the data of the '70s and that I had to change my mind. I don't want to be understood as thinking that there is some larger satisfactory version of the Phillips curve which can absorb the observations of the '70s.

So could you simply tack on a variable to the equation for the Phillips curve?

Actually, you probably could. Every so often I get a paper in the mail that does that with some success. The problem goes deeper. Even if one could, I still think that it is an intellectually dangerous thing to do. I could verify the existence of witches if you give me the chance every other year to tack on some variables in a regression.

It is possible to draw from the experience of the '70s the conclusion that the stable Phillips curve of the '50s and '60s was an optical illusion. That may be so, but I am not convinced of that. I accept the possibility that in the '50s and '60s there was a stable Phillips curve and that it was destroyed by the prolonged inflation of the late '60s and the '70s. As long as the rate of inflation is variable from year to year and not too large, I entertain the possibility of a stable Phillips curve. There are people who regard this as nonsense; a doctrine that is true once should be true forever. My answer to that is if economics is limited to doctrines that are true forever, then I am afraid that there is nothing to economics at all [laughter]. Economies change over time in ways a poor economist cannot understand.

There is still a third version of monetarism that I want to mention, and that is the Lucas version. There, I balk fundamentally because, in that case, all of the loopholes that provide some fuzziness in the vertical long-run Phillips curve are taken away. Then, it no longer makes empirical sense to me at all.

But the controversy between the two approaches was not settled.

That's right; they weren't settled. Why was that? I do not think that it is possible to settle these arguments econometrically. I do not think that econometrics is a powerful or usable enough tool with macroeconomic time series. And so one is reduced to a species of judgment about the structure of the economy. You can always provide models to support your position econometrically, but that is too easy for both sides. One was never able to find common empirical ground.

To give you an example, I, like Tobin, kept interpreting original monetarism in terms of the slope of the LM curve, but Friedman would never, to my knowledge, agree that that was the key to the disagreement. There are certainly passages in his work in which he says that the interest elasticity of money could be any number; but for better or worse we, Milton Friedman and I, have never been able to get the data to provide any interest elasticity that is significantly different from zero. That says in my language that the LM curve is vertical. Obvious evidence against that position is that everyone else who has tried to determine that elasticity has found a finite non-zero interest elasticity of the demand for money. That seemed to me to be strong evidence against the first version of monetarism. As I saw it then, Milton kept backtracking: he would not accept that as the key test. At that stage of the game it seemed impossible to narrow down what the critical empirical question was.

Another challenge to your work was made by the post-Keynesian economists. What did you think of that challenge?

I am very unsympathetic to the school that calls itself post-Keynesian. First of all, I have never been able to understand it as a school of thought. I don't see an intellectual connection between a Hyman Minsky, on the one hand, who happens to be one of the oldest friends I have, and someone like Alfred Eichner, on the other, except that they are all against the same thing, namely the mainstream, whatever that is.

The other reason why I am not sympathetic is that I have never been able to piece together (I must confess that I have never tried very hard) a positive doctrine. It seems to be mostly a community which knows what it is against but doesn't offer anything very systematic that could be described as a positive theory. I have read many of Paul Davidson's articles and they often do not make sense to me. Some of post-

Keynesian price theory comes forth from the belief that universal competition is a bad assumption. I have all my life known that. So I have found it an unrewarding approach and have not paid much attention to it.

ABOUT NEW CLASSICAL ECONOMICS

Let us talk about new classical economics. What do you think it is?

I just mentioned new classical economists as the third incarnation of monetarism. Perhaps that is an unprofitable way of thinking about it. I think of new classical economics as being a macroeconomics which sets itself the task of interpreting the contemporary world as a moving Walrasian equilibrium. It starts from the assumption, and I think it is no more than an assumption, that what you see is the result of the intersections of a lot of supply and demand curves. All markets or all of the most important markets clear nearly all the time. The intellectual problem of new classical economics is to determine how one can make the size of observed fluctuations in employment compatible with the belief in perpetual Walrasian equilibrium. I suppose there is more than one way that can be done, but the way that Lucas, Sargent, and Barro, who I suppose are the intellectual leaders of that school, have chosen to do it is with the notion of misperception or the ubiquitous inability to read macroeconomics signals correctly.

I have come around to the belief that the habit of labeling new classical economics as the rational expectations school is a bad and a misleading habit. All of the strong propositions that one associates with that school of thought come, not from the hypothesis of rational expectations, but from the hypothesis of market clearing. There are now examples of macroeconomic models which have rational expectations but which are very Keynesian in behavior because they are not market clearing. These models have unemployment and even allow regular oscillations. They simply do not have a Walrasian auctioneer who clears markets at all times. Some of this I have done myself, in lectures, but I have never bothered to publish it. I have shown, for example, that in a model in which: (a) prices are fixed (in a Malinvaud sort of way), (b) markets do not clear, (c) optimization occurs over multiple periods, and (d) rational expectations apply, rational expectations can *enhance* the effectiveness of monetary and fiscal policy.

I'd like to add something about the implications of the different ways in which schools of thought choose to formulate problems. Suppose you ask a new classical economist, "What is the central problem of macroeconomic theory?" I think the answer would be "to explain how nominal disturbances can have real effects." New classical economists wonder why rational people do not always see that a 10 percent increase in the money supply is equivalent to a 10 percent increase in every price overnight and that all real things remain in the preexisting equilibrium. I think that they have managed to sell to large parts of the economic profession that statement of the fundamental problem of macroeconomics.

I began to realize in the last few years, especially in thinking about what I should teach students, that is not what my teachers thought of as the fundamental problem. They thought that the main problem was to understand why real disturbances to the economy have such prolonged real effects and are capable of generating oscillations or fluctuations which last for a long time. Schumpeter, for example, was not at all concerned with the money supply; he was concerned with real shocks like inventions or innovations.

It seems to me that the formulation of nominal shocks, that Lucas and Barro prefer, is favorable to their own view of the world, in the sense that the one kind of disturbance that you can imagine as having occurred to the economy without much real effect is a pure nominal shock. But there is no way that you can say that if a real shock occurs, say the invention of television or the computer, everyone in the economy could be able to figure out what the new equilibrium is and go there and save the economy from having a recession or some other "pathological" interlude. No one in his right mind could believe that everyone can figure out how such inventions change real wages, relative prices and all that. It really is a question of how an economy that is disturbed gets back to a new equilibrium, or whether it ever will get back. This is much more like the old business cycle type of question.

In a reaction to a paper of yours [Solow, 1980], *Neil Wallace criticized you for not being rigorous in the application of the rationality postulate and using ad hoc assumptions to account for rigid prices. What do you think of that criticism?*

I think that there is some justice in that. It is certainly descriptively accurate in that when I have tried to do economic dynamics, I have tended to invent plausible—but you certainly could say ad hoc—disequilibrium dynamics, which is certainly not the solution of some vast, intertemporal optimization problem. My response to that criticism comes along several lines.

In the first place, I have to admit that I don't adopt the notion of rationality as an axiom beyond which one is not allowed to proceed. I am an eclectic. I have often argued with people like Herbert Simon because it seemed to me that his notion of satisficing rationality gave up too easily in describing business firms. It seemed to me that business firms actually work pretty hard to maximize whatever they can. On the other hand, someone like Simon is completely hostile to the notion of rationality at all costs, as you just described it, saying that it is descriptively false. At this stage, I am more on Simon's side. One ought not to insist on rationality where rationality becomes so excruciatingly difficult that it is hard to believe that that is how economic agents behave. That is point number one. (To qualify by saying that unspecified costs of calculation have to be included is to empty the notion of rationality of all content.)

Point number two is one with which other neo-Keynesians do not necessarily agree. Even if I were to accept rationality, I would not be inclined to accept the specification of what it is that people try to maximize and what constraints they believe they face. I would not accept the conventonal descriptions, certainly not in a market like the labor market. Relationships among workers and between employers and workers are socially complicated. It doesn't seem possible to accurately describe labor market behavior in the way economists describe spot markets. People have notions of equity, fairness, and conventions which play a very important role.

The third argument that I would make against Wallace is that I see things happening which do not look to me like the playing out of a multistaged game; it rather looks like friction dragging against adjustments, that is to say, it looks like a disequilibrium phenomenon, situations in which people did not contemplate being at the start of the game.

To what kind of observations are you referring?

I think of things like unintended inventory accumulation in the automobile industry; that does not seem to me to be the playing out of a strategy that the automobile industry foresaw. See, it is conceivable that I would have preferred to do *anything* but talking into your tape recorder, and still, here I am. Nevertheless, the new classical economists would say that I am in equilibrium.

But that is because you act under certain constraints.

Yes, I wanted to get to that. When they regard me as being in equilibrium, since I solved a constrained optimization problem, they stress the standard constraints of general equilibrium theory, primarily technological, budget, and some legal constraints. The main constraint I am working under might be, however, that I want to be polite; I want to behave in a way that I think is appropriate so that I wouldn't be ashamed if my mother saw what I was doing. Once you inject those — and they may be very important — then the sorts of results that equilibrium theorists like would not come.

The assumption of conventional rationality has to earn its wings every day, as Mr. Borman of Eastern Airlines would say; and if it doesn't earn its wings it is not entitled to fly [laughter].

Did the rational expectations hypothesis earn its wings?

It has a natural habitat, like most hypotheses. I think that the hypothesis makes good sense in securities markets. For complicated situations — for example, real shocks like earthquakes and the outbreak of wars — the hypothesis seems to be entirely inappropriate. Let me be exact. If I ask myself what I could legitimately assume a person to have rational expectations about, the technical answer would be, I think, about the realization of a stationary stochastic process, such as the outcome of the toss of a coin or anything that can be modeled as the outcome of a random process that is stationary. I don't think that the economic implications of the outbreak of World War II were regarded by most people as the realization of a stationary stochastic process. In that case, the concept of rational expectations does not make any sense. Similarly, the major innovation cannot be thought of as the outcome of a random process. In that case the probability calculus does not apply.

This is like Frank Knight's old distinction between risk and uncertainty. In the case of uncertainty, rules of thumb may be useful. My colleague, Modigliani, says that he is prepared to believe in not obviously irrational expectations, and that seems to be sensible in case of nonstationary phenomena.

So you allow some kind of ad hoc-ness to deal with such situations of uncertainty.

Yes, I don't see any better way. I don't have a good way of dealing with Knight's kind of uncertainty, as distinct from risk. Maybe there isn't one.

Let me give another example. Sargent said in a talk here last year that it is simply a methodological mistake to regard any macroeconomic policy action as an isolated episode. The only legitimate way to think of economic policy is as if the government adopts a policy rule (which may have a random element). What he meant was that he can't apply his methods to isolated policy episodes. My reaction is that the man in the street or even the man in the corporation boardroom, looking at the US Congress making macroeconomic policy, regards it as a possibly unstable episode. He doesn't know how it is going to come out. He not only doesn't know how it is comes out, he doesn't imagine it to be the application of a policy rule plus a random error. It is simply not that kind of event. There are 500 crazy people down there with worries about getting reelected; they don't know what the public wants; they don't know what they want; they don't know what will work or how it will work. God knows what they will do.

New classical economists say that we should follow rules. . . .

Not only that we should follow rules, they also say that it is the only reasonable way to think about policy. I have argued against that. I would further argue that you can obviously advise a government to follow a rule, you might nearly succeed in that, but that a strong case has not been made for such advice. If the Federal Reserve had been stuck to a preset rule concerning the growth of M1, the policy probably would have been worse than it has been now. That is a conclusion of positive economics.

Do you get ever upset about the policy proposals of new classical economists?

Upset? Well, I have a short fuse, but no, I don't think I get upset, because it seems to me to be so very far from reality.

What do you think of the new econometrics that the new classical economists have developed to test their propositions?

What I think about that should not be taken seriously, because I am not a skilled econometrician. I read the stuff, though. I have two problems with Sargent's econometric work. Problem one: the methods that he proposes to introduce, because of his wish that what one observes is the realization of a stationary stochastic process, are excessively heavy artillery. I am not much devoted to those methods, because I am not much devoted to the assumptions on whch they were based.

Problem two: many of the empirical things that the school has done strike me as unserious in the particular sense that the results are so fragile, so tied to particular sample periods, particular methods, and so on, that even the authors of the papers don't really tend to believe in their results. They are writing these papers to get across the message that it can be done technically; that's all.

I am not sure that some of the econometric work done by Keynesians is any better or is any less fragile, but that is not what you asked, and raises some very complicated questions.

Do you think that you are on the defensive right now, compared to the '60s?

No, I thought that I was a few months ago, but now I think that the tide is turning. If the tide is turning, it is partly for justifiable reasons, partly for unjustifiable reasons. The unjustifiable reason is that, for better or worse, the ideas of the new classical economists and political conversatives (there seems to be a connection there, at least at the moment) have been tied to the success of Reagan administration. The Reagan administration has generated a bad outcome, and they have been tarred with that brush. I suppose that that is unjust, because Bob Lucas could honestly say that he never advised Reagan and that the Reagan policies are not an exemplification of his policies. That is fair, but there is also a lot of truth in the notion that his ideas got some of their popularity because of the inflation of the early '70s, and that was not the fault of Keynesian economists, but Johnson's and Saudi Arabia's fault.

The other, and fair, reason is that more and more economists have come to realize that you cannot give a believable account of macroeconomic behavior in Western capitalist countries on the basis of market-clearing and misperception type of assumptions. Common sense rejects that.

My perception is that a lot of young economists are running away with it.

Yes, I agree, but I only said that the tide is turning, not that it has turned. I think that the number of young economists who are attracted to new classical economists is decreasing. Let me be concrete.

Last term I converted my part of the graduate macroeconomics sequence at M.I.T. into a course of lectures designed to give the analytical underpinnings of the sort of things that I have tried to describe to you. I also taught, later that term, more or less the same courses at Stanford. (By the way, I describe to my friends what I taught on those occasions as countercultural macroeconomics.) My object was to explain what my analytical objections to new classical economics are and to show them there is intellectually respectable work to be done outside the framework of new classical economics. I would not immediately describe it as Keynesian, but it is not market clearing economics. I was stunned with the response that I got. I cannot tell you how many students here and at Stanford came up to me and said, "Oh, I really am enjoying this course a lot; I felt all along that something was wrong with that stuff, but I wasn't able to articulate it and to see the alternatives. Now I have a much better idea." So I am convinced that many graduate students have misgivings about new classical economics, and for good reasons. It does not give them an adequate explanation of what they see.

But most of the graduate students seem to be enchanted with the rigor of new classical economics. . . .

I do think that is right. The main attraction of new classical economics is that it is analytically very nice. The analogy that has occurred to me is the scientist's attitude toward the hydrogen bomb. Oppenheimer is quoted to have said, "There is no doubt in my mind that we would have made the bomb no matter what, because it was technically so sweet." I think that is one of the reasons why new classical economics did so well: it is so technically sweet; it involves all those sophisticated techniques. Students have to learn something new that other people do not know. It is hard to learn, but you can do it. But I don't think that it will make people happy forever.

I try to show my students that there are other neat and interesting things you can do. They are perfectly rigorous, but they start with different assumptions and reach different conclusions. Students want to see that. You can only replace one shiny toy with another. That is all right. I think my toy looks more like what I see when I look at the real world, and I think lots of students share my feeling.

ABOUT DOING ECONOMICS

You agree with the statement that economists disagree. . . .

Yes, evidently they do. They disagree primarily as to the sensible assumptions to make. They also disagree on policy proposals, of course.

We cannot settle those disagreements, can we?

That bothers me. The resolution that I have come to in my own mind is this. We tend as economists to ask econometricians to settle questions which are too refined. We have to learn to ask cruder questions and recognize that the prime virtue of any econometric procedure is robustness. We also have to be prepared to consider a wider range of evidence. I would be very surprised if we cannot get convincing empirical evidence on important questions, such as whether the labor market typically clears or not, or whether unemployment between January '82 and January '83 can be regarded as intertemporal substitution. You might get it from investigating time series, but also in other ways. For example, I do not see anything wrong in asking unemployed workers direct questions on their actions. I am sure that you could pretty soon show that misperception of the real wage is an unlikely explanation of very much. If you can't, I would have to reconsider my own beliefs. Maybe the laboratory science is an overoptimistic model for economics. We can still be "scientific" in a meaningful way.

Did you ever try to talk with Lucas and Sargent?

Yes—not often because I don't see them very much.

How does it work when you try?

It doesn't work very well. There are two reasons for that, I guess. One reason is that we really start from very different assumptions about the economy, so it is very hard to communicate seriously. Frank Ramsey, a philosopher, once said that many conversations strike him as analogous to the following conversation: "I went to Grantchester today." "That is funny, I didn't." [Laughter.] After you have said that, there is not much else to say. If we had time, we could sit down and try to start with the crude assumptions and ask each other about them. It may be that we come to recognize that we have different sources of evidence. Sargent does not believe that people could conceivably behave the way I believe people behave.

The other reason is that in any conversation between say Lucas or Sargent and me, there is an element of game playing. There is a tendency to grab a debating point whenever you see it.

Why is that?

I suppose that each of us has self respect to maintain. No good motives, only bad motives. If we were all better people it would not happen. We have positions and we want to defend those, not merely seek the truth.

Really.

Oh sure, come on. Everybody is like that, at least some of the time, especially in situations structured like duels. If I were a colleague of Lucas's and we saw each other every day, I suspect that we would pretty soon find ourselves in fundamental disagreement about the underlying mechanism of what happens in the world. I don't know . . . maybe we could agree on some experiments or empirical investigations.

I suspect some annoyance on their part with the jokes that you tend to make in those conversations.

I know; I tend to react to many situations by making jokes. It comes naturally. Sometimes I think it's a flaw in my character, and I ought to fight it. But there's another side, too. Suppose someone sits down where you are sitting right now and announces to me that he is Napoleon Bonaparte. The last thing I want to do with him is to get involved in a technical discussion of cavalry tactics at the battle of Austerlitz. If I do that, I'm getting tacitly drawn into the game that he *is* Napoleon. Now, Bob Lucas and Tom Sargent like nothing better than to get drawn into technical discussions, because then you have tacitly gone along with their fundamental assumptions; your attention is attracted away from the basic weakness of the whole story. Since I find that fundamental framework ludicrous, I respond by treating it as ludicrous—that is, by laughing at it—so as not to fall into the trap of taking it seriously and passing on to matters of technique.

Look at it from my side of the fence. Lucas and Sargent refuse to discuss their market-clearing-equilibrium assumptions seriously. They'll go in forever about optimizing agents and partial information, covering up a little there too, because they really want to specify *what* those agents are optimizing. But when you ask them how they can justify assuming that all prices move flexibly to clear markets essentially all the time, they stonewall. Lucas's typical response is: "What's the alternative?" That's just a diversionary tactic. You don't have to be a genius to know that the alternative to the assumption of perpetual Walrasian equilibrium is either disequilibrium or some other nonclearing market concept of equilibrium. It's possible to say, and probably this is what they must mean, that the notion of market-clearing flexible-price equilibrium is the best worked-out concept of equilibrium we have. But if that framework is, as I think it is, a basic distortion of what actually happens in economic fluctuations, then the fact that it has been well developed — for other purposes, by the way — is not a strong argument for using it. I think they do not mind consciously discouraging students from working on other, more realistic, equilibrium or disequilibrium concepts. After all, some alternative concepts do exist: the quantity-adjustment equilibria of Dreze and Benassy, for instance — needing further development, of course, but what doesn't? In any case, if "Keynesian" economists are looking for a non-Walrasian description of the economy, it's a funny sort of criticism to say that what they're doing is inconsistent with Walrasian equilibrium. That's a joke too.

The other, more or less ludicrous thing I find in Lucas is his unwillingness or inability to imagine that social institutions and attitudes and concepts of fairness have *anything* to do with the way people interact in markets. After all, I don't argue that there would be unemployment in every artificial textbook society, only in ours.

Does this mean that conflicts of personalities intervene in economic intercourse?

That may be true in personal conversations, but it has little or nothing to do with the literature. I read things by people about whose personalities I know nothing.

I wonder now . . . If I give a talk in a seminar and if the seminar were occupied mainly by new classical economists. . . It happened to me once at the National Bureau of Economic Research; it didn't go very well. The reason that it doesn't go well is, I think, that I say something within my set of assumptions, and Barro will say in effect (but not in those words) that it is absolute nonsense, meaning by that it is nonsense on his assumptions. So I will say in return, "That is funny, I did not go to Grantchester." I am not the only one with that experience. I have heard Barro, in particular, say to others, "You can't possibly believe that." The third time that something like that happens I will probably reach for an outlandish example, and make a joke.

Still, I do not think that these problems are very important. Communication through writings is what moves economic thinking. I also should say that I remain positivist and believe that we should subject our theories to empirical tests as much as possible. Personal characteristics should not intervene.

Do you think that the differences are mainly philosophical?

Insofar as the basic assumptions express a philosophical vision, yes. But I certainly don't think that they cannot be settled, in principle at least, empirically.

What about disagreements on what constitutes good economics?

No. There may be some small differences, but I do not think that it is essential. Let me give you an example. Arrow and Hahn, who are the authors of a standard book on rigorous general equilibrium analysis, are both opponents of new classical economics.

I happen to believe in simple models rather than complicated models. But I believe in simple models with absolutely airtight argumentation.

But your models may not be as neat as new classical models.

Yes, there are some differences in style of reasoning. I am less happy with a model whose inner workings I can't understand. Other people may be more comfortable with those models, but those differences are inessential.

PART THREE

Conversations with Neo-Keynesian Economists: The "Younger Generation"

8

ALAN S. BLINDER

Lucas and Sargent speak of a generation gap, suggesting that the "older" (Keynesian) economists have difficulties keeping up with the times. How, then, does a "younger" neo-Keynesian economist look at new classical economics? Blinder appeared to be a good choice. His articles attest to his technical expertise, and he is not averse to the rational expectations hypothesis, as his recent work shows. Despite this, he remains an outspoken advocate of Keynesian policies. For a taste, one can read his monthly column in the *Boston Globe.*.

Receiving his Ph.D. from M.I.T. in 1971, Blinder was a student of Robert Solow. Subsequently, he returned to his undergraduate college, Princeton University. We talked in his office in July 1982.

BACKGROUND

Why did you start studying economics?

I, like many people who study economics, came in, at a very early age, interested in math. When I first came to college, I thought I was interested in math, but that's largely because kids in high school don't know what math is. When I came to Princeton as a student, I learned what math really was, and I really wasn't interested. But I was interested in applying quantitative, mathematical, and scientific methods to social problems. That only leads to one place for the most part, or it used to [laughter], and that's to economics. Sociology is really very underdeveloped. Anthropology is a whole different thing. I think of that more like history than like a contemporary social science. I'm not sure why sociology is underdeveloped; maybe it's because they haven't been able to quantify things as well as we have. A lot of things they [the sociologists] deal with are more elusive and harder to get measurements of. And if you don't have measurements, you don't have science. That may be the reason.

I took what in those days was a lot of mathematics. Economics has become so mathematized so fast that what was thought of as a lot of mathematics to study economics when I as an undergraduate in 1963–67, is certainly not any longer. I took eight or nine math and statistics courses when I was in college.

Were you good in math?

Yeah, I was good at math, but not in the serious abstract math they teach at Princeton. I remember when I came here as a young man I never felt like I was very good; I always felt like my head was under water. But I was getting As in the courses, so I'm not sure how to answer the question [laughter]. I think the answer is that nobody was very good at it. Relative to my peers, I was doing just fine; but I didn't really feel I was.

Excuse me for my curiosity, but the amount of articles that you have been able to publish is amazing. How do you do it?

I don't think it's that many—35 or 40 articles in twelve years. They're not all great [laughter]. If they were all great I would be more amazed. You've been looking at other people's vitaes also. I don't think that's unusual for a full professor in a top department. I bet Tom Sargent has a lot more than that. I work a lot [laughter]. Not that much—my wife says I work more than I actually do. I guess I typically work a 50–55 hour week. I always work evenings; I don't work much on weekends. It's not extraordinary.

It must mean, though, that you are committed to economics.

Yeah, I'm also pretty efficient. I write fast. One thing I did in college was newspaper work to help pay my way through, and that taught me to write, and to write fast and well. So, I write pretty quickly once I sit down. That helps. I don't really struggle over the writing. I don't know anyone except Baumol who can write faster than I.

What is it that you find attractive in economics at this time?

I think it's the same thing that attracted me originally when I was 18 years old. The way the profession has turned in the last 18 years has been away from that. It is turning much more toward a priori reasoning, much more toward mathematical models that have very little anchor in the real world, very much against empirical work, very much against concern with social problems. How many things do you read in the top journals these days that are concerned with social problems, as opposed to concern with technique? The elevation of technique over substance very much distresses me. I don't like that about what's happened in the discipline in the last decade or so. . . . The social aspects in economics are very important.

I have the impression that you are a true Keynesian at heart.

Yeah. I don't shrink from that label. I think it's right.

How did you become a Keynesian?

I was weaned on it like everybody else. Bob Lucas was also weaned on it; I just never threw away the baby bottle [laughter]. It tasted good, it still tastes good.

Who are the people that influenced you in the Keynesian direction?

My first economics book was Samuelson's *Economics*. That made a lot of sense to me, so he influenced me indirectly, even though I never met him until I became a graduate student at M.I.T. about six years later. Burt Malkiel, who taught me at Princeton, was very influential in attracting me to economics. His approach, the way he taught, the way he explained things, the way he weaved common sense and mathematics — he was just very good, a very good expositor. Originally I was interested in things having to do with corporate finance, which is what he taught. Bob Solow, in graduate school, was very influential. He has a very compelling personality, just a wonderful guy. It's impossible not to like him. He's also a superb teacher; and he makes a lot of sense. He hasn't been swept away by these recent fads either. I worked a lot with him; he was my thesis advisor. After I finished the thesis, we started working on the survey piece that eventually appeared in the Brookings book; and out of that came the famous *Journal of Public Economics* piece on fiscal policy. That was a spin-off of the Brookings piece, an idea we had while working on the Brookings survey.

Were you considered a promising student?

[Laughter] I think so, yeah. You should ask Bob Solow [still chuckling]. Yeah, I think I was. The good students distinguish themselves. There were a couple of really top people in my years at M.I.T. and I guess I was one of them. . . . I felt I was one of them . . . I think the faculty felt I was one of them.

Were you highly motivated?

I've been very much self-motivated. I've never needed anyone to push me — it's my Jewish overachieving background. You can hardly help but notice the great number of Jewish professors in many disciplines. A Jewish upbringing has always put a very high premium on education, and it sort of drives you to hard work. It's part of the culture. Some of this hard work shows up in the business world; it shows up mainly in areas in which Jews were not discriminated against. In academia, there was some discrimination but compared to many other walks of life there was relatively little discrimination against Jews. And so, all over academia, you see a huge number of Jewish people.

Did you get a lot of support from your family?

When I was young I got a tremendous amount of support — "Go to the best college, study and do well" — that was very much encouraged. My father was a businessman and went to college for two years. My mother didn't go to college. They were married very young. I was brought up in suburbia. I had the median family background for American Jewish middle-class kids brought up in the suburbs of New York. Most of us come from the suburbs of New York and get a lot of energy from that.

The other thing is that most of these kids grew up with liberal political views. It used to be (although it is getting to be less so) that the American Jewish community was very liberal. The milieu that I came out of was very much liberal politically. It's left a permanent imprint on me. On some of us it left only a temporary imprint. Robert Barro comes out of the same background, and he is extremely right wing.

What does liberal ideology mean to you?

To me it means one thing more than anything else: sympathy for society's underdogs. Almost everything else spins off of that. For example, greater concern for unemployment rather than inflation. We know who pays the cost of unemployment, and it's not the upper-middle-class people.

Were you affected by the '60s?

No, I was a little too old for that. It was the students at the very end of the '60s and the early '70s—like my two brothers. I was already finished with college in 1967; I was married in 1967. I really never got into the student movement in any way. In fact, I've never been involved in any political movement.

ABOUT HIS ECONOMICS

What do you consider the main issue in your research?

Early on, and I still carry an interest in it, the distribution of income. The main question is why it is so unequal. The next question is what are the ways to make it less unequal—that's what motivates the interest. And then unemployment and inflation. . . When I came to Princeton, I started teaching macroeconomics, though I hadn't really specialized in that direction in graduate school. This myth about the positive interaction between teaching and research is true when you come to graduate teaching at top universities. Teaching the graduate course in macro theory kept these things on my mind. I just kept getting ideas for research in macroeconomics. Also the market pulls you that way. There was, and still is, a great demand for people to come to a conference with a paper on topics in macroeconomics, not in income distribution. Third, there were colleagues here in macroeconomics, other people doing work. In income distribution there were very few; you were talking to yourself. I felt that no one was ever reading anything I wrote. That turned out to be wrong: my book on income distribution was much more widely read than I ever thought in the early years. But I still get more reaction about that book from abroad than from this country.

My interest in macro issues just sort of evolved. I got involved just as the soup was getting stirred; the thing was fermenting. I felt it my duty to protect the truth [laughter]—the Keynesian truth. A number of the research issues I settled upon came out of the courses I was teaching. My interest in inventories came out of the experience of the United States in the '73-'75 business cycle. I was struck that the whole show was inventories. So, I started looking into this. I'd never been taught anything about inventories, and I hadn't taught my students about it either. So I started looking into it, and I found out that the '73-'75 experience was typical. I discovered that most of the ball game in business cycles was inventories, and it wasn't just then, but had been so in the past.

There had been a lot of interest in inventories in the US in the '40s and '50s, but it died. I decided somebody ought to start reviving it.

Does your getting into an issue like that mean endorsement of the Keynesian position?

Not particularly, no. I may start with an a priori belief that understanding what's going on in business cycles is terribly important, that it's a terrible social problem. After that, the ideology leaves my mind. There may be some moral imperative in studying that subject rather than another one. But after that you try to forget the moral imperative, act like a scientist, and find out what's really important: What are the important phenomena? What do we need to understand? What do we know about them? What do we not know about them? The moral aspect is gone, and you're looking for truth, for an explanation, and letting the chips fall where they may. These chips may or may not lead to "support" for Keynesian policies.

In general, your conclusions lead up to Keynesian conclusions.

I don't think that's true. I like to think I'm one of the few economists who has published research results that are hostile to his ideology. I'll give you two examples. My book on stagflation was published two years ago, but I circulated the preliminary results six years ago in a paper on wage-price controls which was very hostile to wage-price controls. (This article was subsequently published in the *Journal of Monetary Economics.*) If you think in terms of people on the left or right of the spectrum, it is mostly the people on the right who argue that the controls didn't work. They argue that prices bounced back to where they would have been anyway, and that the whole controls program was a waste. I believe that, too. But that position is hostile to a left-leaning ideology. Another example is my paper in the *Journal of Political Economy* in 1975 that argued against the view that poor people have a substantially higher marginal propensity to consume and, therefore, if you want to raise consumption, you should redistribute income in favor of the poor. This is an old Keynesian argument, but I couldn't find any evidence for it. So, I just changed my thinking.

None of this affects my ideology, though. The fundamental bedrock is sympathy for the underdog. If it's the case that they have the same marginal propensity to consume as everybody else, then forget about that; it's irrelevant. If it's the case that wage-price controls don't improve the inflation/unemployment trade-off, and in fact make certain things worse, then forget about that. That doesn't change the bedrock ideology that's in the back of your mind all the time. It's important to keep clear the ends and the means. If things that are supported as means to the right ends are really not means, then you have to jettison them. This is something that politicians can never understand. They think minimum wages are a good way to help poor people; that's wrong. What you want to do is help poor people. If that means sweeping away the minimum wage, even though that brands you as a right-winger, then you support that. And I always have.

In your inventory work you also join the recent fad of trying to establish the microfoundations of macroeconomics.

I think establishing the microfoundations of macroeconomics is a good idea. We're not really going to understand what's going on in the macroeconomy until we understand the micro. What's important to me is that we construct empirically relevant microfoundations, not play games with silly models which seem to have very little to do with what's going on in the real world. I am thinking of the assumption in some new classical models that people do not know what the money supply is. Everybody who cares to know, knows what the money supply is, within a small margin of error. This can't be why we have business fluctuations. But, on the other hand, inventory behavior can explain, indeed must explain, a lot of the business cycle. So, getting the right microfoundations to explain the macro data is very important.

The problem in all this is aggregation. Take my model in the *American Economic Review* [1982] on inventories. That model will aggregate nicely only if everybody has the same technology. It assumes a quadratic objective function, so it has linear decision rules; and linear decision rules aggregate nicely. Now, maybe the world's not like that, and in that case the aggregation problem is more difficult.

The problem I dealt with in the *Brookings Papers* [1981] was not a stock adjustment linear decision rule, but a so-called "S, s" model. It's a model where you have a lower limit "s" and an upper limit "S." The policy is to let your inventories fall until they hit "s," and then build them back to "S." That's optimal under certain technologies. But the upshot is that different firms will react very differently to the same stimulus. A firm that's in the middle range that gets a positive sale shock will still stay within its range, and so won't react at all. It won't order anything.

But a firm that's near its "s" boundary will get pushed over and make a finite reaction. In such a world, you really have hard micro-foundations. It is very difficult to go from that to an aggregate macro equation.

In general, though, if you want to do macroeconomics you simply have to learn to live with a certain amount of error and ambiguity that's introduced by the aggregation problem. For, generally, the aggregation problem is not analytically soluble. I think similar problems emerge in many branches of physics and chemistry — a good micro structure and not such a good macro structure. But it works for them, and not as well for us. I have sympathy for the microfoundations drive, but I do think that it's exaggerated — and not only because of the aggregation problem. The upshot is that the problem will never have a perfect solution.

What is Keynesian economics, according to you?

Keynesian economics is the economics of nominal rigidities basically, nominal rigidities everywhere. Fully anticipated money does affect output. Everybody can see that! So, it's right. The fact that it's not as theoretically tidy as Lucas's *1972 Journal of Economic* Theory paper is not a reason to throw it away. That's become a minority view in this profession, unfortunately. It wouldn't have been in the '60s.

What else, besides nominal rigidities, characterizes Keynesian economics?

Unemployment: that it's a real and long-lasting phenomenon. Government policies can do something about unemployment, albeit in the face of the short-run trade-off with inflation. That's the positive economics. And then there's a normative proposition that says the government should do something to limit recessions.

ABOUT NEW CLASSICAL ECONOMICS

New classical economics has undermined the hegemony of Keynesian economics. Some people speak of a Kuhnian revolution in macroeconomics. What do you think?

The story in Kuhn is that one scientific paradigm gets thrown away after some anomaly is discovered, and a new paradigm arises to replace it. This is not at all how Keynesian economics was discarded in favor of new classical economics. There are empirical anomalies which

Keynesian economics has difficulty with, but in none of these cases does new classical economics do a better job, in my view. This was a case of a victory of a priori reasoning over empirical observation. The model was appealing. Young people who are coming into economics, but who really are closet mathematicians, latched onto it. It swept away Keynesian economics. But not in the Kuhnian way. . .I can't think of any good parallels to Kuhn's story, but that's the way it went.

I just wasn't swept away [laughter]. I'm not persuaded by the line of argument that says that which is theoretically neater must be true.

Do you sense major disagreements among macroeconomists?

[Laughter.] Doesn't everybody sense that?

No.

Who doesn't?

Sargent, for example.

Tom Sargent is a bit out of touch with the real world up there in his office in Minneapolis. A lot of the disagreement is ideologically based, though certainly not on Tom's part. I see this by talking to people. Certain people have a capacity for ignoring facts which are patently obvious, but are counter to their view of the world; so they just ignore them.

Maybe people say the same thing about me, but I don't see it that way. You see things through your own eyes, certainly. Some of the new classical economists are extremely ideological. If you give them evidence, for example, that fully anticipated money matters, evidence counter to their world view, they say that you're wrong. And if you say that their evidence is wrong, they'll say you're wrong again. I give up! Barro once said to me that there isn't any evidence in the world that fiscal policy is effective. Just open your eyes and see episodes of tax cutting and government-spending increases. How about World War II? That had big effects on real output. His response? . . . He sometimes shrugs, he sometimes gives a clearer alternative explanation.

Sargent is much more serious. He doesn't come to these economic views from a rigidly maintained ideological position. He's a sort of tinkerer, playing an intellectual game. He looks at a puzzle to see if he can solve it in a particular way, exercising these fancy techniques. That's his thing, so to speak.

I think Lucas is a blend of those two, actually. He's not as extreme as

Barro, he's more open. And he's not quite as technical as Sargent. The reason he rejects disequilibrium, for example, is that there isn't a nice theory of it. You get the impression that if there were a beautiful theory of disequilibrium encased in a jewel box, he might actually accept it. His view is "Look, I have a nice theory of equilibrium. You say 'disequilibrium,' but all that is is 'non-equilibrium'." I believe that if there were a nice disequilibrium theory based on maximizing behavior, and all the loose ends were tidied up, he might accept that. I wouldn't expect such a reaction from Barro. But, of course, we don't have that theory and probably never will.

Do you consider these three people as your major opponents?

Yes. Milton Friedman is less active in this new classical debate. But in the old debate about monetarism he still is a major actor. I don't think of him as an adversary because he is so much older than I am. In "Monetarism Is Obsolete" I didn't mention him, but he is in between the lines. I don't meet him much. Lucas, Sargent, Barro — they are the economists I meet.

At the moment you are in a very defensive position with Keynesian economics. How did that happen?

I believe that the younger economists were attracted to the techniques that came out of Lucas and, later, out of Sargent. Many younger economists didn't give a damn about the substance; they just love the techniques and all jumped onto the bandwagon. And that's the reason that it took the profession by storm: it was an elevation of technique over substance. There is a pressure to conform, but some of us resist.

You don't talk about disagreements with the post-Keynesians and the Marxists.

You mean Paul Davidson and Sidney Weintraub, people like that? I guess they've been much less involved in the debates. Those guys have a much lower profile in the profession. These are not the ones you see at conferences. I think they actually may have something valuable, but I'm not very well read on this. For example, the finance constraint: lately I've been thinking about that a lot more. Their concept about uncertainty has never been formalized and mathematized, and there also isn't empirical evidence to go with it that I'm aware of. These things are important to me. And a lot of it is semiincoherent. You read something of this literature, and a few sentences will strike you as really right on the mark. Then there'll be 30 other sentences you can't make any sense out of.

The Marxists, I think, never had any good ideas and still don't; the only difference is that no one pays any attention to them anymore. In the late '60s a lot of people were paying attention. It was hot, and a lot of people swung to the left — society went to the left. Now it's swung to the right and so they're out. I never paid much attention to them in the late '60s and I still don't. I think there's something to the dual market hypothesis. I'm not very comfortable with the concept of struggle and conflict, but that's my intellectual upbringing. I feel comfortable with budget constraints, stuff like that.

What do you think new classical economics is?

Really, it's the economics that restores the principle of market clearing. Rational expectations was a smoke screen, although not intentionally. People thought for years and years, and a lot of people still do (it takes a lot of time before the truth reaches the people), that it was a debate about rational expectations. It's not at all. We're perfectly willing to accept rational expectations as a working hypothesis — as long as it's kept as a working hypothesis. I really think expectations probably are not rational. Likewise, I think people don't really maximize utility. But it may be moderately close, and certainly for long-run issues it's the only reasonable hypothesis.

But the debate is not about rational expectations. We now know that none of the queer conclusions of new classical models came out of the assumption that expectations are rational; they came out of two things, namely, the assumption that markets clear all the time and, secondarily, out of the so-called Lucas supply function, which states that what drives output is mistakes in estimating the price level. I believe that both of those ideas are totally wrong.

The Lucas supply function goes wrong right at the beginning. I think it has nothing to do with the supply of goods in the modern economy. Everyone who wants to know it, knows what the money supply is. I think you'd be surprised how little many people care about what the money supply is. They care about how much they can sell, what their costs are. There are lots of things they care about a lot more than the money supply. If they want to know what the money supply is, they read it in the *Wall Street Journal* every Friday. The idea that you're not quite sure what your relative price is has a ring of plausibility, but I also think that's ridiculous. The CPI was announced for June this morning. Up until this morning, I didn't know what the price level was in June and I still don't know what it is in July. I don't know what the price level is in July, so when I sell my consulting services, I don't actually know my own relative price. However, I know it within 1 percent. I cannot be off by more than 1 percent for July. A 1 percent error is a 12 percent annual rate on the rate of inflation. How could I be that far off? So that means that when I translate my nominal consulting fee into real terms, the most I could be off is .5 to 1 percent. Can anyone believe that that kind of error can result in cyclical fluctuations of the magnitude that we observe? It's totally absurd to think that. It's on those grounds that I totally disagree with it. I just find it totally unrealistic.

What do they mean by market clearing prices?

I think they mean that the price level in period t adjusts to shocks that hit the economy in period t so as to clear all the goods off the market. But that also has to be ridiculous. Somehow, some people are able to look at the world and not see involuntary unemployment. I think I see it all over the place during cyclical downturns. I also think I see unsold goods all over the place, like in automobile lots right now. I see houses and apartments sitting empty. I don't think it can be the consequence of mismatching. I think of the Keynesian factors, rigidities of various sorts and the multiplier problems in case of a downturn . . . I think of the basic Keynesian ideas. They say that Keynesians don't have a good theory of why the nominal wage is rigid. But that does not lead me to the predisposition to assume, until the day I have a good theory of why it's rigid, that the nominal wage is flexible when I see that it's rigid.

I just don't accept the epistemological point of view that until you have a good, solid, theoretical explanation of a phenomenon you have to ignore the phenomeon. That's very wrong . . . I don't accept the view that, until we know why, we have to ignore it. That's the part I don't accept. I'm perfectly happy to accept the idea that we should always try to know why they do what they do, and that's why I do believe we should try to find the microfoundations of macro. But I don't believe that until we find them we have to assume some silly model.

When did you realize that you had to deal with their argument and that rational expectations . . .

. . . is here to stay. I was a little slow. I resisted it. I dismissed it as quackery for a few years. That turned out to be a bad mistake. I was very slow getting into the new things, so to speak. I had the mistaken attitude that it was just a matter of a few crazy papers and that it would largely be ignored by the profession. It was probably '75 or '76 before I really started to pay attention. It had been around since '72 . . .

Some people around me were reluctant to adopt rational expectations, some weren't. John Taylor is an example of a guy who is the opposite of me. He saw that it would be important, and he latched on to it quite early. He writes good stuff, much better than some of the others.

Did anyone in particular convince you that the new classical argument was worth your attention?

No one in particular introduced me to it; it was just the whole profession. I don't, or I try not to, live in a vacuum. The whole profession was moving that way. There were two or three early papers. That became 20 or 30 and then 300. You could hardly ignore it. That applies also to the notion of rational expectations, which, I still believe, is tertiary to this debate. I originally rejected it as silly. Half of me still does, but the other half of me finds it an attractive idea. The half of me that likes to think of people deciding what to consume by finding the tangency of budget lines and indifference curves also says that expectations are rational. The other half says people don't really act that way, and that these are all ad hoc assumptions, which are in the long run related to those sort of things, but which in the short run aren't. That half says expectations aren't rational. But that's different from where I started. I started by rejecting it as a silly behavioral hypothesis.

You have done some modeling with rational expectations in particular in your model on supply shocks [Blinder, 1981].

I had been debating what would be the proper monetary response to a supply shock. I finally decided that I would try to do it on their ground rules. I wanted to see if I could address this issue in a model with rational expectations, that is, in a model congenial to their way of thinking. I wondered whether I could still come to the same conclusion, which was that the monetary authority should have provided more monetary accommodation to the supply shocks of 1974. I don't think I was very successful. The conclusion is that within the framework of the Lucas model the scope for monetary accommodation is rather small. It gets bigger if you get into a nonmarket-clearing, Fischer-type framework, but still maybe not as great as my prior beliefs were. It was basically an exercise motivated by the idea that if they don't want to talk about it on my ground rules, Keynesian ground rules, let me try to talk about it on their ground rules.

How would you talk about the issue, according to your ground rules?

On my ground rules, what happens in a case like that is that prices get pushed up by costs, since they're a markup over costs in the short run. The money supply doesn't increase, so you have a monetary squeeze. You also have a passive fiscal squeeze because the tax system isn't indexed, and real taxes go up when prices go up. So monetary and fiscal policy both unintentionally tighten. In addition to that, there's a redistribution of income toward high savers and away from high spenders. This is an international phenomenon. All these things are happening on the demand side. On the supply side, there is a contraction of potential output at the same time.

The monetary accommodation is aimed at not letting the supply-shock side contaminate the demand side. I think that, in the short run, it was the demand contraction induced by OPEC that was the far more significant thing in causing the recession of 1973–75. And that's where you need the monetary accommodation. If it were just a supply shock, and none of these demand-side things were happening, it may turn out that the optimal policy is not to accommodate at all. After all, you can't fight the reduction in potential output.

There's also the question of how permanent the supply shock is going to be. I, like many people, didn't believe in 1974 that it was going to be as permanent as it turned out to be. If it had been a transitory drop in potential output there would have been more reason to ignore it and to try to keep output temporarily above potential. How permanent you thought it was going to be was relevant, and I think I had bad judgment on that issue . . .

Your position favors discretionary policy. Sargent and Wallace, among others, believe that all economists agree by now that rules are more effective than discretionary policy. Where does that leave you?

[Laughter.] Tom says a lot of things. I don't believe that's a meaningful statement, because I don't believe there's such a thing as rules — except some extreme ones. I can't think of any, actually. Monetary policy is not following any rule now. We use rules in theoretical models, but policy-makers don't use them. A policy-maker follows a certain policy, and any time he thinks there is a reason to deviate from it, he will. So unless you've written this rule into the Constitution, which I think is a reckless thing to do, and have written it very tightly into the Constitution, the Congress or the Fed or whoever it is will find ways to end the rule. I don't think it's a real issue.

The rules in a model shouldn't be taken seriously. When I teach these models, I rarely put in a monetary rule. I usually just leave anticipated and unanticipated money as two variables and try not to explain the rule. The rule indicates the anticipated part of the money supply, but in my teaching I don't say much about the rule.

But don't we have to know the rules in order to determine the optimal policy in any given situation?

The debate about what rule is optimal is almost meaningless, because we're never going to have rules: we're only going to have discretionary policies, and the question is what kind. New classical economists talk about rules as policy. That's one of the very naive things in the writings of new classical economics. The argument in Barro [1976] and in Sargent and Wallace [1975] shows that lagged feedback rules can't have any effect. In the second stage, they introduce monetary noise and conclude that that can only be bad and therefore — and this is a very transparent syllogism — the best rule is constant money. Yes, it's true under the assumptions of the model . . .

The new classical argument is that we have to take into account the effects of current policy on the future. Discretionary policy is ineffective as people will try to anticipate its future consequences. Moreover, erratic policy will increase uncertainty.

Regarding the future shock argument — that if government policy is erratic, people will be more uncertain — what makes better sense is the related statement that if economic performance is more erratic, then people will be more uncertain. But few people really care about what government spending is relative to GNP. Most people care about general economic performance. If the economy is erratic without unstable government, then you have a lot of uncertain private agents.

One important aspect of the debate is about how stable the economy would be without an active government . . . Look at a time series chart (in my stagflation book) of the year-to-year fluctuations of GNP. They are remarkably smaller in the '50s and '60s, the "Keynesian" years, than they were before. Once I put this to Barro. I said, "Look at this, buddy, and tell my why this is." I think I know why it is. I claim I know why —

that there was active fiscal and monetary policy to iron out business cycles beginning after World War II, but not before. So I think discretionary policies have been used and they have often worked. They haven't always been perfect; lots of times they've messed things up, but by and large they have been salutary and have resulted in less uncertainty for private economic agents.

I think the best case for rules is political. There's a political argument that the political forces will very often do the wrong thing, make the wrong decision. There's something to be said, then, for replacing them with rules. But that's a conceptual argument. As a practical argument, you're not going to have the politicians stand by and say, "You economists give us a rule and we'll put it in place," and not do anything else. That's silly! My theoretical work doesn't answer this question; it's a political question. My theoretical work tells me that if politicians do the right thing, it is better not to have a rule; if they do the wrong thing, it is better to have a rule.

ABOUT THE EMPIRICAL ARGUMENT

New classical economists severely criticize the use of large-scale models by neo-Keynesian economists. Lucas in particular argues that the notion of rational expectations renders their simulations of alternative government policies unreliable. What do you think of this criticism?

The critique of large-scale models holds; it is unquestionably valid. The only problem with it is that its empirical importance is not yet established. This is a case where people have latched on to a criticism. All you have to do in this country (more than in other places) right now is scream mindlessly, "Lucas critique!" and the conversation ends. That is a terrible attitude. The Lucas critique may be correct, but I have seen no persuasive evidence in any sphere to indicate that it is empirically important. The empirical case is yet to be made. The big question is whether changes in policy regimes cause large changes in coefficients. Maybe they cause just very tiny changes. Maybe people don't know that there has been a change in policy regime; they only slowly adapt, as they are very skeptical that the world is ever going to change.

Sargent and Sims seem to have developed a new style in econometrics with two components. One of these components focuses on time series and uses a minimum of theory. The other uses very elaborate theory and focuses on cross-equations restrictions. What do you think of this work?

I'm not big on the empirical work of either of these components. I'm very much against the vector autoregressions, or the methods that scramble the data so that they don't look like data that came out of the real world. It rejects the idea of testing the relevant structure. I am just very negative about this methodology.

As far as the other component is concerned, the issue is, I think, very simple. If you really know the right theory of the world and have good data, then doing the econometric work the way Tom wants to do it is the right way. However, if you don't know the right model — and the problem of aggregation suggests that you never will — then imposing this structure on the model can make the estimates worse, and that's why I don't like this stuff. I wrote a little criticism of Sargent, but I haven't tried to publish it yet. It's addressed exactly to the new econometrics as Sargent conceives it.

ABOUT DOING ECONOMICS

What do you think are the criteria of good work?

It's easy to say, but not easy to achieve. It should have good theoretical foundations and often, but not always, be grounded in maximizing behavior. (Some people say always, I say often.) It should make correct predictions about behavior. It should be founded on realistic assumptions. (This is a violation of the Chicago methodology.) It should have good microfoundations; it should make empirically correct predictions; and should be empirically validated.

Easy to say, right? The problems are several. First, the world is messy; it does not fit into any nice theoretical mold. For some issues that may not matter, but for some it does. Second, the data are never quite what we want them to be. We have to make do with testing our theories with empirical proxies, bad data, data with measurement errors, data that do not really measure the right conceptual variables that we'd like to measure. We usually have to test micro theories with macro data. We don't often have data on individual people or individual firms. That's the aggregation issue. I don't think our econometric techniques are bad; it's just that the data are troublesome. If we had the right data, we wouldn't have to worry so much about funny econometric techniques. Many experimental scientists use very rudimentary statistical techniques; they're not nearly as sophisticated as we are . . .

How important is the distinction between normative and positive economics for you? Does the weakness of the empirical argument undermine the foundation of positive economics?

There's a line between normative and positive economics in my work. I try to make that clear. Empirical work should be objective. I'm a little optmistic, maybe naive, that empirical work can be objective. You used to see it more, now not so much.

The argument with Barro over the effect of anticipated changes in the money supply is an example. There's been a lot of work done by various people on this issue. I'm not sure that Barro will agree, but I think it's almost over; almost everyone agrees that those anticipated changes do have real effects.

How do you view the role of economists in this world?

You mean the real world, not the academic world? You have to keep plugging away. An academic doesn't want to repeat himself. You always have to think of something new and different to say. But to have influence in the public policy sphere you have to repeat, repeat, repeat. I've learned that recently from the new right. They finally got their way; they repeated; they plugged away; they said the same thing over and over; and they finally convinced people to listen.

In the long run, ideas may have influence. In the short run, I think politicians do what they want, and if they can latch on to an idea that justifies it, they do. There's an old cliché that economic policy has always been considered too important to be left to economists. I think that's true.

Your editorials in the Boston Globe *show   a strong urge to stand up and yell.*

It has gotten stronger in the last couple of years.

Why is that?

I guess I'm naturally a loudmouth. Part of it goes back to the attitude I had when I was 18 years old and first discovered economics. I saw social problems and thought the economics could contribute something to overcoming them. I feel more passionately involved recently because of the movement to the right, the election of Reagan, and the politics that Reagan has brought in. I have become more of an activist than I ever was before. I am writing columns for the *Boston Globe* and *Washington Post*; and I am involved in an organization called the National Policy Exchange which, while it doesn't want to be described as a Democratic think tank, really is.

All this is new to me. I never would have gotten involved before, but now I am. I used to keep quiet, but if we keep quiet and the right wingers keep yelling, what has happened will keep happening.

9

JOHN B. TAYLOR

In 1981, Lucas and Sargent published a selection of empirical contributions to new classical economics. All the papers were written by economists who are directly associated with new classical economists except John Taylor. His work is generally critical of new classical economics. For example, a well known article that he coauthored with Phelps (1977) states the importance of contracts and rejects the equilibrium assumption of new classical economics. Nevertheless, his inclusion by Lucas and Sargent certainly indicates an affinity between his work and that of new classical economists. We will want to explore this tension.

Like Blinder, Taylor was an undergraduate at Princeton. He earned his Ph.D. at Stanford in 1973 and taught at Columbia and Princeton. He served on the Council of Economic Advisers in 1976–77 and is now at Harvard University. We talked in Princeton in November 1982, while he was then professor of Economics and Public Affairs.

BACKGROUND

Why did you get interested in economics?

I majored in economics as an undergraduate and got very interested in the chance to apply scientific ideas to problems that seemed very real. It seemed to give an understanding of which factors determine economic conditions in the world. I was very fascinated by the whole thing.

I wrote a thesis at Princeton, where I was an undergraduate, on monetary and fiscal policy for stabilization purposes. It was very quantitatively oriented. I developed numerical models which allowed me to do simulations.

Was any faculty member in particular stimulating?

No, I think that it was more the faculty as a whole. Phil Howrey, who is now at the University of Michigan, helped me quite a bit. He was interested in time-series analysis at the time. Burt Malkiel was stimulating; I took a class with him on corporate finance.

Then you went to Stanford.

Yes. One of the reasons I was attracted to Stanford was their heavy emphasis on quantitative and econometric techniques. My thesis was almost as much on econometric theory as it was on things that are useful for macroeconomics. It was on ways to learn about the economy by estimating econometric models at the same time that you try to use these models for policy purposes. That is what you call a joint problem of estimation and control.

Why were you so interested in the quantitative aspects of economics? Was it because you were good at it?

No, I wouldn't say so. I was interested in the problems. It seemed to me that quantitative economics is an area that needed a lot of work and had a lot of open questions. It is on the forefront of the connection between theory and the real world. Economics is a quantitative science: it deals with quantities.

There is also a sense of excitement, because you seem to make a lot of progress in understanding substantive issues using mathematical or quantitative techniques.

Progress?

Economists have been studying economics for hundreds of years, and in some sense the basic principles of economics have not changed very much. What has really changed is the methodology. You can now address the issues more rigorously, more systematically, and in more detail. You can say what you mean and you can document what you say. People can check whether what you are saying is true much more easily. That all is very useful.

If the same principles still apply, what is then the substance of the progress? Do we, with the improvement in techniques, understand better how the world operates? What did we learn?

The underlying assumptions about economic behavior have not changed. There are criticisms of this approach, but in general economists still rely on the maximization postulates. The progress is in the application of techniques. The development of computer technology has been very helpful. There are also much more data.

It seems that Phelps had an important role in your career. For example, you wrote an article with him and acknowledge him in many of your other papers.

Yes, he was a colleague of mine for seven years at Columbia. We interacted a lot. Without question he influenced me. I guess it was his interest in macroeconomic questions. He is an imaginative thinker, and he thinks about substantive issues such as inflation and unemployment.

ABOUT ECONOMICS AND ECONOMISTS

How would you describe yourself as an economist? The conclusions you draw in many of your papers would suggest that you belong to the neo-Keynesian camp, or at least the younger generation in this camp.

I find it very difficult to use such terminology, quite frankly. I like to focus on the improvement of models, and in particular how macroeconomists model expectations. There is a big difference between modern macroeconomics and macroeconomics before the 1970s. For example, there is a much better understanding of how we can model expectations, both quantitatively and theoretically.

The term "new classical" usually refers to a type of modeling which not only includes better treatment of expectations but also a description of the way in which markets behave. It is the latter part of new classical economics that I do not think is acccurate or particularly helpful. But I have used the rational expectations part for as long as I have been doing work in macroeconomics, at least since I left graduate school. I think that the expectations approach is very helpful. It is not always right; sometimes it is not realistic at all. But it is a big improvement.

There is much more to the progress in macroeconomics than just stating that expectations are rational. When you study business cycles, you consider behavior over a long period of time. You are asking questions about how the economy would respond to different types of policy systems over 10 or 15 years. The questions concern strategy. There is more concern in macroeconomics with the details of how markets work, for example, how flexible prices are. I am spending a lot of my research efforts trying to design improvements over the assumption that markets always clear, and that prices are perfectly flexible.

In your article with Phelps you suggest that your conclusion that stabilization policy is effective implies a victorious restoration of an old doctrine. That is neo-Keynesian, isn't it?

I think you use the word "Keynesian" in a way that is not appropriate. The paper that I wrote with Phelps attempted to show that monetary policy, even if anticipated, would have an effect on the economy. That is true for most Keynesian models. It is also true of monetarist models, and for that matter, it was true in Irving Fisher's view of the world before Keynes. Of course, you have to go back and try to interpret what early economists actually said. Because they were never quite as explicit as economists tend to be now, this is not easy. It seems to me that the idea that even anticipated changes in money affect the economy is not exclusively a Keynesian idea, though Keynes helped us understand why that is the case. Phelps and I wrote the paper in response to the Sargent-Wallace paper to restore this idea.

In which sense do you differ from people like Blinder and Tobin, who do not resist the label of neo-Keynesian?

I think that you have to read our papers carefully to get a feeling for that. I have great respect for both Blinder and Tobin. We don't see eye to eye on everything. I might put more emphasis on expectations; I also have different views about government policy. But I don't think you want to divide people up along what their view is on government policy. You also want to consider their view as to the way the economy works and the useful strategy of doing economics. I have no major disagreements on the scientific approaches of either Blinder or Tobin or, for that matter, with those of Lucas and Sargent.

How did you get into rational expectations? You were quick in picking it up, unlike many others.

I thought that it was an important modification of conventional ways of doing macroeconomics. The importance of expectations seems very clear after the work of Phelps and Milton Friedman. In the late '60s there was increasing interest in models of expectations and the effects of expectations on the economy. So it was a very important development, one that needed a lot more research and that would be useful in helping us to explain behavior.

What do you think are the major characteristics of the work of Lucas and Sargent, apart from rational expectations?

They have done a lot of things. It is really impossible to describe all the work that they have done in a short interview like this. Part of Lucas's work is on the way the Phillips curve works; it is based on informational problems. I think that that is a major contribution: it showed a way to model a puzzling feature of economic behavior very logically, very rigorously, with an emphasis on uncertainty and on the problems that individuals have because they don't have perfect information. Lucas has also done a lot of important work on investment theory and, more recently, on financial economics.

Do you know Lucas and other new classical economists?

Yes, I do. I have discussed my work with Lucas. I talk a lot with Sargent and Barro; we are working in the same field. It would be very unusual if we would not discuss our work.

You disagree with them, though. What is the disagreement about?

I do not think that you can accurately model macroeconomic behavior assuming that prices are perfectly flexible. That is an element of disagreement which is still there and which will be solved somehow, maybe empirically.

Do new classical economists really assume perfectly flexible prices? I thought they allow for the role of contracts.

If you take their models literally, they assume that prices are perfectly flexible. My understanding is that they feel that if contracts are designed optimally, they have characteristics that would duplicate a world of perfectly flexible prices. Then the assumption of perfectly flexible prices seems warranted.

I don't think that contracts can be designed to mimic a world of perfectly flexible prices. In the real world we see contracts that are not designed that way, for various reasons. Because these contracts exist, I think it is impossible to model accurately economic fluctuations without taking them into account.

Don't you risk the criticism that your modeling of contracts becomes ad hoc if you do not make them consistent with the postulates of optimal behavior?

My general view is that there is a lot more optimality about existing relationships than an economist can see at first glance. So it is quite likely that many characteristics of contracts are optimal. We may at a certain point be able to see that apparently suboptimal contracts are not in fact suboptimal.

The bottom line in Lucas and Sargent's thinking is that we should explain why agents choose to do what they do in accordance with the postulate of optimizing behavior. You don't do that.

My reaction to that kind of criticism is that at some point we always will have to impose what appears to be arbitrary restrictions. Lucas and Sargent restrain the information that is available to people, but that is arbitrary. If the information barrier is so important you would expect that people find a way to get around it. I think that such a restriction is just as ad hoc as the assumption that prices adjust slowly.

Also, models that use the assumption of perfectly flexible prices and market clearing are assuming, implicitly, that there is an auctioneer. And there are no auctioneers in many markets. This is another example of an artifical imposition or restriction in that style of modeling.

I would say that as a general guiding principle for research that I would like to minimize the extent to which we rely on such arbitrariness. It seems to me that economic progress can be described as moving further and further away from such devices. I think that is a good way to proceed. It is misleading to say that one style of macroeconomic modeling has a lot more of that than others. To some extent it is a matter of taste. I certainly don't like everyone's style. But that is natural.

The difference between your style and that of new classical economists seems to be responsible for different conclusions.

That is right. The different assumptions generate different conclusions. Strictly speaking, the models with which I work show that government instruments can have stabilizing effects on the economy. Going from that to designing stabilization policy is another matter. One view is that the political system is too complex to use these instruments effectively.

Is rules versus discretionary policy an issue?

That depends on the group with which you are talking. I think that it is very important to try to emphasize macro policy as a rule, as a system, rather than as discretionary changes in the instruments. That is a very useful way of thinking about macroeconomic policy. The more that is done, the better. It encourages a longer view.

There are, however, limits to this. You can never plan for all contingencies. There are unique events that require discretion. But it seems to me that a lot of events are recurrent, for which you can make contingency plans.

How do we account for 10.4 percent unemployment?

The attempt to reduce inflation, which was too high in the opinion of a lot of people, required a contractionary policy. According to the model with which I work, such a contraction in money growth will cause a recession. That gives us the major part of the explanations for the high unemployment. There are also some demographic factors; the population is changing. But a large fraction of the high unemployment is explained by the contractionary policies.

PART FOUR

Conversation with a Monetarist

10

KARL BRUNNER

The relationship between monetarism and new classical economics is intriguing. One would expect it to be close because of certain similarities in conclusions. Both Bob Lucas and Thomas Sargent profess their indebtedness to Milton Friedman, a main figure in the monetarist approach. Nevertheless, a merging of the approaches has not occurred, and monetarists continue to stand their own ground.

Karl Brunner, with Friedman and Allan Meltzer, represents the core of monetarism. His role in the world of economists is remarkable. Apart from being a prolific writer, he organizes annual conferences at Rochester, New York, and is the editor of the *Journal of Monetary Economics*. In addition, he is the initiator and member of the Shadow Open Market Committee. His recent writings bear the marks of the new classical influence on macro discourse, yet he maintains his distinctly monetarist views.

Brunner received his doctorate from the University of Zurich. He came to the US in 1949, first visited Harvard, and subsequently moved to the University of Chicago. He later taught at U.C.L.A. and Ohio State University. Since 1971, he has been a professor at the University of Rochester. Our conversation took place in March 1983.

BACKGROUND

Why did you study economics?

When I finished high school, I didn't know what to do. I started off with history, but I decided that it offered no real attraction. I felt that it was a good subject of investigation, but not a discipline. Purely by chance, I began to read some economics and became fascinated by it. It seemed to give me a better understanding of the problems of society and history.

I studied at the University of Zurich and one year at the London School of Economics, where I spent most of my time in the library. It gradually dawned on me that what I heard at the University of Zurich was quite unsatisfactory, so I continued my private studies after returning to Zurich. I read economists like Marshall, Edgeworth, Pareto, Cassel, Wicksell, Wicksteed, and von Bohm-Bawerk. The university offered little encouragement in this respect, but I did it anyway.

Then you left for the United States . . .

After some interruption during the war, I started my career at the Swiss National Bank, but I realized that there would be very little chance to develop my professional interest in Switzerland. So I went to the US.

Which people were important to you during the beginning of your career?

I first came on a Rockefeller fellowship to Harvard University. The only professors there with whom I could talk were Haberler and a young man by the name of Richard Goodwin. He later left for England, I believe. They were the only ones encouraging some interaction. I was very disappointed with Harvard: the people there were mainly interested in the "Washington circuit," and I found few opportunities for intensive scholarly discussions. But I was very fortunate to have met Schumpeter just before he died.

Chicago confronted me with a very different intellectual atmosphere. It was really alive. People constantly talked with each other, arguing about ideas and the proper interpretation of the world. They would talk in seminars, of course, but also over coffee and during lunch.

Was Milton Friedman important to you in Chicago?

Yes, he was very important for me. I never really developed a close personal contact with him, but I learned much from him and also from the whole group around him. It was, in some ways, a shocking experience for me, as I was totally unprepared for what I found. They took economics very seriously. They really alerted me to price theory and its potential application to the problems of the world. I was fascinated. This contrasted with my accustomed background. I had been conditioned to consider price theory—best reserved to textbooks and classrooms—as a clever but irrelevant exercise and to rely on "sociology" when talking about the "real world." It dawned on me that price theory offered an intellectual discipline and a framework of analysis substantially superior to the pervasive sociological allusions.

Who else was important for you at that time?

I think Lloyd Metzler and Frank Knight were also important. Frank Knight was a very impressive, knowledgeable person. We had all kinds of discussions over luncheon and on occasional Sunday afternoons. I remember one afternoon that he began to talk about the wandering of Germanic tribes at the end of the Roman Empire. That subject happened to be my hobby, so I knew quite a bit about it myself. He also probed, with an inquisitive and searching mind, many ideas in philosophy and theology descended over the centuries. On one occasion he checked with me to find out whether I knew the difference between Karl Barth and Emil Brunner in contemporary Swiss theology. Frank Knight was a rare intellectual, one of the great ones of this century. Let me also add to my list Aaron Director, who conveyed a remarkable insight how to use price theory to understand our world.

Then you went to U.C.L.A.

My encounter with Alchian was very important; the many discussions with him ultimately shaped a clearer vision of what economics was all about. I had been somewhat intrigued with mathematical economics and impressed by its cleverness. It gradually dawned on me, ironically also as a result of discussions with mathematicians at U.C.L.A., that economists might usefully address the problems of the world. Alchian is a man with a remarkably perceptive and subtle mind, a paramount example that you can be subtle and substantive in your analysis with relatively simple means — you need not always have a complex analytical structure in order to say something useful and penetrating. It was very stimulating to see how he applied his economics to what we observe. My discussions with him initiated my interest in an extensive application of economic analysis. I began to understand, as a result of my probing discussions, how price theory could be applied to an analysis of institutional problems.

You also met Allan Meltzer at U.C.L.A. Your collaboration with him is quite a phenomenon within the economic profession.

Well, Allan was my student. It was exactly 30 years ago that I met him. He was certainly one of our top students. He worked with me on his dissertation, and from there on our collaboration started. We like to discuss things with each other; we both benefit from that. We talk about all kinds of topics. We find that we can be very productive as a result of a continuous exchange of ideas.

Another important person for me at U.C.L.A. was the philosopher Reichenbach, who unfortunately died too soon. He really contributed to the final clarification in my mind. I was still wondering at that time what the criteria of relevant and useful work really were. It seemed to me that you could do all kinds of things, but the point of it all was not clear. Reichenbach provided an analytical clarification. He helped me to understand the general nature of the cognitive endeavor. I spent much time subsequently studying analytical philosophy.

What effect did the Keynesian Revolution, taking place at the time you studied, have on you?

Between '44 and '46 I studied Keynes very, very seriously. For several years, his ideas influenced me quite a bit. Then I started to think further about these issues. I was not yet much influenced by Friedman at that time. The gradual renunciation of Keynes' analysis came in the early '50s through my interactions with Alchian. Meltzer joined us in the middle of this process.

Did your choice to withstand Keynesian economics evoke resistance?

See, that is what I always appreciate in the US. It is much easier to be an odd beast here than in Germany, France, or Switzerland. The US offers greater opportunities for "odd beasts." Even so, a Marxist may be more acceptable on some occasions than a monetarist, or for that matter an economist using price theory in his approach to socio-political problems in lieu of some sociological allusions.

ON HIS ECONOMICS

When did you become a monetarist?

That is hard to say. My views developed gradually, and critical awareness became more clearly formed after 1953. I find it actually quite interesting in retrospect to retrace the questions in my discussions with Alchian. One line addressed what I later called Keynes's "London City Syndrome," expressed by the idea that monetary influences on the economy are totally channeled via capital markets. This idea appeared increasingly dubious and difficult to reconcile with observations that monetary shocks and events pervasively affect economies with stunted or practically nonexistent capital markets. The development of this idea eventually led us, by the early 1960s, to reject the IS/LM framework as a paradigm for monetary analysis.

The labor market formed another important focus of our questioning, particularly under Alchian's insistence. We felt that there was really no adequate explanation of unemployment, neither in classical nor in Keynesian theory. Keynes emphasized the persistent occurrence of a discrepancy between the marginal disutility of labor and the marginal utility of the wage product. The observed persistence suggested the absence of any social mechanism resolving this discrepancy on the market. This was recognized as an inherent flaw of the market mechanism. Keynesians usually shifted to sociological allusions in order to provide some background for the assumption of predetermined money wages, required for their purposes. We felt that Keynes wrestled with a serious problem which could not be dealt with by inherited price theory. This theory, as formulated, failed to integrate important institutional dimensions built into market processes. But we also felt that Keynes and Keynesians attempted to cope with the problem by moving from economic analysis to "sociology," i.e., replacing an incomplete analysis with no analysis. The search for an answer needs to proceed, in our judgment, by developing a more-complete price theory. This required, so we felt, more attention to the role of transaction and information costs. These discussions are clearly reflected in the first edition of Alchian's textbook. Their occurrence explains many important institutional arrangements incomprehensible in the context of a price theory bereft of information and transaction problems.

What are the basic tenets of monetarism?

The basic tenet of monetarism is the reassertion of the relevance of price theory to understand what happens in aggregate economics. Our fundamental point is that price theory is the crucial paradigm — as a matter of fact, the only paradigm — that economists have. You can use this paradigm to explain the whole range of social phenomena. I do not believe in a sort of "shoe box approach" according to which you distribute problems over the different disciplines, such as political science, economics, and sociology. That does not make much sense. These divisions are essentially arbitrary historical products. The classification does not refer to alternative disciplines. It can usefully be understood as referring to different ranges of problems — different subject matters — approachable with the same basic social analysis evolved in the context of economics.

So you think that economics provides a universal method for solving problems that can also be applied to problems that are usually associated with sociology or political science?

Yes, indeed. This idea can be recognized already in Adam Smith's work. Its reemergence over the past decades occurred in the spontaneous thrust of research efforts pursued by many economists.

But let me proceed beyond this fundamental methodological point, which of course must eventually survive critical assessment against alternative paradigms as, for instance the Marxian scheme or the traditional shoe box methodological rule. Such rules are ultimately assessable in terms of their cognitive consequences.

In the narrower context of monetary theory, the following themes characterize monetarist ideas: First there is the nature of the transmission mechanism. We emphasize that money is basically a substitute in all directions; it is a substitute for any financial asset, but also for any real asset. It operates, therefore, in all directions throughout the economy. It operates not so much through the real balance effect, as Patinkin emphasized, but it operates dominantly by adjustments in relative prices. These adjustments involve relative prices between assets, between assets and their yields, and between existing assets and their new production. The implication is that money works via a much vaster range of channels on the economy and is not confined by a narrow interest mechanism, as the Keynesians still argue.

The relevance of normal output or normal unemployment forms another issue. The market system functions as a shock absorber and tends to establish a normal level of output. This means that we consider the market system to be inherently stable, in contrast to the Keynesian position that attributes to the private sector a basic instability. The normal level of output is, moreover, not determined as the Keynesian "full output" by technology and tastes. It sensitively reflects institutional constraints. The production function is not only affected by changes in technology, but also by changes in organizational forms and in the structure of property rights. The institutional dimension also affects the normal level of unemployment. This aspect involves serious political consequences. Many politicians, responsible for the institutional changes raising the normal level of unemployment, misleadingly interpret the result as an expression of a deficiency in aggregate nominal demand.

The third point concerns the comparative role of monetary impulses. My position on this issue changed somewhat over the last ten years. My views on the previous two issues also changed under the influence of ensuing professional discussions. We need to distinguish for our purposes more carefully between the transitory and more permanent components of movements in price-level and output. The comparatively more-permanent strand expressed by a trend in price level movements is dominantly controlled by monetary impulses. The more-transitory (stationary) component is much influenced by real shocks. Real shocks generally do contribute to the (stochastic) trend in price levels but do not dominate its pattern. The movement of output is similarly divided into a trend and a stationary deviation. Most important is the recognition that the trend also emerges from a stochastic process. It is dominated by real conditions and shocks summarized by technology, preferences, and institutions. The last category includes the nature of both the fiscal and monetary regime. The stationary component of output movements jointly reflects the operation of misperceived or unanticipated real changes or monetary shocks arising in the context of a given regime.

The last point which I would like to stress addresses central issues in the political economy of societies. We do confront here a fundamental issue which Keynesians, like Tobin and Modigliani, apparently do not wish to face. The disputes about the role of government and the range of political institutions as social coordinating devices involve more than ideology. The easy interpretation of such disputes in terms of ideological differences misses the crucial issues completely. Two very different substantive views of the world determine the nature of the conflict. Keynesians are prone to approach nonmarket situations and social institutions in terms of an essentially sociological perception. Roy Harrod recognized this pattern with his reference to the prevalent "Harvey Street Syndrome." We reject, on the other hand, an escape into sociology which offers no relevant analytic framework. We maintain that socio-political institutions are the proper subject of economic analysis. This entails an entirely different view of political institutions and their operation. The sociological view typically supports a goodwill theory of government and yields conclusions favoring a large and essentially unlimited government. An application of economic analysis, in contrast, alerts us to the fact that politicians and bureaucrats are entrepreneurs in the political market. They pursue their own interests and try to find optimal strategies attending to their interests. And what is optimal for them is hardly ever optimal for "public interest."

This is a radically different view of the role of political institutions, in particular of the role of the Constitution which limits political activities. The sociological view underlying much of Keynesian sociopolitical thinking hardly sympathizes with the conception of limited government. This essentially Keynesian position is excellently revealed in Okun's book *Equality and Efficiency: The Big Trade-Off*. He accepts the economic hypothesis of maximizing men resourcefully coping in their interests in the context of markets. The socio-political context seems to form a very different world and requires a totally different hypothesis. Men are, so we are told, self-interested in the marketplace and public-interested in the public sector. I could paraphrase a comment made by Tobin at another occasion and call this a "sophomoric" distinction. Surely, it has no foundation in our reality. The "Keynesian position" fails to recognize that private property and wealth are only one dimension of self-interested behavior. We can also think of the role of influence, power, and interest in the control over resources and the political apparatus offered by every political context. A hard and nonromantic look at social interaction yields little support for the "sociological dichotomy" of men's behavior. We argue that the basic pattern of behavior is not affected by the institutional context. This context, however, does influence specific aspects of behavior.

How do you use your monetarist ideas to explain the current recession with its high unemployment rates?

Let us consider the high unemployment rates. We recognize that several components constitute the total unemployment: the basic normal rate, the intermediate-run component, and the cyclic component. The basic normal rate of unemployment reflects a comparatively more permanent phenomenon shaped by the incentives of the prevailing institutional structure, expressed by the fiscal policy, the welfare system, and labor union policies. This first component probably doubled from about 3 ½ percent in the 1950s to about 7 percent by the end of the 1970s. The second component results from the reallocation of resources between major industries in an economy. Massive reallocations have been imposed over the past years on all Western nations and most particularly on our economy. Last, the shift from inflationary policies to a disinflationary policy in 1980 produced the recession of 1981–82.

Am I right in saying that you believe that fluctuations in the money supply are the major factor that explain the transitory component of unemployment?

Yes, in the present case. The recession is the result of monetary deceleration.

What policies could have prevented the recession?

The recession was almost unavoidable at this stage. Let me put it this way. We do not say that you get out of inflation by first creating a recession. Inflation is not brought down *because* you create a recession. Inflation is brought down by lowering monetary growth. Whether or not this produces a recession depends very much on the conditions under which the change in monetary regime is carried through. The greater the credibility of the change in regime, the greater the incentive for all price and wage setters to adjust their behavior. The resulting recession will remain comparatively short and small under the circumstances.

If the change in regime, on the other hand, attracts little credibility, agents experience little incentive to modify price- or wage-setting behavior. I would be a fool as a union negotiator to adjust my wage demands when I strongly suspect that the change in monetary policy is, at most, temporary.

The monetary authorities in the US began to decelerate the growth in the money supply, but their unreliable and unpredictable procedure expressed by their commitment to a discretionary policy raised the social cost. We predicted two years ago that there would be a recession. We criticized the Reagan administration for its incoherent implementations of some basically sound ideas, but cautioned against the exaggerations of the "supply siders." However, we also argue that the social costs of permanent inflation would be substantially higher than the social costs of a maintained anti-inflationary policy. The political economy of permanent inflation does not produce a stable pattern of fully anticipated inflation; it produces a highly erratic policy of monetary expansionism. This fact has been observed all over the world. Permanent inflation is thus associated with intermittent losses in output due to repetitive attempts to cope with inflation.

Do you believe that it is incorrect to associate monetarism with conservative politics?

Yes. This characterization really reflects some sloppy intellectual habits and requires some clarification. I find the American terminology, to say the least, quite misleading. My European background does play a role at this point. I grew up in an environment in which you would differentiate between socialist, social democratic, liberal, and conservative positions. The socialist position, well represented by the programs of the British Labour Party, proposes a vast nationalization of resources. The socialists want a society controlled by the state. The social democrats argue for an extensive welfare system with comparatively little nationalization of resources. This position dominated, for instance, the German SDP after the formulation of the Godesberg program. The liberals are concerned with a small and limited government, with a constitutionally constrained government thus contrasting with the social democrats, who opt for a big and open-ended government. Conservatives basically want a corporate state with a large government. They view the state as the guardian of moral principle to be enforced with its apparatus. The American terminology, beloved by the media, lumps rather different positions together. The "philosophic" foundation of socialists and social democrats (i.e., "liberals" *à l'Américaine*) are, however, often much closer than the respective foundations of liberals and conservatives (i.e., "conservatives" *à l'Américaine*).

In terms of the differentiation advanced there is a connection between monetarists and the liberal position. I should note, however, that I have encountered monetarist Marxists. The "liberal component" in monetarist ideas is most particularly expressed by the constitutional approach to a limited government.

ABOUT NEO-KEYNESIAN ECONOMICS

Keynesians object that your theories are unrealistic and emphasize market failures, such as price rigidities, in their argument. How do you react to these objections?

We should consider two aspects about the issue of market failures. First, the Keynesians simply state the fact of the rigidities, as Keynes did in the *General Theory*, but they offer no explanation. But let us be clear that "inflexible prices and wages" do pose a serious challenge to our intellectual efforts. This pattern has been recognized in monetary analysis for almost 200 years. Monetarist analysis explicitly acknowledged this fact. Monetarists also consider "inflexible prices" a major task problem for future research efforts to be explained systematically in terms of economic analysis. They question both the relevance of the Keynesian interpretation of the fact as a "market failure" and the "neo-classical" attempt to disregard it. Both positions fail to understand the emergence of a wide array of social institutions as a rational response of interacting agents confronting serious information problems. Institutions appear as devices contributing to the solution of social coordination problems in a context of substantially incomplete information.

The interpretation of inherited price-wage processes reveals the difference between Keynesian and monetarist positions most effectively. Both recognize the occurrence of such processes. Keynesians deny, however, the dependence of these processes on policy regimes or the structure of exogenous processes, or deny the operation of feedbacks from policy regimes within any relevant time horizon. We would assert, on the other hand, that the inertial processes are crucially affected, over an intermediate run, by the policy regime and the state of the economy. There seems to exist, for instance, a good reason for downward inflexibility of prices. For over 30 years the economy has continuously experienced accommodating monetary policy. The institutions adjust to that experience.

The second point with respect to market failures is more general. The argument is that because of the market failures, the government has to intervene. That is a classical example of the goodwill theory of government. It expresses a belief that the government will find the proper solution to maximize social welfare and will act to achieve that solution. But "government failure" characterizes the reality of political institutions. The goodwill theory of government offers us little guidance to understand our socio-political world. The "government failure" can frequently be much worse than the alleged "market failure" when assessed in terms of the public's welfare.

One last comment on the use of the term "failure." It typically appears to describe a deviation from some ideal state projected by a theory. This theory often omits, however, the operation of relevant costs or describes quite generally an irrelevant situation. The normative suggestion associated with the use of the word is thus quite dubious and misleading.

Do you talk with neo-Keynesians about these issues?

Oh, yes we do, with some, and we are willing to discuss this with anybody.

Nevertheless, the communication breaks down. At which point does that happen?

That is indeed an unfortunate problem. It is, however, not uniformly distributed. Meaningful communication is hopeless with the demagoguery of the Arthur Laffers or Lester Thurows. But serious communication problems seem also to exist with scholars of the Keynesian establishment. It seems centered around fundamental questions of political economy and spills over into a wide range of policy problems. I have found it particularly regrettable to observe the easy disposition to impugn character and motives of the intellectual opponent. Keynesians such as Modigliani and Tobin frequently seem to suggest that our position is essentially "ideological" or "doctrinaire." But the fact remains that detailed substantive arguments bearing on the underlying issues have been developed. They refuse to recognize these arguments and fail to deal seriously with them. An interested reader may usefully compare Buchanan's and Tobin's contribution to a Symposium on the President's Economic Report 1982 published in the *Journal of Monetary Economics*.

Communication seems also impaired by misleading attributions or plain logical illiteracy. Tobin persists, for example, with a critique of a "positive economics" attributed to monetarists. Two lines of the critique need our attention. This methodological position is supposed to hold, first, that reduced form tests are as a matter of "principle" the only way to proceed, and that, secondly, the realism of assumptions need not be considered. The critique misses, on both points, the crucial issues. Reduced form tests are quite relevant and appropriate, not as a matter of principle, but whenever properties of *classes* of hypotheses (in contrast to properties of *specific* members of the class) are under consideration. Such properties are uniquely related with the coefficients of the reduced form. A "structural" approach adds nothing under the circumstances. This argument has been repeatedly made and simply disregarded. The second line of the critique fails to appreciate a basic fact about the logical structure of hypotheses. This structure determines that hypotheses are confirmed or disconfirmed on the basis of their observational implication. When economists talk about "assumptions" they either mean specific classes of the hypothesis, boundary conditions controlling the relevant test conditions, or higher-level hypotheses. All these assumptions have a function, but the validity of a hypothesis cannot be assessed by reduction to the validity of such assumptions. Carnap, Braithwaite, Nagel, and other logicians of science elaborated this point in detail.

Many other examples could be addressed. They all raise an unresolved question: How can we explain this particular social phenomenon? We may have to recognize that all our intellectual endeavors occur in a socio-political context exposed to the incentives of the game of power and influence. And most particularly, this social process invokes strong emotional forces buttressing the beliefs supplied in influence games. Still, we should not despair. There remains a range of communication among committed scholars of diverse emphasis. So let us enjoy this opportunity.

ON NEW CLASSICAL ECONOMICS

Do you consider yourself a new classical economist?

The answer is no. Let me put it this way. I admire the work of Lucas, Sargent, and Barro. Their work offered important contributions to monetary analysis, which benefitted us and which affects permanently how we think or approach some issues. But I also have strong reservations about crucial aspects of their "equilibrium approach."

But new classical economics is often considered a mathematical version of monetarism.

To an extent it is. They have formalized much more technically some of the ideas we already had for some time. To give you one example. Twenty years ago we emphasized that, in contrast to Keynesian analysis, monetary growth exerts no real effects. We stated that monetary growth is already accounted for in the movement of the price level. Only accelerations or decelerations, i.e., variations in monetary growth, would exert real effects. These effects would be temporary, however. New classical economists have sharpened our understanding and offered new insights with the aid of an explicit formulation of the information process. They explicated the idea of unanticipated and unperceived monetary impulses. That was a very useful contribution and moved our discussion further.

Are adaptive expectations dead?

Not necessarily. Jack Muth already demonstrated that adaptive expectations are the consequence of rational expectations applied to an "augmented random walk." Adaptive expectations may appear rational also in some other contexts. See, for example, Ben Friedman in the *Journal of Monetary Economics* of 1978.

Quite generally, the idea of rational expectations is something that will remain. Even Tobin acknowledges that. I do not expect that it will remain in its present form. Some of its current aspects, such as the idea that agents have full information about the stochastic structure, are hard to accept. But the basic idea of rational expectations does not depend upon this.

So what is wrong with new classical economics?

Their interpretation of equilibrium analysis seems dubious to me. This *specific* kind of equilibrium analysis implies that *all* prices are market clearing relative to *all* shock-realizations. Prices reflect all ongoing shocks irrespective of their duration, irrespective of whether agents perceive shocks to be quite transitory or very permanent. My reservations on this central point tie in with an issue discussed before. Incomplete and diffuse information is basically associated with, and conditions the emergence of, a wide array of social devices in the spontaneous interaction between coping agents. The problem is to determine the social arrangements with their conditions yielding prices that do not respond to all shock-realizations expressed by any modification in market conditions. Some prices change every day, but most of the time transactors find it useful not to change prices to reflect all temporary shocks, but to change them when the changes are judged to be more permanent.

But they don't deny that. They would refer to transaction costs or problems of information to account for price inflexibility.

This may be, but their analysis does not say this. We should note that contract theory yields no answer to our problem in its present form. It is an interesting piece of analysis, but is essentially expressed in real terms and fails to explain the relative inflexibility of *nominal* values. And this is the crucial question.

Lucas and Sargent say that the reliance on any disequilibrium mechanism means the reliance on some ad hoc assumption concerning the behavior of agents and that you always get an equilibrium when you specify, in the right way, the constraints under which agents maximize.

I agree partly with that statement. The problem is the relevant constraints, however. We think — and I remember particularly the discussions with Alchian back in the early '60s — that they omit some relevant constraints. They introduce uncertainty through the introduction of stochastic processes and assume that people enjoy full information about those processes. We encounter, however, a much more extensive information problem recently reemphasized by Phelps and his colleagues. We also observe the operation of serious transaction costs.

We are still wrestling with these issues. We probably accumulated in our professional discussions an intuitive comprehension. But we need to move beyond that stage to an analytic explication. The intuitive comprehension suggests that if relevant constraints contain information and transaction costs, we will find that the resulting equilibrium reflects those constraints. They may be responsible for relative inflexibilities in nominal values. We must recognize, however, that the constraints gradually move over time. It is here that stochastic economics made a major contribution which has affected us all. We should, in particular, realize that equating relatively inflexible prices with some market failure expressed by agents' failure to fully exploit all mutually gainful trade is simply incorrect. The fact that we have such rigidities does not mean that agents are irrational or markets fail. On the contrary, such rigidities probably reflect social devices which do exploit all opportunities, given the serious information problems confronting agents. The problem that we face at this stage, I think, is not so much the intuitive idea developed in many of our discussions, but to find a proper analytical formulation of that idea.

I understand that your reservations with new classical economics do not so much concern the rational expectations hypothesis as the formulation of the constraints.

I do not think that the narrow conception of market clearing incorporated in the new classical economics offers a viable approach to observable problems. We need a broader analysis involving an equilibrium concept defined relative to the relevant constraints associated with the information problems. Against the background of neoclassical analysis it is very hard to explain many of the institutional arrangements that we observe (inventories, middleman, order backlogs, contracts in nominal terms, etc.).

So you disagree with the ways in which new classical economists reach their conclusions, but am I right in thinking that you basically agree with those conclusions?

Some of their conclusions are very important. There are several major conclusions that are down the line of our thinking. One of them is the importance of unanticipated and unperceived changes in monetary growth. We would add an extension to misperceived or misinterpreted monetary events. The difference between the three categories rests with the relevant information structure. Unanticipated events involve expectations formed on the basis of past information, unperceived events result from expectations conditioned on past and current (incomplete) information and, last, misperceived events follow from expectations conditioned by complete past and current information about data, but incomplete information about their interpretation (e.g., transitory or permanent events). Let me add that the last category permits explications of the credibility issue not accessible to the standard rational expectations analysis.

Another conclusion to be mentioned here is the emphasis on the role of policy regimes and, in particular, the idea that the structure of the economic system is not invariant with the policy regime, or more generally with the structure of exogenous processes.

But was the later conclusion already in your work before Lucas began talking about it?

We did not talk about this, but the question intrigues me. My retrospective judgment is that we had no coherent or systematic analysis bearing on this point. I seem to remember the occurrence of some puzzling inconsistencies. Lucas's work really helped me to overcome some of these problems.

I very much agree with the emphasis on policy regimes versus policy actions. What this involves is that the central problem is not what you specifically do today or tomorrow or what you have specifically done yesterday. We emphasize the *institutional* aspects of policy. We basically argue that there should be institutional arrangements controlling policy so as to minimize the unexpected or misperceived shocks. This emphasis on an institutional approach is designed to lower the burden of the information problem imposed by discretionary policy-making on agents. The two Economic Reports prepared by the Reagan administration so far [1982, 1983] offer the interested reader a remarkable contrast bearing on this issue. The 1982 Report's chapter on monetary policy reflects an essentially monetarist position, whereas the 1983 report takes a conservative, Keynesian position.

An interested reader may find our emphatic distinctions between specific action here and now, or then and there, on the one side, and institutional arrangements or procedures on the other side very explicitly formulated in the study jointly prepared in 1963–64 with Allan H. Meltzer for a Congressional Committee.

Do you feel that new classical economics will increasingly appeal to young economists at the expense of monetarism?

Several aspects need to be distinguished: the flexible price analysis, the Cartesian fallacy, and the requirement of formalization. We have discovered the first strand, and I suspect that we may experience a turn on this point more attuned to our basic position. But let us consider the second strand. The Cartesian tradition insisted that all statements be derived from a small set of "first principles." "Cogito ergo sum" and everything else follows. This idea has had a strong influence on philosophy but also on the program of the new classical economics best represented by Neil Wallace. Anything not derived from "first principles" does not count as knowledge. You are not allowed to talk about money if you have not derived from "first principles" a specification of all the items which are money. This methodological position is quite untenable and conflicts with the reality of our cognitive progress over history. Science rarely progresses by working "down from first principles"; it progresses and expands the other way. We begin with empirical regularities and go backward to more and more complicated hypotheses and theories. Adherence to the Cartesian principle would condemn science to stagnation. There are, moreover, as Karl Popper properly emphasized, no first principles.

Do I hear here the suspicion of a heavy emphasis on rigor that you learned from Alchian?

Well, this is my third strand. I have an intermediate position in this regard. There is, indeed, merit in the attempt to formalize, and I would not discourage anybody from coping with better explications. The history of economics over the past two centuries demonstrates these benefits. The evolution of monetary analysis over the past ten years offers more confirmation. We should wrestle with the explication problem. I am worried about a new trend, most particularly among young economists. This trend reflects an attitude more or less implicitly legislating that whatever is not explicitly and rigorously formalized does not count, and cannot possibly contribute any relevant knowledge. I do maintain that we can gain some understanding even with incompletely

formalized ideas and hypotheses. The requirement of total formalization frequently leads us to discard the essential characteristics of a good
problem, and to reduce it to a triviality for the benefit of manageably
rigorous treatment. The insistence on the methodological requirement
imposes a high trade-off of relevance for rigor.

ON ECONOMICS AS A SCIENCE AND ON DOING ECONOMICS

*From your writings it is evident that you support the distinction between positive
and normative economics. Positive economics relies on the ability to discriminate
between hypotheses through testing. However, testing appears to be problematic.
What does that mean for the distinction?*

The point is that comparatively little work addresses systematic assess-
ments of alternative hypotheses. Most of the work attempts to find some
hypotheses, but it rarely attempts a test of that hypothesis against an
alternative one. I could stress the need for a systematic way of
appraising theories. There is no reason why we should not be able to assess competing hypotheses more insistently.

Have you ever reversed a position?

Yes, I have. Statements made twelve years ago bearing on the nature of
the transmission mechanism, and the dominant impulses operating on
the economy, do not reflect my current thinking. The same applies to
my position on aspects of political economy held twenty years ago.
Last, by the time I left Switzerland I was a staunch Keynesian. I can
appeal to Hayek and Haberler as witnesses for that. One more point in
this context. I did occasionally indicate the pattern of observations
which would make me dubious about a statement advanced.

Do economists do that very often?

No. I am inclined to say that if people develop a hypothesis, they
should be obliged to state, on some occasion, under which conditions
they would give up the hypothesis in preference for a systematic
alternative, or at least about reservations or doubts.

Do you think you will ever give up your monetarist beliefs?

That is possible and holds many propositions. Let me use the simplest
case. Suppose, for instance, that we find again and again that a monetary acceleration over two to three years does not produce an increase in
the rate of inflation. I would indeed have to change my views.

Would Keynesians support such a relationship?

Let us consider it. Yes, some Keynesians would, especially in the US. We should mention, as a small sample, Fischer and Blinder. They acknowledge the interaction between monetary shocks and the rate of inflation. But Keynesians in Cambridge, England, for example, would deny such an interaction. We should be careful in our labels. There is a large variation in positions. Also, within the inflation problem we do differ to a more or less greater extent in the interpretation of inertial processes. This affects, in particular, the assessment of disinflationary policies.

Blinder still disagrees with many of your monetarist ideas.

Yes, of course, and most of all on aspects of the political economy. This will loom, in my judgment, as a major issue in the future.

How good is the communication among economists?

There is communication and also a serious problem. Substantial communication evolved in the Carnegie-Rochester conferences that we organized since the early '70s. We do appreciate an open door, and Keynesian and "neutrals" are welcome.

My impression of conferences is that people present their story but do not really listen to others. The communication does not seem to lead to much agreement.

Conferences are not designed to reach agreements, it would be rather naive to expect that. I think that the objective of a conference is to expose economists to each other's work. I also think that the discussions have some influence. I would argue, moreover, that substantial changes occurred over the last ten years. If you look at the presidential address of Modigliani in 1977, you'll see that he abandoned major Keynesian positions of the '50s. My current views also differ in many ways from those presented ten or twelve years ago. The changes were certainly influenced by my discussions with and work by many colleagues at a variety of universities.

What do you mean by your statement that economists play language games that hamper mutual understanding?

The multiple use of language frequently creates problems. The cognitive requirement imposes several constraints on the use of language often violated by our conditioned impressionisms. One famous example may be useful. It was widely held that in order to assess a hypothesis, we have to assess the "realism of assumptions." From a logical point of view this argument makes no sense. Milton Friedman was right in his "Essay on Positive Economics" when he argued that the realism of assumptions offers no answer to questions bearing on the cognitive status of a given hypothesis. I have developed this point in some detail in a paper published in a philosophy journal. Unfortunately, Friedman sidestepped an explicit logical analysis of the structure of statements involved and argued in terms of more or less intuitive metaphors.

Do you mean that the opponents of Friedman's argument focused on his examples such as the one concerning the billiard ball?

That is exactly what I mean. One focused on the idea of "as if" assumptions, and that was simply beside the point. It sidetracked the discussion from the logical issues involved.

So is your argument one of logic that states that a theory cannot be assessed on the basis of the realism of its assumptions?

This is correct. We use the term "assumptions" quite ambiguously. An examination of the language used reveals at least seven distinct meanings with very different logical functions. Some "assumptions" are open clauses in a general implication and function as a device to screen out irrelevant observations. These assumptions basically state that extraneous influences may occur under which the hypothesis does not apply. They are usually not made explicit. In addition, there are the boundary conditions occurring as molecular statements which specify a particular condition within the range of application of the hypothesis. It is also possible that an assumption of a hypothesis refers to a higher-level hypothesis. None of these three types of "assumptions" can be used in accordance with the standard argument to determine the cognitive status of a hypothesis. The "realism" of the second type determines the relevance of its use without any effect on the truth or falsehood of the hypothesis. And as to the last type mentioned, the truth of a higher-level hypothesis does assure the truth of all implied lower-level hypotheses. But this hardly bears on the confirmation process. The latter starts with observational implications and moves opposite to the direction of logical deductions. Logicians made this point time and again. I find it thus remarkable how people immediately attributed to Friedman a sinister ideological motive for his correct rejection of the prevalent argument.

Ultimately I argue here that we should assess more explicitly the logical structure of our analysis.

Do you think that if economists get more precise in the terms that they use and in the econometric testing that they do, they will reach some form of agreement at the end?

One thing needs to be said. During my fourteen years as an editor of a journal, I have watched a remarkable progress in the technical aspects of the papers. A paper that would have been considered good fourteen years ago would have great difficulties being accepted today. I recognize also some problems with this development. The content seems occasionally to suffer under the insistence at rigorous formalization.

But I see no reason why we would not move closer on *some* issues. I doubt whether we shall ever reach a general agreement on all issues, though [laughter] and most particularly whether we ever will reach any agreement on issues bearing on aspects of political economy.

PART FIVE

Conversations with
Nonconventional Economists

11

DAVID M. GORDON

The preceding conversations indicate that conventional economists have very little to say about Marxian economics. The professional respect that they give each other, despite their disagreements, is not extended to Marxists. By talking with David Gordon we may see how it looks from the other side.

David Gordon, a prominent Marxist economist, has a special interest in the labor market. In 1982 he published, with Richard Edwards and Michael Reich, *Segmented Work, Divided Workers*. With Samuel Bowles and Thomas Weisskopf, he recently spelled out a radical perspective on the American society in *Beyond the Waste Land: A Democratic Alternative to Economic Decline* (1983a). He plays a significant role in the Union of Radical Political Economics (URPE) and currently teaches at the New School for Social Research and the Labor Institute, which provides instruction to union members. His family background is intriguing: the Gordon family has been described as "the flying Wallendas of economics." His father, the late Robert Aaron Gordon, was a professor of economics at Berkeley and was president of the American Economic Association in 1974–75. His mother, Margaret S. Gordon, now retired, served as associate director of the Institute of Industrial Relations at Berkeley and also as associate director of the Carnegie Council of Higher Education. The Gordons' other son, Robert J. Gordon, is professor of economics at Northwestern University.

We talked in November 1982 in his office at the New School.

BACKGROUND

Why did you study economics?

That is a question about which few economists believe my answer. The assumption in the profession is that my brother and I must have started economics because we had two economists as parents. In my case the order of determination was somewhat different. I graduated from college as a fledgling new left political radical in 1965. I didn't know what I wanted to do after college, so I spent a year trying to figure that out, thinking that I wanted to do something that would allow me to combine some scholarly and writing work, some political work and some government work. This was during the Vietnam War; I was still too chicken to declare myself as a conscientious objector, but I certainly didn't want to be drafted. So I thought I needed to enter graduate school in order to get a deferment. Everyone told me that the two graduate degrees that would best keep open the career possibilities that I wanted were either law or economics. I assumed that either would be equally boring and equally tailored toward preparing one for participation in the establishment. I wanted to choose the one that would be least imposing. That is where my family background came in. At that point I realized that although I had studied little economics as an undergraduate, I would have an advantage in that I would be more or less familiar with the names that are important in the profession because I had heard about them at the dinner table.

So I chose economics primarily as a convenience. It was only during graduate school that I started to explore the linkage between economic analysis and radical politics. Then I began to take economics seriously as something that one could pursue with commitment and seriousness rather than holding one's nose.

Why do you think that many radicals, such as Michael Piore, Samuel Bowles, Herbert Gintis, and you, came from Harvard?

In the student community as a whole there was an enormous amount of radical political ferment in the mid- and late '60s and that was because Harvard, like other good universities, taught us to think. Anybody who bothered to think about issues like racial inequality or the nature of the war in Vietnam would be bound to find those phenomena problematic. So it is not surprising that an established institution that provides critical education, in a classical sense, would foster a lot of radical movement. Within economics itself it was only around 1966 and 1967 that a fairly large number of people, some of whom were junior faculty, began to work together and hold weekly luncheon meetings.

Virtually all of the discourse was outside of the economics department, that is, among ourselves and through URPE, the Union of Radical Political Economics, which was also formed in 1968. It was an entirely independent beginning. It was only around 1970 that mainstream economists thought that we had become noticeable enough that they needed to make comments on the legitimacy of our approach. At that time they were sharply critical of what they described as the rhetoric and politics embedded in our work. Finally, by the mid-1970s, it appeared that they had decided that it was no longer worth attacking us and returned to a stance of relatively neutral neglect, ignoring us and leaving us to ourselves.

Which people of that period do you recognize as being important radical economists?

There is a fairly large number. The ones with whom I still work most closely are Steve Marglin at Harvard; Sam Bowles, Herb Gintis, and Rick Edwards at the University of Massachusetts at Amherst; Tom Weisskopf at the University of Michigan; and Michael Reich at Berkeley. There is a history of overlapping work among most of these people. There are other Marxist and radical economists who have somewhat different perspectives and would define themselves with a slightly different emphasis and tradition than the group of us. I am thinking of people like Anwar Shaikh at the New School, Donald Harris at Stanford, and Duncan Foley at Barnard, who have done very important work that is clearly distinguishable from the work that we have done. It is not yet clear that we are prepared or equipped to draw those lines adequately or properly.

At Harvard you must have been taught neoclassical economics. How did you deal with that?

We studied it very carefully. Our attention for neoclassical economics was a product of two factors. One was a personal impulse to do well in the competitive environment of American academics. The other factor was that we firmly believed and continue to believe that if one wants to criticize neoclassical economics or any other analytical framework, one has to know it from the inside. You have to know it as well as the people who do it. That belief continues to frame the teaching that we do at our own separate departments. We stress very strongly the need to know neo-classical economics. And since it is hard for us to attract good neoclassi-cal economists we have to do a lot of the teaching ourselves. I think that I myself teach neoclassical labor economics at least as well as it was taught to me at Harvard. It is also very important that people know quantitative methods; without that expertise one's work can be too eas-ily dismissed. This, of course, imposes a double burden. Sometimes our students moan about that burden, but in general they agree with us.

Did you have any mentors?

No, not in economics. All of us were largely self-taught.

Did your parents play any role in all this?

I think that what I learned from my parents that was useful in econom-ics was more methodological than substantive. That was enormously valuable. What I learned, and I assume my brother did also, was the necessity and possibility of clear, detached, rational inquiry, of being clear about one's presuppositions and one's method of discourse as part of any kind of discussion — whether it is at the dinner table or at school. I also picked up from my parents a traditional liberal concern for in-equality, for inequity, and for injustice. That obviously motivated my politics. In my case, I learned nothing from my parents about econom-ics itself. So the spirit of their economics was important, not the substance.

Your brother took the spirit in a different way. How do you understand that?

He didn't interpret the methodological approach differently. If you put us together you would probably have as rationalist as any two brothers one could find in the US these days. We think that the difference in our politics, and therefore largely in our economics, is a joint product of differences in our early childhood, which we don't understand very well, and from the fact that he went to college three years before I did. Just that three-year difference meant that I was exposed to and became part of new left politics. This is not a sufficient explanation, but it was clearly important.

HIS ECONOMICS

How would you describe a radical economist?

Most of us would describe ourselves as Marxist economists. That means that we relate to a significant tradition that runs through the history of economic analysis. What it means substantively, and here I have to simplify grossly, involves two entry points, one of which is methodological, the other analytical. The methodological entry point is a commitment to a mode of analysis which draws on the insights of historical materialism, that is, the importance of material (or objective) determinations of people's economic and social lives, the importance of attention to potentially conflictual and contradictory relationships and structures influencing historical developments, and of attention to the extraordinarily complicated relationships between material determinations and people's subjective appreciations of things like work. This is a starting point which can be differentiated from neoclassical entry points.

Analytically, it involves an approach to the study of capitalism as an economic system which defines relations of both production and competition quite differently from neoclassical economics. Relations of production are presupposed as conflictual, and whether one grounds that analysis in one version of the theory of value or another, Marxist economists have in common an attention to the conflicts of interest between those people who work for a living and those who own the means of production.

As far as competition is concerned, many Marxists argue that competition is more like warfare than mutually beneficial exchange. That presupposition warrants an analysis of disequilibrium or crisis more than of equilibrium situations.

How do you apply the Marxian perspective to current macroeconomic problems?

Starting backward from the issue of inflation, some of us would argue, following what we now call conflict theory of inflation, that the rate of inflation is a function of the difference between the rate of growth of productivity (that is, the rate of growth in available supply of goods) and the rate of growth of economic actors' claims on that supply of goods. This is simply a more-careful reformulation of the traditional notion that inflation results when too much money chases too few goods. That becomes a Marxian analysis if and when one develops a determinant Marxian analysis of the rate of growth of productivity, on one side, and of the factors affecting the rate of growth in claims on aggregate output, on the other side.

We would argue that, in any case, the more important of the two determinants of the rate of inflation is the rate of productivity growth. We have recently developed an applied social model of aggregate productivity growth in the US in the postwar period. [See Weisskopf, Bowles, and Gordon, 1984.] We are not yet finished, but we feel confident that the Marxian perspective provides a better starting point in this area than what we have seen of the available mainstream analysis, which either eschews the analysis of the political realm altogether—relying on purely technical factors—or emphasizes harmony of interests. We emphasize additional determinations of aggregate productivity growth which are left out in a more-traditional analysis. There are two that are most important. One involves a careful analysis of the determinants of variations in work intensity, which itself is probably best approached by operationalizing some kind of conflict model of the labor process. We have been able to show that a substantial amount of annual variation of aggregate productivity growth can be attributed to a vector of variables affecting work intensity.

The second additional determinant of productivity growth, which seems to be equally important, is that conditions of competition are themselves variable. There is no such thing as either perfect competition, or therefore, a constant intensity of competitive pressure. We call this the Schumpeter effect. It tells us that the intensity of innovative pressure on enterprises is variable over time, in particular over the long cycle.

Another difference between our work and mainstream economics is that we have treated as endogenous certain kinds of variables which are largely regarded as exogenous in neoclassical economics. For instance, a question for us is how one explains the OPEC shock. We would choose to explain it with respect to a model of conflictual relationships in the world economy. Another example is the obvious influence of the Vietnam War shock. Again, neoclassical economists prefer to treat that as an exogenous event. We prefer to treat it as a part of the challenge to US domination in the world economy.

In general, neoclassical economists seem to treat current problems in the economy as temporary and as remediable without changes in the structure of the economy. If the shocks come from a domain which is outside the economic system itself, then one could argue that the economic system is not flawed and that there should be a more stringent set of limits on government policy that better respect the private sector and the market economy.

You talked about the conflict theory of inflation awhile ago. I am not sure what you mean by that.

The conflict theory of inflation is an analysis of the mediation of the potential inconsistency between the two rates of growth. Given a rate of growth of productivity, it is a theory about what happens to the rate of growth of claims. But if one asks for a simultaneous determination, the conflict model of inflation is a set of hypotheses about the consequences of imbalance between the two rates of growth.

Can the conflict theory be interpreted as saying that different groups compete for a share of limited income and that this competition brings about an upward pressure on prices?

Yes, but we would add that one cannot take the rate of productivity growth as exogenous. We can argue the converse, that the rate of growth of productivity is endogenous to the larger process of political economic conflicts, but we can only make that argument if we develop an alternative model which reveals the influence of those dimensions of conflict. (For the full historical argument, see Bowles, Gordon, and Weisskopf, 1983.)

Is the connection between inflation and unemployment as close in Marxian analysis as it is in neoclassical analysis?

There is actually a fair amount of debate, or I would say uncertainty, on the nature of that relationship. It is something that I have not yet explored well. There are two somewhat competing perspectives on that relationship. One is a more traditional Marxian analysis with an emphasis on the reserve army of unemployment. That model should suggest that variations in the intensity of labor market competition would affect the rate of growth of nominal and probably real wages and therefore, ceteris paribus, probably also the rate of growth in prices. This position is closely related to Phillips-curve–type models. On the other hand, Marxists have paid enough attention to institutional or post-Keynesian accounts of wage-price-employment determinations in advanced capitalist economies to be sensitive to the idea that, in the core sectors of the economy, it is quite likely that there would be, at least in the short run, a fixed output-employment coefficient, and therefore that the level of the intensity of competition in the labor market would not affect the level of the demand for labor, and also that the rate of growth in the real wage would be trend-determined. From that vantage point one argues the independence of the real wage and the level of employment. Those are two substantially divergent analytic expectations.

Resolving them requires additional work which we simply haven't done yet. We could add that the degree of the sensitivity of the growth of real wages to the level of unemployment will vary by stages of capitalist development.

ON COMMUNICATION WITH NEOCLASSICAL ECONOMISTS

Do you communicate with neoclassical economists about your research efforts?

For a long time there was relatively little contact and, from our side, relatively little effort to communicate our own ideas and our own approach directly to neoclassical economists. I think that has changed, largely because we are further along in our analysis and policy perspectives and are therefore able to formulate some of our analyses in terms that are commensurable with the terms that neoclassical economists use. A number of us are involved in launching an economic research institute, the Economics Institute of the Center for Democratic Alternatives, that would aim explicitly at communicating an alternative left perspective about the macroeconomy and policy. In doing that, we obviously have to formulate our ideas in ways that permit their comparison with the dominant perspective. For if one doesn't, the ideas become policy-irrelevant.

So there is an attempt to communicate on our side. I can't say that is reciprocated. We sense that there is very little interest on the part of neoclassical economists in communicating with us. But one has to be careful here about what one defines as neoclassical economics, because it is obvious that, in the erosion of the grand neoclassical synthesis, one has witnessed a splintering within the profession. There are very large numbers of economists coming out of the centrist and liberal traditions who believe neither in perfect competition nor in the choice theoretic approach to the micro foundations of macroeconomics, which dominates, for instance, the rational expectations school. Nor are they convinced that macroeconomics should exclude all institutional considerations. So, from the center of the Keynesian tradition to the left, or the group that calls itself post-Keynesian, there is substantial amount of interest in questions in which Marxists are also interested.

Who are the conventional economists with whom you do communicate?

There is a fair amount of communication, but not as much as we would like, between Marxists and post-Keynesians such as Paul Davidson and

Alfred Eichner. Many people at Cambridge, England, are also very important for us. John Eatwell, for example, is teaching here at the New School, at least partly to help improve that bridge. There are representatives of the institutionalists, such as Michael Piore, with whom we have been in close communication. There is the tradition both created and represented by Wassily Leontief, with whom we have tried to improve the communication. There is the more-traditional Keynesian tradition represented by people like Tobin and some of the people at Brookings; we are interested in increasing communication with that tradition. It is likely that this will take place more with younger people in that tradition than with the older generation. And then there are people who practice a very traditional neoclassical analysis, but who are interested in alternative developments. Kenneth Arrow, for example, is very supportive of our efforts, but his work involves other issues.

HIS CRITIQUE OF NEW CLASSICAL OR NEOCLASSICAL ECONOMICS

What is new classical economics, according to you?

I think that the strand of recent macroeconomic analysis represented by the rational expectations school is obviously only a part of broader traditions and tendencies within neoclassical economics. It is easier to characterize some of the commonalities in neoclassical economics in general these days than to start with the particular work represented by those figures.

It seems to me that the critical transition in neoclassical economics took place in the period between the mid-'50s and the late '60s when neoclassical economics completed its historical transition from being the science of market allocation of scarce resources to the science of individual and institutional choices about resources, whether those allocations take place in markets or in other institutional domains. After that transition, it is much more relevant to refer to neoclassical economics as choice-theoretic analysis than as an analysis of market determination of resource allocation. It is, therefore, as much a product of that transition that microeconomists now develop analyses of hierarchy within the firm, of fertility decisions, or of investment in human capital, as it is that many are developing new microeconomic foundations of macroeconomics.

So the most important characteristic of neoclassical economics over the past 25 years involves a decision to formalize economics as a study of choice modeled as maximization subject to constraints by any individual agent, and therefore to move away from conceiving of economics as the analysis of particular institutional actors. That has permitted an enormous number of developments which, from a neoclassical perspective, have been enormously fruitful.

The way in which the most recent neoclassical analysis of the microeconomy reflects that same tendency is that the new classical economists have sought to treat, even more rigorously than before, the macroeconomy as an aggregation of individuals maximizing current and future opportunities subject to existing constraints and, therefore, to try to place as little importance as possible on the effectiveness of the government in the determination of the operations of the macroeconomy, and to try to attribute as much as possible to operations of individual producers, consumers, and savers. In that sense, the rational expectations insight represents a natural extension of an effort to treat as much as possible through the choice-theoretic perspective. The extraordinarily simplifying and totally unrealistic assumptions which enter into that anlaysis, such as the assumptions of instantaneous adjustment of price expectations and perfect information about the future, which characterize much of the work, represent a necessary consequence of the effort to try to attribute essentially everything to the consequences of individual choices. Obviously, when one wants to pursue that analytical project one has to assume that individuals are in possession of both as much information as one could possible assume and as many degrees of freedom as one could assume. In that respect it seems to me that the debate between the rational expectations school and a whole array of alternative approaches basically involves a debate about the degrees of freedom available to individuals.

What do you mean by that?

From the Marxian perspective, one can treat economic decisions as a product of two kinds of determinations. One kind involves structural limits on the range of options available to people; the other involves individual actors' choices within the boundaries set by those structural limits. So one of the main differences in almost any analytical domain has involved the stringency or openness of structural limits on individual actors' choices. For example, if, for large portions of the working population, real spendable earnings remain relatively close to what is historically determined as basic subsistence, then models of substitution among available commodities are much less interesting than basic models of the level of real earnings. If one assumes that people have substantial discretionary decision making within their consumption, then the traditional neoclassical model of consumption is much more interesting because there are more degrees of freedom in the kinds of choices in that case.

We argue that much of the crisis results from a narrowing of the range of macroeconomic opportunities available as a result of the growing friction in the postwar corporate system affecting all actors and effectively limiting the decision-making opportunities available to all actors. The starting point of neoclassical economics and increasingly of the new classical macroeconomics is a tendency to treat all of the determinations of the environment as given and to derive all of the analytical hypotheses from models that have individuals respond to things that are, according to us, endogenous. Rational expectations seems to me to be a most-recent manifestation of that neoclassical tendency.

What do you think of the equilibrium strategy that new classical economists have developed?

A stochastic equilibrium model involves two methodological inclinations. One is that it is meaningful to treat the economy as generating a succession of equilibria; second, that it is meaningful to treat individual outcomes in the economy as if they are the outcome of stochastic processes. The first presupposition seems to me incomplete and therefore misguided, unless it is treated as a hypothesis against the null-hypothesis of disequilibrium. The problem with the neoclassical inclination, in that regard, is that it borders on the tautological, that it presupposes axiomatically a sequence of equilibrium outcomes without testing the relevance of that presupposition.

Think about the macroeconomy. For example, by the NBER's definition of business cycle turning points, the U.S. economy spent exactly half of the years between the Civil War and 1980 in a recession or a depression — 58 years out of 115, to be precise. That suggests to me that the most-promising hypothesis is a hypothesis that capitalist economies experience continuing cyclical disruptions. One can generate models of the business cycle that are based on equilibrium models, but at the least one ought to compare their explanatory power with models which treat contraction, recession, and depression as disequilibrium processes. We have tried to work toward an analysis of longer-term stagnation and crisis as a product of the failure of the short-term business cycle to correct frictions that develop. [See also Gordon, Weisskopf, and Bowles, 1983b.]

The second issue about stochastic processes can be related to the narrowness or openness of individual actions, which we discussed earlier. In fact, from the point of view of probability theory, it is only meaningful to treat individual decisions as the outcome of stochastic processes if one assumes that the limits imposed by structural factors are so broad that those structural determinations have very little explanatory power in explaining individual outcomes, and that one can treat individual outcomes as largely a product of individual and random variation in choices. On the other hand, if one works with a model of strict institutional determination, a model of stochastic determination would be irrelevant; a reductionist institutional view of the determination of micro and macro variables would generate averages with no variation around the averages. If this defines a spectrum of analytic inclination between fully institutional determination of outcomes and fully stochastic or relatively independent individual determination of outcomes, then Marxists would argue that where one falls on that spectrum depends on the time frame, and on the geographic extent of the analyses. The broader the extent and the longer the time frame, the greater the importance of institutional determinations. That suggests that one's choice of model depends enormously on the questions asked and the horizons of observations.

How would you summarize your critique of new classical economics? Is it unrealistic, unscientific, or irrelevant?

I think that neoclassical economics is surely scientific. Much of the work involves a careful attempt to derive results from axiomatically grounded models and to test hypotheses carefully derived from those models. So, it is not an issue of whether neoclassical economics is scientific or not, although one has to say that much of their policy conclusions are in fact not adequately grounded in neoclassical theories.

I guess that, at the most-general level, I would criticize neoclassical economics in three respects. The first overriding criticism is that its behavioral propositions are remarkably simple-minded and essentially unrealistic. Every time in the history of thought that neoclassical economics has had to make a choice between preservation of its choice-theoretic approach and alteration in order to gain some degree of realism, it has always chosen to preserve the theory.

The reasons for such a choice reflect two other tendencies of which I am critical. One tendency is that it eschews any dialectical analysis of conflict in relationships and has sought, wherever possible, to model behavioral choices as reflecting a harmony of interest among economic actors. That seems to me one of the main ways in which neoclassical economics is influenced by its political predilection to emphasize the advantages of capitalist economies. For example, the market process presupposes that its outcomes are always mutually beneficial for all participants, because both parties to the exchange have the option of not completing the transaction. We would argue that many of the exchanges *cannot* in fact be avoided; people are forced into them because they have no options. That takes us back to the issue of the limits on individuals' decision-making.

The second tendency of which I am very critical is the tendency to be ahistorical and universalistic. Wherever one looks, there is an effort to formulate models which are generalizable to the full history of market economies without regard for their institutional arrangements. One has the opportunity to develop more elegant and robust models that way but one loses everything in institutional relevance. The explanatory power of these models is limited.

One can argue that neoclassical economists consistently make choices which lead to less-realistic assumptions than are necessary in order to emphasize either the harmony of interests or the universalism of economic operations. The effect of those choices is an analysis that appears to argue that we are better off under capitalism than we would be under some other conceivable system, in spite of all the obvious problems with capitalism.

The new classical criticism of Marxist work is that it is global, vague, and unscientific. It even seems that they get quite annoyed with your historical approach.

Much of the work that has been done in the Marxian tradition is sloppy and, particularly in earlier generations, also dogmatic. One can also say that much of the work done under the umbrella of neoclassical economics has been sloppy and dogmatic. It is true for any tradition. In the neo-Marxian tradition, we would argue, the problems of scientific inquiry are taken very seriously; we pursue our work very carefully.

Wherever possible, we compare the explanatory power of Marxian models with that of alternative models. We think that much of the current work stands up to any kind of scrutiny at least as well as other work, and provides some very important analytical advances. We have made progress in modeling conflicts between, say, capital and labor, and testing hypotheses about those conflicts.

I would add that a lot of recent neo-Marxian work is more scientific than a lot of parallel neoclassical work, because we have indeed compared our models with corresponding neoclassical and other models. In that respect, we have honored the scientific imperative. One would have to say in fairness that remarkably few neoclassical economists hav been interested, over the last 15 years, in comparing their work with that of others working in different non-neoclassical traditions.

What do you think about the predictive performance of alternative models?

One can only speak about particular instances for which one can compare the predictive performance of alternative models. The example that I know best is the case of recent aggregate productivity growth. A relevant standard would be an ex-post forecast of the annual rate of growth of aggregate productivity since 1974, based on a model estimated for the period up to 1973. Though we still have to make some more refinements in our model, it has, nonetheless, dramatically outperformed a state of the art, neoclassical model of aggregate productivity growth.

ON BEING AN ECONOMIST

What do you perceive your role as an economist to be?

Better to redefine it as what is our role as political economists in the society. I think that any science is rooted in a relationship between theory and practice. In the end, and this involves a very profound criticism of the tradition of positivism in the social sciences, one can never fully evaluate the explanatory power of any idea until one acts upon that idea. In that respect, any science has to be evaluated by three criteria: its internal logical coherence, its observational consistency, and its practical effectiveness in either reproducing or changing the world one lives in. I hope to change the world because I don't think that, as Keynes put it, "capitalism is either just or beautiful," but I think that one can only hope to do that if one grounds one's change efforts as scientifically as possible with as clear and as rigorous analysis as possible. Therefore, it seems to me that my political and scientific roles are integrated. The role of a radical political economist is one in which one pursues the objective of a more-decent and just society. I can't think of any other definition of an economist, and I think that neoclassical economists would, by and large, agree that the objective of their science is to try to reproduce a set of relationships that they regard as both efficient and just. In the end, the differences are not so much in the degree we adhere to traditional scientific standard (they would disagree with this), but that we disagree both about alternate political objectives and the models that best illuminate the world and have the best practical effect. Defined in those ways, these are differences that could foster more communication between the traditions than there has been and that should warrant more communication. Given the current crisis of both the economy and of economic theory, I would expect much more communication in the future.

12

LEONARD A. RAPPING

This conversation is of particular interest. It was Rapping who collaborated with Lucas to lay the foundations for new classical economics. Rapping was a full professor at Carnegie-Mellon in the '60s, but a different Rapping now teaches at the University of Massachusetts and writes articles that fit into the post-Keynesian or institutionalist tradition. The change is radical, and we may well wonder why that change occurred and what personal and social consequences it entailed.

We talked in Amherst, Massachusetts, in May 1982.

BACKGROUND

Why did you choose economics?

I went to U.C.L.A. between 1952 and 1956, a period dominated by the Korean War, McCarthyism and prosperity. When I arrived in '52 I was a green kid from West Hollywood with a worldview shaped by the same forces that produced Lenny Bruce, the comedian and social critic. I had spent most of my time in high school gambling and playing basketball. I hadn't paid much attention to my studies, but I knew enough to get the necessary grades for admission to the university.

At U.C.L.A. I met an economist named Warren Scoville, who taught the history of economic thought. He was a Texan, a big Southerner about 6'2" with a barrel voice, loud and passionate — an impressive man. He was my role model. By the way, I've always admired Populist Texans ever since my encounter with Scoville. In any event, he seemed to have a good life. In my background, education and teaching were highly valued, so I decided that I wanted to be a teacher. I also' met Karl Brunner, who taught me monetary and macroeconomics. It was the first time that I had met a European professor, and I was impressed with the style. He was very well organized and I learned a great deal from him about model building, about monetary theory, and about monetary institutions. He liked me and recognized that I was ambitious and hard-working.

What quality attracted him to you? Was it that you were bright, or good in math, or eager?

The latter. I was very eager, very energetic, and very hard-working. He would say I was good raw material. I was a good student, a straight-A student. I did not have any money, and I wanted to go to the best graduate school. I made Junior Phi Beta Kappa. I am proud of this because I started from scratch, and I achieved this in two-and-a-half years.

As a student, were you a conformist?

That is a very hard question to answer. At one level I was very conventional. Whatever I was taught, I learned. I was desperate to learn, and I learned in an uncritical way. I was amassing a tremendous quantity of information. I learned about philosophy, history, economics, and mathematics. I always liked history and hated mathematics. After meeting the real pros at this business at RAND and Carnegie-Mellon, people like Kenneth Arrow and Bob Lucas, I know why. In any event, I was not a conformist in the sense that I didn't want to go to business or medical school, as many of my friends did. They wanted to make a fortune in Los Angeles which, of course, turned out to be easy in the boom days of the postwar prosperity. But I didn't like California — it was like Sodom and Gomorrah to me, desert and all. So, I guess I was a non-conformist in the sense that I wanted to get out of California. I was a non-conformist in the sense that I didn't want to be rich, or at least I didn't want to spend my life getting and protecting money.

THE CHICAGO DAYS

Then you went to Chicago . . .

I was offered financial support from Harvard, Yale, Stanford, and Chicago. I chose Chicago because my father was from Chicago and his side of the family lived there, so it was a return to his home. I also knew that Chicago had a very good economics department. They trained me very well. The university was, of course, a great intellectual center. I heard lectures by Frank Knight, Von Hayek, Hannah Arendt, Bruno Bettelheim, and others. I was stimulated to work and learn.

Which professors were important to you at Chicago?

Gregg Lewis, a labor economist, helped me a great deal. I learned applied econometrics from him. I also learned from him self-confidence and how to take my work seriously. He was a great teacher. As a result of my association with Lewis I became a labor economist with a technical bent.

I have often heard that he is like a father figure for his students. Do you agree with that?

Yes, I guess so. He provided a clear model for what a dissertation should be, so a young person knew what had to be done to finish or to succeed. It was just a question of doing it. Unambiguous procedures are critical. Otherwise graduate students, who in most cases are apprentices, will spin their wheels. By the way, Lewis was also on Lucas's thesis committee.

As far as general economics is concerned, I was influenced by Milton Friedman. Friedman was a charismatic figure. I took his price theory courses for two semesters. I was impressed with his ability to get so much mileage out of an extremely simple view of the world. He was very smart. Friedman was a debater as well; he was in the verbal tradition. I was a good debater, too, and I was drawn to his style.

Was?

Well, I still am, but in New England the opponent is politely embarrassed, not demolished for faulty logic. I admired in Friedman that he was so articulate and quick thinking in public appearances. He was a very effective teacher. He argued that capitalism and individual freedom were closely associated, an important part of his appeal to a young idealistic American in the years after the US helped to defeat the German Devil. So I became a Friedmanite. That was true for most students. But I studied with Lewis from whom I basically learned how to do econometrics. Lewis is a master at econometrics unlike many who are practicing now. He is a methodical, careful, thoughtful, and meticulous person.

Did you read radical economics at that time?

No. I didn't read it then. As an undergraduate, I read some Marx but I found it tedious. At the time that I went to Chicago, economics training was fairly technical. By the mid-'50s they were cleaning economic history out of the curriculum.

Why was that done?

Why was it done? [pause]. Economics was becoming very technocratic. Economists viewed their discipline as scientific, and science means progress. All you have to study is the current techniques and solutions, not history. A person of average intelligence who went to graduate school would need four years just to learn basic economic theory and econometrics. There was really no time to do history or related subjects. Anyway, for a while, at least, the big questions were settled by World War II. We were in the "American Century."

Were you familiar with the methodological argument that the realism of assumption does not matter?

This issue was critical. It was critical in two senses, I think. As a debating technique, it was very valuable. But it was also an ideological assumption. Friedman would say that the assumptions do not matter because you can go from false premises to true conclusions. However, it is in the nature of human beings, and the Chicago students prove this point, to forget after a time that the assumption may be false. You start thinking that it describes reality. Repetition not only makes perfect, it makes believers. Many Chicago people would argue that the world is, in fact, competitive. They tend to believe their own pragmatic myth.

You also thought and argued that the world was a competitive one in which people maximize profits and utility?

Right, that is how you thought and how you argued. I always believed that it was more than just a convenient assumption; I believed that it was descriptively accurate. People, myself included, can't stand the idea that we can draw true conclusions from false premises. Of course, a lot of people argue that you want to start with realistic assumptions. Friedman's position is too extreme. The students, in the end, can't stand to live with that position, so they solve the problem by seeing the world as competitive and making the assumption "true."

Friedman, however, does not refer to his essay on "Positive Economics" anymore. Do you think that argument is still important for him?

On yeah, it is the key. That article is a work of extraordinary psychological insight. Either by design or by accident he hit on an argument that was incredibly powerful. What seemed an innocent point in logic and scientific methodology is, through the workings of the mind, transformed into a description of the world for his students.

What were your political beliefs at that time?

I accepted the view that the US was making the world safe for democracy, that the US would develop the Third World, and that the US was basically a liberal and progressive state. I believe that it was a land of opportunity. In those years, there was good reason to be optimistic in America. The war had ended; the US had won a military victory against evil. You don't often get a chance to defeat the devil. The country was very self-confident and optimistic. I believed that a strong military was necessary to deter Soviet aggression. I accepted all of those arguments.

I was conservative. Friedman's book *Capitalism and Freedom* was very important to me. I believed in it. The thing that impressed me most about Friedman was his emphasis on freedom. His view was consistent with the American dream, the dream about a land of freedom and opportunity. I must say that I did feel free until the late 1960s.

CARNEGIE-MELLON AND HIS COLLABORATION WITH LUCAS

Before Carnegie-Mellon, I was at RAND for two years. There I learned about the problems of rationalizing logistical and procurement processes in the military bureaucracy. I traveled a lot. Met many interesting people. A valuable learning experience. Later I often consulted at the Pentagon and worked as a special assistant to the then Assistant Secretary of Defense, Alain Enthoven. I maintained a working relationship with RAND until 1969.

After RAND I went to Carnegie-Mellon. I got a job there because George Shultz recommended me. He was a teacher of mine at Chicago—he later became Secretary of Treasury and is now Secretary of State. At Carnegie I learned about the corporation and business problems; I interacted with corporate executives; I consulted in Washington. For 11 years Herb Simon was the dominant intellectual figure in my life. He is a genius.

But Simon's ideas are not reflected in the paper that you coauthored with Lucas.

Oh no, the Lucas-Rapping work is in the Chicago tradition. The Carnegie influence had not yet taken root in me. It is in my current work that many of the Carnegie ideas appear. Lucas incorporates the Carnegie influence on him when he turns to Muth's idea on rational expectations.

When did you start working with Lucas?

I came to Carnegie in '62, Lucas came in '63. We were friends from the beginning. We spent lots of time together. I expect that we talked once or twice every day from '63 till '68. We talked about everything: about economics, about politics, about business school problems, just about everything. We would have coffee from about three until five. We were the two people who would always be at the afternoon coffee hours. Everyone else would be back at their offices. Yes, we got along very well.

Lucas gave me the impression that you were a mentor for him.

That may be, but I was not that much older than he was, only a year or two. Bob was rather shy; I was more of a hustler. I did a lot of consulting and a lot of traveling to California and Washington, D.C. Bob didn't like to travel. He was a devoted father and husband. He was also fairly systematic in his research. I was more impatient and always wanted to move on to the next issue.

We started early on to discuss the problems that came out in our 1969 paper. We were always discussing the issues of unemployment, inflation and real wages. The paper did not take long to write once we began to write it. The whole project did not take more than nine months once we seriously embarked on it.

What assumptions did you make in that paper?

As I said, we were in the Chicago tradition, so we assumed perfect competition and profit and utility maximization. Every single proposition had to be consistent with those assumptions. There were certain rules of logic that had to be followed, and the discussions were very tight and logical. We would try to explain everything in terms of the competitive equilibrium models. (We had learned that from Friedman. Friedman impressed his students because he got so much mileage out of those assumptions; they explained so much.) That paper was nothing more than an attempt to explain the supply and demand for labor in conventional terms. Sometimes I think that the paper wrote itself, but that's probably because Bob was doing a lot of the writing.

Did you get much criticism?

Yes, several people expressed scepticism. Our way of dealing with unemployment was a problem; we knew that. Mike Lovell nearly had a heart attack when he saw the paper. He was a student of Tobin's. He thought that we were defining away the problem of unemployment.

Was the controversy political?

Yes. It was very political, but I liked the controversy.

Did it disturb you to be labeled a conservative?

Well, I started minding it because other issues started to become important for me. Perhaps I never fully understood the paper's full implications, that is, its policy and methodological implications. I do not think that they were perfectly clear to Lucas, either. I think that we were groping with those ideas and trying to get them straight. This is evident in his subsequent papers. They are an effort to clarify a lot of issues that were raised in our paper. For example, we knew that there was a problem with adaptive expectations because it did not give us Friedman-like results. So we had to introduce a shift in expectations at one point.

The equilibrium modeling was unconventional at that time, wasn't it?

We just thought about writing down a demand and supply for labor, which was the easiest way to proceed. Later when we got it all worked out, we noticed that we did not have any unemployment in the model. We worried about that, of course. We knew this was always a problem with demand and supply models. One day one of us said, "Look, let's define unemployment in this way." Then we noticed that the equation that we defined was a Phillips relationship. It was sitting right there.

How important was econometrics in this paper?

Econometrics was very important for us; it was one of the things that tied us to the literature. We had learned from Lewis that any single econometric study is not very convincing. It is only when you take large numbers of studies that examine the same set of problems from different perspectives that you are able to gain some empirical insight into the world. It seemed important to us that the empirical results relate to the literature and be consistent with that literature. So we included in the article long discussions about how our results related to the literature. We thought that we were testing in the sense that we tried to determine whether other empirical efforts, using different bodies of data and different time periods, were consistent, in some rough way, with our results. In fact, like all researchers, we were doing the econometrics while we were working out the theory.

Were you aware of Muth's hypothesis of rational expectations at that time?

Muth was at Carnegie-Mellon until '64. His idea was discussed throughout the '60s but we did not see its possibilities then.

By the way, Tom Sargent was at Carnegie-Mellon when Lucas and I were writing that paper. He came from Harvard and stayed for a year.

Did you talk a lot with him?

I did some. He was quiet. He did not pay much attention to what Bob and I were doing. He did not talk with Lucas much.

How did he fit in at Carnegie-Mellon?

He must have been aware of the factions at Carnegie at that time. He was considered part of the Harvard group. The Chicago people tended to have reservations about liberals, and the Harvard people were liberals. Do not forget that Chicago has always been like an intellectual outpost on the western frontier and has always had an inferiority complex with respect to the prestigious schools of the east. So there was a conscious attempt among Chicago people to prove themselves. I was affected by all this because it was in the atmosphere. There were controversies over Keynes. Harvard was thought of as the American home of Keynes, probably because of people such as Alvin Hansen and Seymour Harris. Finally, Chicago was anti-elitist, and Harvard and Yale were seen as elitist schools.

You and Lucas also published an article in the American Economic Review *of 1970, but Lucas does not seem to like that paper anymore. What is the story?*

Bob did not reproduce it in his latest book [Lucas, 1981a]. It was a further empirical examination of short- and long-run Phillips curves. We wanted to test the proposition that there is not a long run Phillips curve. We adopted a new expectations assumption, a somewhat more flexible one than adaptive expectations. It gave us one more parameter to estimate. We estimated long- and short-run Phillips curves for three subperiods, namely 1918–1929, 1929–1939, and the post-World War II periods. It didn't work. The conclusion of that paper was that in the period 1918–1929 we had a classical mechanism; we had a short-run Phillips curve and a vertical long-run curve. The reason we got that result was because of the '20–'21 recession which was a classical recession—short, deep, and effective. Inflation ended and sustained growth emerged. In the '30s you get garbage; in the post-World War II period you get ambiguity. That paper suggested that there might have been a fundamental structural shift in the system between the '20s and the '40s and '50s. But we were operating under the assumption of structural stability over long periods of time. When I met Lucas lately in Washington he claimed that I had pushed the publication of that paper. In later work, he argues that the approach in that paper was improper. Maybe so.

A PERIOD OF CHANGE

What happened afterward?

Bob and I remained friends. But I became interested in the issues revolving around the war in Indo-China and became increasingly involved in the anti-war movement. I began reading a lot about Indo-China; I started looking for an explanation of the war. I also realized that there was something very wrong with the military build-up. And, I began to see the nuclear problem as *the* social and economic problem of our time. I had learned about this problem during my years at RAND.

Lucas was not interested in that?

He was not interested in where I was going. I pretty much began to disassociate myself from most of my colleagues. My involvement in these issues was embarrassing to a lot of them. I was already a full professor and had a lot of privileges. I was well paid; I had a light teaching load. I was teaching in the program for executives, and I was connecting up with many corporations and foundations. There was a profound contradiction between my privileges and my beliefs. I quit Carnegie in 1973, because I couldn't stand the dissonance any longer. I was lucky to have another job. I could afford principled positions.

You must have discovered that something was wrong with Chicago economics.

I discovered that the war was wrong: I came to the conclusion that it was an illegitimate war and America was an imperial power. That disillusioned me. In all my training at Chicago there was no serious mention of the global system. Chicago training, like training elsewhere, was closed economy training. I knew that the Chicago world vision was inappropriate for the problems I was concerned with, which were the problems of foreign policy, of military power, and of the war. I did go back and reread Henry Simon's work. He was very clear: you cannot have a democracy at home and an empire abroad (that was in 1938). Simon was the guru of many Chicago people. But Friedman never mentioned anything about foreign policy or defense spending or an American system. So I did the only thing I could: I jettisoned Chicago economics. But that left me in an intellectual vacuum.

How did you feel during this intellectual and personal transition?

It was an awful experience. Very difficult. I had never experienced depression before; I did then. It took me many years to recoup from that. For about six years I just read; I didn't write anything. It was a dark and painful period. It was hard. I was afraid. Everything that I had learned seemed inadequate, given the war. I concluded that I was inadequately educated and that I had to search further for the truth. I searched to the left and read and thought about that point of view. But I would never again embrace an extreme ideology.

To understand the experience you could think of a football player who suddenly decides that football is not his cup of tea and tries another game. The adjustment was tremendous. For a long time I was without any defenses. I was intellectually exposed. I disassociated myself from a whole set of personal friendships developed over a 20-year period. Every time I made a move I was accused of inconsistency or disloyalty. I was frozen out of the "money river." I felt like a pariah.

Did your colleagues and friends treat you differently?

Well, I pretty much walked away from them; I didn't have much contact with them anymore. That is the way I dealt with it.

Did you continue speaking to Lucas?

Little, very little. We have had some friendly correspondence, but we clearly went different ways. The friendship has not been lost; it has been discontinued. Yes, it was a very difficult period. I also got divorced during that time, so I lost my job, my family, and my career.

So you started out new.

Yes. I recently remarried. My children are doing well, my work is progressing, so I guess I've recovered from those difficult times.

Was the decision for you to leave Carnegie-Mellon a hard one for you to make?

I don't know. Life is funny. You kind of trip into things; events often make it difficult to think carefully about the implications of every decision. The reason that I left Carnegie-Mellon was that I had lost my sense of purpose. As a young boy I was very much affected by the Holocaust experience. For a young Jewish boy it was a profound shock to discover that there are people in the world who track you down and murder you in the grotesque way devised by the Nazis. I had at the time of the Vietnam War the vision that the Vietnamese were murdered in a way that reminded me of what happened in Germany.

Why did you go to the University of Massachusetts in Amherst?

I had been offered the chairmanship of the Economics Department in 1971. And I knew people in the area. Later, when the department hired several radicals and anti-war activists, I felt it was the right environment for me. The department was ecumenical. Ideologically diverse points of view were represented. It was the perfect environment to enquire about the world. This was the beginning of a profound education for me. Without the experience of changing values I would not have grown intellectually and morally. I am more aware of right and wrong now. I know the moral dimension of the human condition. I also began to think in broader terms. My article on inflation [Rapping, 1979] is a good expression of that broader mind set. I could not have written that article ten years earlier.

I tell you, the reconstruction of a worldview is a long, slow process. It is also a wrecking experience. The process is never completed. I am eclectic and sometimes inconsistent. It is hard to be consistent because you have to accept certain constraints on your thinking. And I don't want to do that; I have never chosen another ideologically constraining framework. I do have a lot of respect for Keynes. He was a pragmatist. I am sympathetic to the post-Keynesian framework. I would say that my politics are social democratic. In a nuclear age, consensus and compromise is the advisable way.

With whom did you work and associate with, at what time?

I worked with Jim Crotty, who was a student of mine at Carnegie-Mellon and who came to the University of Massachusetts a year after I did. But otherwise, no one in particular. In the past five years, I've basically worked alone. I was somewhat active in URPE. I met Steve Hymer, who had gone through much of what I went through. I liked him. Unfortunately, he was killed in an automobile accident in 1974. That was a loss. He was a free thinker.

There were actually four economists that I know of who "defected." There was Ellsberg of the Pentagon Papers; and there was the chairman of the City College of New York, the husband of Adrienne Rich, a famous feminist poet—Conrad was his name. Unhappily, he committed suicide in about '72. And there was Steve Hymer. The war was a great shock to the American society, very great. It changed or destroyed many lives.

ON NEW CLASSICAL ECONOMICS

What do you think about the current work of Bob Lucas?

It is very abstract and formal model building. Like any general approach it has limitations but it is one of many ways that we attempt to comprehend the world. For me it's too general, too removed from reality. However, for its genre, it is the best, I guess.

Rational expectations is a flexible idea. It opens up a lot more possibilities than adaptive expectations. I think it introduces a new dimension into the way economists think about the economy. It had a great impact because of its psychological possibilities. Of course, it need not be combined with monetarism or general equilibrium.

The business cycle in Lucas's models results, in part, from the way in which people perceive the world. This opens up the possibility of an interaction between people's thought processes and material reality. This is very much different from a theory of business cycles based on technological change, or an oil and other raw materials relative price changes, or on population changes. This psychological vision of the process is probably one reason why the approach is so popular, or at least it would be the reason, if people thought about it.

But what is the psychological content?

Rational expectations assume that people behave rationally; they can't be fooled; they have a strong sense of where things are going. Each player is a prophet. This approach gets around the Von Neumann-Morgenstern problem of finding a solution to a game with two rational players. Of course, their approach permits the government, by shrewd manipulation, to influence the market. In Lucas's model it can't, or at least it is very difficult.

Now, I think that psychology is very important to understand the economy. In the current era, economic parameters are changing rapidly. This is the age of mirrors and propaganda. Institutions are changing rapidly; they change in unpredictable ways; the system is disordered and uncertain. In such periods people are subject to a herd instinct. People act as if they are trapped; they run in one direction and find the door closed. Then someone shouts "Run in the other direction!" and everyone does. There is a constant search for a way out, but there is no way out. It is not quite panic, but it is herd behavior. Psychology begins to dominate the movement of many variables, such as the exchange rate or the interest rate. Keynes knew this. He was insightful.

For example, let us assume that the Federal Reserve wants to lower the interest rates. How much paper does the Fed have to buy in order to drive down the interest rate? It depends on whether the market in general believes that the interest rate will go lower permanently. Before the Fed enters into a policy of open market operations, it prepares the ground by engaging in a propaganda campaign—that is, by engaging in what was once called moral suasion—to convince everybody that the Fed's efforts will be effective. It is not just a matter of selling bonds; it also means dinner meetings, lunches, cocktail parties, and news releases to get the word out. I do not think that back in the '50s it took the Fed nearly as much convincing as it does now. In an earlier period, people believed the Fed. The reactions are now more psychologically elastic. This is because of the uncertainty that now exists. So we have to think about the ways in which people form their perceptions. It is in the sense that the rational expectations notion is useful because it directs attention to a psychological state of the participants. Of course, it does so in too constrained a way, but it does do so.

The second reason why Lucas's approach has become very popular among younger people is because it opens up possibilities for the further use of the mathematical technique. Lucas places tremendous emphasis on technique. But you can become so enraptured with technique that you lose sight of the underlying processes. You ask the wrong questions as you get enraptured by mathematics and mechanical issues; you start to ignore important behavioral processes. This is not an argument against technical training, just against excessive reliance on it.

I don't seriously think that one can explain the events of this decade with exogenous money shocks coupled with the way in which people's perceptions are formed. This ignores the Vietnam War and the revolutions in the Middle East, in Latin America, and Asia. It ignores OPEC and the rise of energy prices, the breakdown of the NATO alliance, the crumbling of Soviet alliances, and the collapse of the Polish economy; it ignores the rise of Eurocommunism; it ignores the weakness of the auto-steel industrial complex. It is just too abstract a vision of what is a very complex historical process. Moreover, it is a closed economy model. But everyone is aware that America is deeply embedded in a global system. The model is limited because, although it accounts for accelerating inflation in the '70s, it cannot explain the stagnation of the 1970s or the persistent high unemployment rates since 1979.

Would the model have been fascinating for you had you not converted to another set of beliefs?

Perhaps. You say that Lucas took the approach that we began to its logical conclusions. I think that is true.

RAPPING'S ECONOMICS NOW

What are the important things in the current economy?

I am worried. I think that the essence of industrial revolution was a substitution of mechanical energy for human energy, and that required cheap fuel. Those days are over. The prosperity of the 1950s and 1960s is now unachievable in the US let alone on a global scale. We have to fundamentally redefine the accepted way of life, or the standard of living. That means major cultural changes, which take time.

How do you look at inflation and the other economic problems of this time?

The high unemployment rate is a structural problem. The inflation is a result of slow growth and the fight over social product. We don't have mass unemployment yet. For that, you need a breakdown of the financial system. And although the financial order is very fragile, it hasn't collapsed yet. It has been kept afloat for a decade. It might be kept afloat for another decade.

Why doesn't unemployment come down, now that inflation rates are coming down?

You understand, I now believe that in troubled times there is a trade-off between inflation and unemployment. I don't take the argument about a vertical curve seriously. Current events indicate that there is a trade-off. [Rapping then draws a graph of the Phillips curve to illustrate to me what he is saying.] What they call a shift in the Phillips curve is a structural break. It is breakdown of a global system. Arthur Burns was right with his inflationary policy in the '70s. It prevented a total collapse of the system. But the correct insight of Lucas's model is that you cannot continue without eventual hyperinflation unless, of course, you have wage-price restraint on a global scale.

As far as the present situation is concerned, we need an investment boom in order to get unemployment down. But around which technology will this investment boom get organized? Not the old metal-working industry. Not housing. The savings and loans are in the process of being dismantled. We do not have the population growth for another boom based on population expansion. Electrification doesn't look promising. It's just not clear.

In any event, we need more political stability. We must have a more-equal distribution of income. We must work out some form of a social contract. Without a consensus you have permanent conflict. The post-Keynesians understand the need for an incomes program which is not a set of numerical rules but rather a political and administrative process seeking democratic consensus.

Your overall pessimism suggests that you do not think that any policy matters very much.

I support arrangements which involve the direction and coordination of market processes. We need some regulation—I do not think we can have a successful market process without regulation. Keynes's work on uncertainty was crucial for me to understand this.

Markets can't work when there is too much uncertainty. For example, in the '20s everyone shared a particular vision, namely that automobiles would be the future technology. People then made their own history. The explanation of why you have confidence in some periods and not in others is complicated. When there is uncertainty—which has as its most important element military and political instability—vision is clouded. This is the situation now. In this situation people are immobilized. They wait. When the right political conditions exist, people come to believe that they can see the future. Of course, they never can; they just think they can.

What is the rationality of this reaction?

I do not think that it is a rational process. When they all come to believe that tomorrow is like today and when they are all confident, then they start to operate with simple decision rules based on financial accounting and numerical calculation. They simply extrapolate. But there are periods of discontinuity like now. In this circumstance, uncertainty prevails.

Do you think that Sargent and Lucas take your work seriously?

No.

Why do you think that they don't respect your work in light of the fact that you are all intelligent people with a common interest?

I have to think about that. It may be that one's thinking gets forced into a certain metaphor and one then must always argue in these terms. However, if you let your mind go, there are many possibilities. But the printed word is very constrained. I think that Bob has a broader vision than his formal work implies.

Do you reject their demand and supply analysis?

I don't use it very much. I am a little bothered by demand and supply. Some of the most important prices, oil prices, the wage rate, and the interest rate, are not determined by demand and supply. They are determined by herd instinct, a social contract, negotiation, dominance, you know, politics and power or just plain speculative frenzy.

How do you analyze that?

Who knows? We try. I don't think that it can be put into a formal model. But that doesn't mean it is wrong.

In this way you make almost any argument with you impossible. How can we determine if you are right or wrong?

I understand the point. I would have made the same criticism in the mid '60s of people like Herb Simon who were thinking about questions of power and social processes. They seemed to be interesting ideas, but unquantifiable. But that doesn't make them any less important to think about and wrestle with. I do not know the answer to your question. It is a fair question. However it applies to formal models, too. They imply more precision than they actually have. People are easily bamboozled by numbers and mathematics.

Do you reject the rigorous analysis that is prevalent nowadays?

I do not think about it much. It probably has its place. I think that formal model building forces you to be too narrow, especially in a period of rapid change. But it is useful for training applied mathematicians and model-building bureaucrats for the corporations and for the government.

But you were passionately involved with all that in the '60s.

The world had changed.

But not for Lucas.

People see the world differently. I guess that the way you see the world depends on your environment. Frankly, I do not think that the rational expectations theorists are in the real world. Their approach is much too abstract.

People trained in his way of thinking will be applied mathematicians. Of course, these people will not be convinced that less "precise" ways of thinking are appropriate. So what? Most of the economists who pick up this stuff are young; the older economists have not embraced it. The younger ones may drive the broad thinkers somewhere else, like to political science or sociology or law. That bothers me about American economics.

Lucas seems to like the game of arguing with other economists, to stand up against established opinions. Does that surprise you?

No. Chicago taught us to contend with positions we disagreed with. Bob is very smart and has built a formidable mathematical fortress. Why not take on the opponents!

PART SIX

Interpretation

13

AN INTERPRETATION OF THE CONVERSATIONS

We have been listening to outstanding and brilliant economists, the very best the discipline has to offer. They nonetheless disagree fundamentally on theoretical and empirical questions, on policy proposals, and on the ways economic issues should be studied and settled. At times, they even have difficulty understanding each other. One may well wonder what this means for economics as a discipline.

Officially, of course (by which I mean according to the prevailing doctrines of a positivist theory of economic science), theoretical disagreements are handled by piling up more and more empirical evidence until the case is settled in the eyes of any "objective" economist. This picture is not borne out by our conversations; relatively little of the argument above can be viewed as a simple citing of evidence. Some might be tempted to react by seeing economics as primarily a subjective or ideological discipline, the great issues coming down to matters of opinion or intellectual preferences. But this sort of subjectivism does as little justice to the rich, multifaceted nature of economic discourse as positivism does. A more promising and fruitful reading of these discussions would, I suggest, focus on the *communicative* or *rhetorical* aspects of economics. This focus leads us to questions such as: How do economists argue or communicate? and, What factors lead them to agree or disagree with a given position? I propose to reflect on the conversations in light of these two questions, and I shall argue that the conversations themselves support such a communicative view of economic discourse.

What emerges is a sense of the diversity of the arguments in economic discourse. Economists do not only construct models and conduct empirical tests, they also argue on what a good model should look like. Moreover, they philosophize, appeal to common sense, and talk about other economists and their work. Economics involves the art of persuasion. In the absence of uniform standards and clear-cut empirical tests, economists have to rely on judgments, and they argue to render their judgments persuasive. This process leaves room for nonrational elements, such as personal commitment and style, and social discipline.[1]

I claim that the conversations support this view of economic discourse, but of course I also bring this view to them. There are other ways of listening to these talks; the scope for the exercise of judgment is wide here as well. And there is a sense in which the conversational format may be said to stack the deck a bit: rhetorical elements are more likely to come to the fore here than in, say, the journals. Here, as in economics itself, we may take different impressions away from the same evidence; my claim for the validity of my perspective is a modest one.

IN SEARCH OF THE CORE CLAIMS

As we listen to new classical economists, we want to know what their arguments are all about; we want to identify the basic statements that distinguish their argument from neo-Keynesian and other arguments. These statements, which I call the core claims of an argument, should reveal the point of gravity of the discussions. Unfortunately, the core claims in new classical discourse are not immediately obvious.

When we ask what the arguments of Lucas, Sargent and Townsend are all about, the easy answer is "rational expectations." As the background picture indicates, however, rational expectations is at most a supportive claim. In addition, the conversations show that the disagreements do not gravitate toward the assumption of rational expectations. All neo-Keynesians and Brunner, the monetarist, acknowledge the merit of this assumption, leaving Gordon and Rapping, the radical economists, as its strong critics. Rather, the disagreement seems to converge upon the claim that new classical economists derive with the assumption of rational expectations: the claim that systematic policy is ineffective, or the neutrality proposition. Lucas and Sargent do underwrite policy ineffectiveness in their work; neo-Keynesians target it in their opposition to new classical economics; and monetarists question its validity in the short run. The neutrality proposition, then, appears to be the core claim of new classical economics.

Nonetheless, the economists interviewed here exhort caution. Both Lucas and Sargent downplay the importance of the neutrality proposition in their contemporary work. Sargent emphasizes that the proposition is an outcome of particular models which "aren't satisfactory" and does not exclude the possibility that other models with rational expectations produce nonneutral effects of systematic economic policy. He notes that others "took the neutrality proposition more seriously than we did." So perhaps the neutrality proposition is too restrictive to be the core claim in new classical discourse. We could look for a more general formulation of conflicting visions. The vision that is manifest in new classical arguments closely resembles the one that earned Milton Friedman his reputation. Like Friedman, new classical economists express faith in the stability of the market. They are suspicious of government intervention and advocate predictable governmental policy rules. Neo-Keynesians clearly disagree. When asked "What is a neo-Keynesian," Tobin responds: "I think the basic issue there is the question of whether there are market failures of a macroeconomic nature in a market economy. . . . A neo-Keynesian thinks there are and that the government can do something about them." The radical economists, Rapping and Gordon, go further and claim the existence of basic flaws in the market system. They champion dramatic remedies for our economic problems, such as national planning and democratic control of investment.

Still, the new classical claim that the market is fundamentally stable is not all that spectacular and cannot account for all controversy. Brunner underwrites it but does not want to be called a new classical economist. It is also conceivable that Lucas and Sargent will accept neo-Keynesian conclusions, at least if they were derived from models that are articulated in a way they like. Therefore, the main disagreement may well be not what to say, but on how to say it; if so, the distinctive claim of new classical economists would concern style, not substance.

Sargent says, "I think the key thing about the new classical economics is a commitment to some notion of general equilibrium and some notion of optimizing behavior, strategic behavior." Both he and Lucas claim to use a new language that dictates precision of expression, in strict adherence to the principles of microeconomics. Brunner is disenchanted with the rigor of Lucas and Sargent's style, and so are Tobin, Modigliani, Solow, and Blinder. They particularly object to the equilibrium modeling strategy in new classical economics. The issue, then, is the style of argument.

The controversial style of new classical economists is manifest in both their theoretical and empirical arguments and it is supported with epistemological arguments. We shall consider these arguments next.

THEORETICAL ARGUMENTS

To the outsider, theoretical discourse in economics may appear to be an esoteric, if not absurd, affair. The assumptions economists use sound unreal, and their technical language deters further reading. Nonacademic economists and new students in economics tend to speak in nontechnical terms about economic questions; the popularity of John Kenneth Galbraith and Lester Thurow is undoubtedly due to their nontechnical, journalistic style. But academic economists usually show impatience with a style that is not, as they would say, "serious." The academics want to talk about questions such as "What are the assumptions?" and "How does a change in assumptions affect the outcome of the model?" Economists look for a systematic theory to expound more clearly the conditions under which an event takes place. A systematic, well-specified theoretical argument is crucial because it allows careful scrutiny of logical consistency and facilitates further arguments in academic discourse. Learning economics is learning how to articulate theoretical arguments in support of one's ideas.

The importance of a theoretical context for the persuasiveness of an idea is brought out in the history of rational expectations. Neo-Keynesians claim that the idea already existed in Keynes's *General Theory*. Modigliani claims that "you can find references to almost anything in the *General Theory*." Even so, Keynes did not articulate the idea in such a way that would compel other economists to incorporate it into their models. We now recognize Muth as the first economist to have presented an effective theoretical argument for rational expectations. Incidentally, the ten years of silence that followed the publication of his article in 1961 makes his recognition seem accidental. Lucas, however, tells us that history is less fortuitous than it seems. He was at Carnegie-Mellon, where Muth had been until 1963, when he heard about Muth's ideas. At that time Lucas did not know how to incorporate those ideas into macro models. Now everyone knows and talks about Muth's hypothesis, because Lucas solved his problem in an effective way. Lucas's style of argument, I maintain, was persuasive.

The new classical style of argument embraces the search for microfoundations of macroeconomics. As Lucas, Sargent, and Townsend emphasize time and again, their models are an attempt to answer the question "Why do people choose to do what they do?" in accordance with the neoclassical postulates of maximizing behavior. The rational expectations hypothesis is one element of their style; the assumption of market-clearing prices another. The disequilibrium modeling strategy of neo-Keynesian economists is rejected because it leaves the rationality of agents ill-defined.

The new classical style entails a new language to describe economic behavior. Sargent says he thinks "about agents as living in a dynamic and uncertain environment and being concerned about strategic considerations." Lucas's image is that of agents placing bets in an uncertain environment. The bets are optimal and, thus, the inevitable mistakes rational. In their models, stochastic variables and imperfect information account for the uncertainty agents face, as well as for the observation of unemployment and business cycles.

In an environment that appreciates precisely formulated macro models with solid microfoundations, the neo-Keynesians appear to be on the defensive against the new classical style. After all, Tobin, Modigliani, and Solow were the front-runners among those economists who tried to combine neoclassical microeconomics and Keynesian macroeconomics; the application of the rationality postulate to expectations formation fits into this scheme. Nevertheless, they resist the radical way in which new classical economists interpret their original intentions. In the end, their commitment to Keynesian macroeconomic prevails; their problem is to make this judgment convincing.

The neo-Keynesian judgment is pronounced in their opposition to the equilibrium postulate in the new classical strategy. Tobin, for example, says he does not understand this facet of new classical economics; even Taylor, who has adopted much of the new classical language, believes it does not make sense. The existence of contracts, they argue, explains why observed prices are not equilibrium prices. Taylor himself built contracts into new classical types of model to reach neo-Keynesian conclusions. The emphasis on contracts characterizes "the economics of nominal rigidities," as Blinder labels the Keynesian approach. When I confront the neo-Keynesians with Lucas's criticism that the rationality of contracts is ill-defined, they shrug their shoulders and appeal to what they see in the real world. A similar interaction occurs with respect to learning. Neo-Keynesians argue that people have to learn before they are able to form rational expectations; new classical economists wonder how learning behavior can be modeled in accordance with the rationality postulate.

Tobin et al acknowledge the criticisms of new classical economists, but counter the charges and point at imperfections in new classical models. Taylor, among others, points out that the restraints those models impose on the available information are arbitrary. Blinder wonders why people would not know what the money supply is, as Lucas assumes in some of his models, even though it is one of the best known of all data. He and Solow do not hide their sentiments when they dismiss the new classical argument that the current high unemployment is due to misperceptions; both think it absurd. The neo-Keynesians also deem unrealistic the new classical assumption that the government follows rules. Here Taylor is the exception.

Brunner, the monetarist, shares the new classical vision of a stable market and a predictable government. Moreover, he appreciates the rational expectations hypothesis and other elements of the new classical approach, such as the assumption of imperfect information and the role of stochastic variables. Despite their similarities, he insists that his approach is not new classical. Like the neo-Keynesians, he rejects the radical way in which new classical economists interpret the rationality postulate; he considers the world too complicated to be captured in new classical models. An important point in his argument is the application of neoclassical price theory in analyzing policy decisions. The optimal policy that follows from such an analysis would be, according to Brunner, to abstain from active policy.

In spite of sharp differences in theoretical perspective, the conversations show that the conventional economists are willing to argue about each others' models. The opposite is true with respect to the unconventional arguments of Gordon and Rapping, so far as the other economics are concerned. Perhaps the conventional economists do not take the work of Gordon and Rapping seriously because concepts articulated by radical economists are difficult to incorporate into nonradical-type models. Lucas admits that the notion of fundamental uncertainty stressed by Rapping makes sense, but blames the limitations of his own techniques for ignoring the issue. For the same reason, Lucas abstracts from monopolistic pricing. Gordon speaks of the historical and social context of economic events, such as inflation, and highlights the economic significance of conflicting situations. Blinder's reaction is, "I'm not very comfortable with the concept of struggle and conflict, but that's my intellectual upbringing. I feel comfortable with budget constraints, stuff like that." A serious exchange on these subjects turns out to be difficult, if not impossible; the communication simply breaks down.

If the conversations make one thing clear, it is that no model, no single argument, is unexceptional and problem-free. When economists talk about their models, they do not pretend that the model in its current state gives *the* answer to the pressing economic questions of our time. They speculate about its possibilities and indicate which direction they want to follow in the future. In other words, they embark on a "journey of discovery," or they involve themselves in a research program. New classical economists believe in the potential of combining rationality and equilibrium postulates and are in the process of exploring the implications of this judgment. Neo-Keynesians and monetarists consider the new classical results unconvincing, and follow different research programs. The Keynesians admit their program has problems, but continue to believe in its possibilities. Accordingly, theoretical arguments are uncertain and their acceptability relies on a judgment which is made plausible with a variety of other arguments.

EMPIRICAL ARGUMENTS

Economists commonly agree that theoretical arguments need empirical support. Thus, they spend much of their time constructing empirical tests and improving the econometrics that provides the statistical backing of those tests. In fact, the demands of empirical research have now become such that it has grown into a specialty. This development has generated the complaint that much empirical research in economics is only related loosely to the theory of economics. Either the econometric models incorporate so many ad hoc assumptions that it is unclear which economic theory they test, or the models are so simple that only the econometrics, and not an economic hypothesis, matters.

The remarks of Sargent can be placed against the background. Sargent, the foremost econometric specialist among new classical economists, considers the lack of a "clear link" between theories and statistical tests a major problem. He notes: "What I mean by the links not being clear is that often times the models that we get have no randomness in them. . . . The statistical model you're using implies there is an environment in which there's uncertainty, whereas the economic model that you're using assumes that away." Sargent credits elements of new classical theory with making the link tighter. The stochastic or random variables in new classical models provides the statistical properties that econometric testing requires; the rational expectations hypothesis introduces the necessary dynamic element.

The new econometrics, as the empirical procedures of new classical economists have been coined, has a fully integrated position. As Sargent confirms, one component of the new econometrics consists of testing elaborate new classical models, the other exploring time series to provide clues for the construction of those elaborate models.

An important point that the conversations highlight is the uncertain and controversial nature of empirical research in economics. Lucas and Sargent use their newly acquired theoretical insights to reject previous tests of the natural rate hypothesis and those with large-scale models. Blinder is not convinced and questions the empirical relevance of the flaws that Lucas and Sargent perceive in the tests with large-scale models. Moreover, Blinder, Tobin, and Solow are not persuaded by the new classical empirical arguments and have doubts about the methods used. Tobin contends that the "results [of new classical models] are outperformed by tests with traditional models all the time."

The disagreements on how to test economic theories indicate that judgment plays a role in empirical discourse as much as it does in theoretical discourse. Just as there is no definitive theoretical argument, there is no definitive empirical argument. Each empirical argument is part of a research program. Sargent, acutely aware of the imperfections of his empirical work, speaks of his "journey of discovery." He apparently considers his journey promising, a judgment not shared by non-new classical economists.

The uncertainty of empirical arguments notwithstanding, the economists in this book affirm their importance. Even Solow, who is very sceptical about the possibilities of econometrics, sees the necessity of empirical arguments. Gordon dispels the notion that Marxist economists are indifferent to testing. He goes so far as to argue that they are more serious about testing their hypotheses against alternative hypotheses than are conventional economists. But, he complains, other economists do not acknowledge this effort.

EPISTEMOLOGICAL ARGUMENTS

The discussion of the theoretical and empirical arguments testifies to the significance of judgment in economic discourse. Much disagreement, as I noted above, concerns the style of argument. Brunner and Lucas, for example, may share the same vision on the economy, but they articulate their arguments differently in support of that vision. Likewise, Taylor's style of argument is distinct from that of the other neo-Keynesians. Epistemological arguments are those arguments that justify or legitimize the vision on how to formulate arguments; they reveal how economists think that they can best improve their understanding of economic processes. The importance of these arguments is usually not acknowledged.

The mathematical style of new classical economists suggests their appreciation of rigor and precision. Lucas and Sargent talk about the importance of technical developments that allow them to be precise in the formulation of ideas at which former economists only could hint. They seem to imply that precision is the foremost standard of scientific arguments, where precision means being specific about the conditions under which agents optimize. Keynesian models are allegedly ad hoc because they do not lie up to that standard.

The epistemological value of rigor and precision is manifest in the pure theory of Lucas and Townsend. Rapping and Brunner, in the conversations, express a widespread suspicion concerning highly abstract theories which seem to lack any connection with reality. The production of testable hypotheses, however, is not the objective of pure theory. Parsimony as to the assumptions is the guiding principle: the challenge is to reach realistic results with a minimum of assumptions. Townsend and Lucas examine, for example, what constraints on the information available to agents are necessary to produce an equilibrium model of business cycles. They attempt to be as precise as possible in the formulation of their models.

The predilection for a mathematical and rigorous style of argument includes a fascination with "neat and elegant" models. Tobin and Solow acknowledge that young economists share that fascination. Solow remarks: "I think that is one of the reasons why new classical economics did so well: it is so technically sweet; it involves all those sophisticated techniques. Students have to learn something new that other people do not know." He claims, however, that the tide is turning in favor of the neo-Keynesian approach.

The neo-Keynesians make clear that they also value rigor and precision. Nevertheless, they opt for relevance when the techniques fall short. They will not abstract from contracts, even though they cannot determine their existence as an outcome of optimal decisions. Their epistemological justification is to attack Friedman's argument that the realism of assumptions does not matter, an argument that they assume new classical economists support. Tobin claims that Friedman's positive methodology "has done great damage." The realism of assumptions does matter, according to him, and denying it only inhibits the development of economic theory. As far as the "ad hoc-ness" of neo-Keynesians arguments is concerned, Tobin responds: "It's too bad."

Lucas and Sargent retort that neo-Keynesian models contain unrealistic assumptions, as well. Lucas wonders why the neo-Keynesians do not criticize the neoclassical theory of utility maximization, which clearly does not describe how people actually make decisions. The disagreement, then, revolves around the trade-off between precision and relevance. The equilibrium models with rational expectation are simply too precise, or too abstract, and not sufficiently relevant to the liking of neo-Keynesian economists.

Overall, the economists with whom I talked support the conventional epistemological argument that empirical tests can and should be the final arbiter in theoretical disputes. They have a high opinion of the scientific quality of economics in comparison with other social sciences. For example, Solow and Blinder do not take sociology as a science very seriously, contending that it does not produce testable hypotheses. Rapping and Gordon do not seem to agree with this judgment, but also they stress the need for empirical tests. This epistemological agreement notwithstanding, there are disagreements over how to do the empirical tests. The discrepancy is similar to the one in theoretical discourse, the neo-Keynesians arguing that the new classical tests are too sophisticated in view of theoretical imperatives and the crudeness of the data.

I should point out that if the perspective I try to develop here is right, the epistemological arguments of economists would give an inaccurate representation of what they actually do. The confidence in empirical arguments, for example, is overemphasized, and the suppression of normative or philosophical discourse only serves to hide philosophical elements in economic discourse. Nevertheless, many of their remarks confirm my perspective. They do talk about problems of communication (although Solow is not convinced of the importance of this problem), and some are acutely aware of the uncertainty of their arguments. Sargent expresses such an awareness in his use of the phrase "a journey of discovery" to characterize his empirical research. We also encounter explicit refutation of the image of a detached scientist. Blinder, for example, acknowledges that he is committed to a particular vision: empirical findings may force him to give up some specific Keynesian ideas, but that does not affect his general beliefs and concerns.

THE PHILOSOPHICAL ARGUMENT

Many debates that start with theoretical issues digress into philosophical discussions. Disagreements often concern human nature, justice, and God's existence. At times even physicists end up arguing about metaphysical issues, as the discussions of Einstein and Bohr show. So, there is reason to expect philosophical disagreements in economic discourse.

Yet, the conversations show that explicit philosophical discourse is relatively poor in the world of economists. The economists in this book are reluctant to talk about why they adhere to a particular vision, and why they ask certain questions and not others. It may be that I did not probe deeply enough, but they are not eager to explore such concepts as the meaning of freedom, the place of the individual in society, or the justice of capitalism; in short, no philosophical topic was discussed in a substantial way. The conversations contain only a few reflections on the vision that is held.

For instance, Lucas and Sargent say they accept the basic message of Milton Friedman's *Capitalism and Freedom,* a book which spells out conservative (or liberal in the European sense) beliefs. Blinder stresses his concern with the underdog. Rapping presents a rather pessimistic outlook on the current system, in which he sees injustice and the prevalence of power. Gordon depicts a world that is filled with contradictions and conflicts, and projects a vision of a better world.

All these philosophical arguments are presented in an off-hand way. Economists also present implicit philosophical arguments through the language they use. One simply has to listen to their concepts to discover that they evoke distinct images. The concept "equilibrium," for example, evokes the image of a world in harmony. It seems reasonable to expect that the persuasive power of this concept will be greater for someone who is comfortable with that image than for someone who senses that something is very wrong with this world. Gordon, who adheres to the latter view, makes this quite clear.

"Rationality" is another value-laden concept. The individual rationality that excites conventional economists is appealing when one accepts Milton Friedman's arguments emphasizing individual freedom and the rationality of capitalism associated with individual freedom. The new classical suspicion of neo-Keynesian models appears to be stimulated by the idea that individual freedom is repressed by governments to which those models assign such a significant role. The individualistic language of neoclassical economists befits these beliefs. The neo-Keynesians do not object to such language, but complement it with a concern for the losers in the capitalistic game. Rapping and Gordon, on the other hand, refuse to use the individualistic language altogether, as it does not express what they want to say. They want to talk about suppression of individual freedom in capitalism and about the social aspects of individual behavior — and they need other terms for that. Yet, as Blinder frankly acknowledges, the radical language of Rapping and Gordon leaves conventional economists uncomfortable.

The uncertainty of economic argument renders language important. The vision that its concepts convey can be a decisive reason for acceptance of an argument. Choosing the right words, therefore, is crucial in economic discourses. In view of this, Solow's critical vision is surprising. In our conversation he talks about his critique of capitalist institutions, but in his writings he uses the conventional neoclassical language and refrains from articulating arguments that support his critical vision. It appears that his vision is repressed by his academic language and has failed to become an issue in economic discourse. His epistemological response to this point is that he is, above all, a positivist scientist, that is, someone who tries not to let his personal beliefs interfere with his scientific work. The experience of these conversations, however, suggests that divergent visions, or beliefs, do play a large role in disagreements among economists. Philosophical arguments, whether they are explicit or implicit, appeal to those visions and increase the persuasive power of the concomitant theoretical arguments.

COMMONSENSE ARGUMENTS

Another way to enhance the plausibility of a theoretical argument is simply to suggest that it makes sense. The mere presentation of highly abstract and mathematical models, uninterpreted, is incomprehensible and lacking in persuasive power. Economists, therefore, tell stories and use plain language to explain what they mean. The Robinson Crusoe story, for example, is a device often used to convey to college students the basic principles of economic wisdom.

A well-known commonsense argument in new classical discourse is the island parable that Lucas uses to render his assumption of imperfect information plausible. Lucas gives another commonsense argument when I suggested that the idea of a well-functioning market is unrealistic. He used Steinbeck's account of the market for cotton pickers in *The Grapes of Wrath* to convince me that the idea makes sense. But what makes sense to him does not necessarily make sense to others. Listening to Gordon, for example, conveys a dramatically different type of commonsense and evokes images of injustice and conflict.

The conversational style in this book undoubtedly reinforces the use of commonsense arguments. Indeed, anecdotes and simple explanations for complicated arguments are ubiquitous. But this is also the style that economists use in informal interactions among each other, in the classroom, and in exchanges with non-economists. Economists obviously realize that their arguments must make sense to be persuasive. In their academic work, however, they prefer to speak another, more-technical language — economists' language.

META ARGUMENTS

Theoretical, empirical, epistemological, philosophical, commonsense arguments — and still that is not all. Economists use even more arguments to sway their audience and get support for what they have to say. Commonly used tactics are to distinguish their own approach from others and to appropriate history. Meta arguments, the formal expression of such tactics, are statements about economists and their work.

One type of meta argument is the distinction between alternative programs in economics through the attachment of labels. Economists speak of "neo-Keynesian," "monetarist," "new classical," "post-Keynesian," and "Marxian" economics to suggest differences in vision and approach. A label is significant in persuasion. Lucas's work undoubtedly gained clout once people began talking about it in terms of "rational expectations economics" or "new classical economics." Brunner maintains an independent position by rejecting the label "new classical." It is also interesting to note that Tobin, Modigliani, Solow, and Blinder have no difficulties with the label "neo-Keynesian," but Taylor does. Taylor's reaction may be a corollary of his commitment to the technical aspects of economics; an outspoken political position does not befit such a commitment. Townsend resists a label, probably for the same reason. Rapping does not know to which school he belongs; such nebulousness, however, may hamper his effectiveness in economic discourse as he himself acknowledges. In general, economists want to know to which school of thought someone belongs, to facilitate their argument. The image of the detached economist begins to fade.

The appropriation of history is another tactic to bolster a position. Lucas and Sargent depict their approach as a "natural" development that began with the classical economists. They are again reading classical economists, like Pigou, and finding them interesting. Keynes's *General Theory* does not fit in their history, although they acknowledge the technical developments that this particular work generated. Friedman is elevated as a major figure. They do not consider the current controversy with neo-Keynesians fundamental, as the young generation is allegedly adopting *their* language. Disagreements, in their account, reflect a generation gap and will eventually die out. Lucas claims: "We think we're using the language of modern economics that, sooner or later, everyone will be using." Sargent foresees an end to the controversy.

This story is quite different from the one that the neo-Keynesians sketch. The Keynes of the *General Theory* still emerges as a giant in their historical account. The '50s and '60s were for neo-Keynesian economists a most significant time, unfortunately culminating in policies implemented against Keynesian advice. For them, the '70s were a decade of retreat, defense, and frustration, but, if Solow is right, the worst times are over, and new classical economics has peaked. Unlike the new classical economists, Keynesians have no problem with the observation that there are major disagreements among economists. Blinder, who belongs to the "young" generation, thinks that denying this is absurd. Apparently, economists also disagree on whether they disagree.

Gordon's meta argument is radically different from the preceding ones. For him, Marx is the central figure, although it is remarkable that he does not refer to Marx's works in the conversation. The '60s were important for him, too, but in a different way than for the Keynesians. He depicts it as a radicalizing period in which Marxian economics came alive again in the United States. He recognizes that conventional economists stopped paying attention in the '70s but gives reasons why this may change.

These meta arguments add a significant dimension to the state of the overall debate. Each community needs awareness of its place in history, economists included.

PERSONAL AND SOCIAL FACTORS

It is important that an extended group of economists can agree on certain basic judgments. When that occurs, we speak of a *research program*. Lucas has obviously been successful in establishing a research program. The introduction of the rational expectations hypothesis appealed to the judgment that macroeconomics be grounded in neoclassical microeconomics. With his emphasis on precision in theoretical analysis, he capitalized on a growing interest for a mathematical style of arguing. Quite a few in the profession are now persuaded that the new classical program is a promising field for further research.

Others clearly disagree with the new classical judgments. A major consequence is a problem in communication. A yawning gap separates the radical economists from the others; Gordon relates his difficulties in communicating with neoclassical economists, who in turn acknowledge that they do not pay attention to radical economics. Conventional economists may read the words of one another, but the communication problems among representatives of separate research programs are revealed in various remarks. Lucas, for example, complains that Solow tends to make jokes when they discuss issues in new classical economics. Solow jokingly suggests that much of the communication among economists has the following form: "I went to Grantchester today." "That is funny, I didn't." In other words, the communication does not go anywhere. Brunner, too, shows frustration with his problem to communicate with other economists.

These problems of communication may come as a surprise to anyone holding the image of detached scientists cherishing open discourse. Anyone who has peeked at or has mingled in the world of economists, however, must have experienced such problems. Being involved in economics is a social and personal process. Social and personal factors enter through the judgments that are inevitable in economic discourse; they are ultimately responsible for disagreements and concomitant problems of communication. If one is puzzled by this, one may want to look at the world of natural scientists — in particular, Watson's famous account of the discovery of DNA reveals the role of extraneous factors (see Watson, 1968).

The personal factor becomes manifest in the passion of economists. Economists generally do not like the term "passion," but surely it underlies much of what they do. I would even contend that an argument is effective only if it succeeds in appealing to one passion or another. In using the word *passion* I do not intend to evoke an image of raging and gesticulating economists. While economists may behave that way at times, passion is more the commitment with which economists adhere to a particular point of view. Passion is also the strong and perhaps overwhelming feeling that a particular idea is right. Lucas tries to instill in his listener that very feeling, even though he knows his arguments remain imperfect. His persuasiveness can be partly attributed to his ability to convey his passion. His personal style, I should add, is modest and soft-spoken. Passion is also felt in the other conversations. For example, Tobin made clear — in more ways than the written word can reveal — his commitment to neo-Keynesian policies and his disapproval of the new classical policy conclusions. These passions understandably may impede productive interactions among economists.

Economics is not only a personal but also a social process. The social factor works within and without the world of economists. The surge of conservative thinking in the outside world undoubtedly has benefited new classical economics, as Solow points out. Although such a relationship between ideas and social events is plausible, it is hard to establish. The conversations contain a few hints. Sargent, for example, refers to his experience in the Army as a reason for his suspicion of government intervention; Blinder recognizes the influence of his middle class, Jewish background; and both Gordon and Rapping mention the importance of the social turbulence in the '60s for their intellectual development.

The social factor operates within the world of economists, as well. Purely individual judgments usually do not count. Only a very few eclectics succeed in being heard and discussed. In general, a judgment carries force when it is shared by a group of economists and is discussed in the context of a recognizable research program. The conversations confirm the view that this social aspect of economic knowledge entails a division of the world of economists. Accordingly, there are the world of new classical economists, the world of neo-Keynesian economists, and so on. The contrast between the worlds is quite sharp; it concerns not only substantive ideas but also values and ways of arguing. Although economists are usually polite to each other and adopt a live-and-let-live attitude, confrontations do occur. Lucas and Rapping give an example when they speak of conflicts between the Chicago and Harvard people at Carnegie when they — Lucas and Rapping — were there. Lucas also remembers how "they were throwing darts" at him when he presented his first new classical papers to neo-Keynesian audiences.

The contrast between the different worlds in economics is especially obvious in Rapping's story. Rapping was a committed neoclassical economist during the '60s, and a conservative at that. He was a prominent scholar with a wide range of contacts. Then he came to believe, for various reasons, that something was fundamentally wrong with neoclassical economics. He subsequently went through what psychologists would call a Gestalt switch: he not only altered his ideas, but also his style of arguing. The process was personal *and* social. He stepped out of the neoclassical world, with drastic social consequences. His story attests to the time and energy that the development of an alternative perspective requires. This may help explain why fundamental changes in position are rare for economists; the personal costs are too great.

One major lesson for good and effective economists is that a detached and neutral attitude does not make an interesting and persuasive economist. As well as having a stance or a vision, a good economist has to demonstrate the ability to argue in terms that other economists can appreciate. It is tempting to argue from commonsense, but one has to speak the technical language of economists to get their attention: empirical arguments, uncertain as they may be, are a necessity. This is the social factor at work. Does the uncertainty mean that economic knowledge is altogether subjective and lacks truth content? We are not sure, but I doubt whether the answer matters much. Do we stop loving or living because of disappointments and the prospect of death? Most of us do not. Likewise, many of us want to understand what is happening around us; we want to talk about economic problems. These are sufficient reasons to probe ideas and come up with compelling and persuasive arguments. The conversations show how fascinating this activity actually is.

NOTE

1. This perspective is drawn from Klamer (1979) and is further developed in a manuscript entitled *The Art of Persuasion in Economics*. It is critical of the views of traditional philosophers of science, such as Karl Popper and Imre Lakatos, both of whom have strongly influenced the thinking about economics as a science. Without denying some form of rationality in economic discourse, I claim a significant role for nonrational elements. The focus on the communicative aspects can also be found in McCloskey's insightful paper "The Rhetoric of Economics" (1983). This paper contains references to the literature relevant for the perspective that I present here.

GLOSSARY OF NAMES

The following list of names is a selection of economists mentioned in the conversations. Much of the information is from *Who Is Who in Economics,* edited by Mark Blaug and Paul Sturges (1983).

Ackley, Gardner (1915–). Univ. of Michigan. Member of the Council of Economic Advisers in the Kennedy and Johnson administrations. Noted for his work in macroeconomics and economic growth and development.

Alchian, Armen (1914–). U.C.L.A. Research on the microfoundations of macroeconomics. Author of a well-known principles textbook.

Arrow, Kenneth J. (1921–). Harvard Univ. 1968–79; Stanford Univ. 1979– . Nobel prize 1972. Made fundamental contributions to general equilibrium theory and welfare theory.

Barro, Robert J. (1944–). Univ. of Chicago 1972–75; Univ. of Rochester 1975– . Contributed first to the disequilibrium approach in Keynesian macroeconomics; currently a major protagonist of the new classical equilibrium approach. His empirical tests of new classical propositions have been subject to much discussion.

Becker, Gary (1930–). Univ. of Chicago 1970– . Known for his application of neoclassical principles to topics like discrimination, crime, fertility, and education. Founder of the "new economics of the family."

Bronfenbrenner, Martin (1914–). Carnegie-Mellon Univ. 1962–71; Duke Univ. 1971– . An eclectic neoclassical economist labeled crypto-communist in McCarthy days, then fascist by radical students in the '60s. His papers are on a wide variety of topics, mainly in macroeconomics.

Clower, Robert W. (1926–). Northwestern Univ. 1957–71; U.C.L.A. 1971– . Made a seminal contribution to the disequilibrium approach in Keynesian macroeconomics. His major research is on the dynamics of business behavior. Currently editor of the *American Economic Review*.

Davidson, Paul (1930–). Rutgers Univ. 1966– . Prominent American post-Keynesian economist. His research is on domestic and international monetary economics. Editor of *Journal of Post-Keynesian Economics*.

Fischer, Stanley (1943–). Univ. of Chicago 1969–73; M.I.T. 1973– . Neo-Keynesian economist. Research on monetary theory and economic policy. Formalized contracts in a model with rational expectations, maintaining Keynesian policy conclusions.

Friedman, Benjamin (1944–). Harvard Univ. 1972– . Neo-Keynesian economist. Research in monetary economics and financial market behavior. Critic of new classical economics.

Friedman, Milton (1912–). Univ. of Chicago 1948–77; Hoover Institute, Stanford Univ. 1977– . Nobel prize 1976. Monetarist economist, fundamental contributions to consumption and monetary theory. Introduced the natural rate of unemployment hypothesis. Columnist for *Newsweek* since 1966.

Haberler, Gottfried (1900–). Born in Austria. Harvard Univ. 1937–71; American Enterprise Institute 1971– . Wrote on international trade and business cycles. Opponent of Keynesian economics.

Hansen, Alvin (1887–1975). Harvard Univ. 1937–62. Known for his exposition of Keynes's ideas in the US during the '40s and '50s. He is the Hansen of the Hicks-Hansen IS/LM framework.

Hurwicz, Leonid (1917–). Harvard Univ. 1969–71; Univ. of California at Berkeley 1976–77; currently at the Univ. of Minnesota. Economic theoretician. Research on the role of information, equilibrium, and game situations. Worked with Arrow. Also wrote on econometric issues.

Jorgenson, Dale W. (1933–). Univ. of California at Berkeley 1959–69; Harvard Univ. 1969– . Provided a neoclassical foundation of neo-Keynesian theory of investment. Has done econometric research on productivity and human capital.

Keynes, John Maynard (1883–1946). Cambridge Univ. Initiated the

"Keynesian revolution" with *The General Theory of Employment, Money and Interest* (1936). Rejected the classical views of Pigou, offered a theory of involuntary unemployment, and advocated active governmental intervention. His ideas are still at the center of the current controversy in macroeconomics.

Klein, Lawrence R. (1920–). Univ. of Pennsylvania 1958– . Nobel prize 1980. Neo-Keynesian economist; pioneer in the construction of large-scale econometric models. Like Hansen, an early advocate of Keynesian economics in the US, known for his book *The Keynesian Revolution.*

Knight, Frank (1885–1972). Univ. of Chicago 1928–55. Influential member of the so-called Chicago School; famous for his distinction between "risk" and "uncertainty." His writings include the philosophy and methodology of economics.

Koopmans, Tjalling C. (1910–). Born in Holland. Univ. of Chicago 1947–55; Yale University 1961– . Nobel prize 1975. Research in econometrics, theory of scarce resources, and economic growth.

Lange, Oskar (1904–65). Born in Poland. Univ. of Michigan 1936–43; Univ. of Chicago 1943–45; Warsaw Univ. 1955–65. Pioneer in the microfoundations of Keynesian macroeconomics. Introduced modern economic techniques in Marxian economics. Wrote on the theory of socialism.

Leijonhufvud, Axel (1933–). Born in Sweden. U.C.L.A. Student of Clower. Stimulated a reassessment of Keynes's original ideas, particularly his notion of disequilibrium.

Leontieff, Wassily (1906–). Born in Russia. Harvard Univ. 1936–75; New York Univ. 1975– . Nobel prize 1973. Laid the foundation for input-output analysis and contributed to the theory of international trade.

Lerner, Abba (1903–). Univ. of California 1966–71; Florida State Univ. 1977–1982. His works deal with socialist economics, welfare economics, employment theory, and international trade theory. Supports a socialist economy.

Lewis, H. Gregg (1914–). Univ. of Chicago 1946–75; Duke University 1975– . Well-known neoclassical labor economist. Major research on union-nonunion wage differentials.

Lovell, Mike (1930–). Carnegie-Mellon Univ. 1963–69; Wesleyan Univ. 1969– . Neo-Keynesian economist. Research on the role of inventories and expectational errors in business cycles.

Marschak, Jacob (1898–1977). Born in Russia. New School for Social

Research; Univ. of Chicago 1943–55; U.C.L.A. 1960–77. Pioneer in the theory of information and decision-making under uncertainty.

Marx, Karl (1818–83). German. Author of *Das Kapital,* a critical analysis of the capitalist economy. Coauthor, with Engels, of the *Communist Manifesto,* probably the most important political pamphlet of the nineteenth century. His ideas underlie the radical approaches to economics as well as to other social sciences.

McCallum, Bennett T. (1935–   ). Univ. of Virginia 1974–81; Carnegie-Mellon Univ. 1981–   . New clasical economist. Theoretical and empirical contributions.

Meltzer, Allan H. (1928–   ). Carnegie-Mellon Univ. 1964–   . Prominent monetarist. Was a student of and is now collaborator with Karl Brunner.

Muth, John (1930–   ). Carnegie-Mellon Univ. 1956–64; Univ. of Michigan 1964–69; Indiana Univ. 1969–   . Introduced the rational expectations hypothesis in an article published in 1961.

Okun, Arthur (1928–1982). Yale Univ. 1952–67, Brookings Institution until 1982. On the Council of Economic Advisers, 1964–69. Neo-Keynesian economist. Wrote about economic forecasting and fiscal and monetary policy.

Phelps, Edmund S. (1933–   ). Univ. of Pennsylvania 1966–71; Columbia University 1971–   . Formulated, simultaneously with Milton Friedman, the natural rate of unemployment hypothesis; constructed the first non-Walrasian models of expectational equilibrium and disequilibrium.

Pigou, Arthur Cecil (1877–1959). Successor of Alfred Marshall at the Univ. of Cambridge, England. Father of welfare economics. Associated with the real balance effect, also called the Pigou effect (which allegedly prevents the persistence of an economic depression.) Singled out by Keynes in *The General Theory* as the leading advocate of the classical view.

Piore, Michael J. (1940–   ). M.I.T. 1966–   . Radical labor economist. One of the originators of the dual labor market hypothesis (explaining structural imperfections in the labor market). Concerned with the problems of inflation and unemployment and migration.

Prescott, Edward C. (1940–   ). Univ. of Minnesota 1971–   . New classical economist. Worked with Robert Lucas. Contributes to the equilibrium theory of business cycles; also writes on game theory.

Robinson, Joan (1903–   ). Univ. of Cambridge, England. Prominent

English post-Keynesian economist. Worked with Keynes. Influential writings on imperfect competition and capital accumulation; major criticisms of neoclassical economics. Did not yet receive a Nobel prize.

Samuelson, Paul (1915–   ). M.I.T. 1940–   . Neo-Keynesian economist. Fundamental contributions to the neoclassical underpinnings of macroeconomics. Author of a widely used principles textbook. Columnist in *Newsweek* during the '70s. Nobel prize 1970.

Schumpeter, Joseph A. (1883–1950). Born in Hungary. Harvard Univ. 1932–50. Widely respected and often-quoted economist. Made important contributions to political economy, the theory of business cycles, and the history of economics. Adhered to a socialist vision but opposed the Marxian analysis of capitalism.

Simon, Herbert A. (1916–   ). Carnegie-Mellon Univ. 1949–   . Research on artificial intelligence and organizational theory of the firm. Well known for his conception of bounded rationality (which implies a criticism of the neoclassical notion of optimizing behavior). Nobel prize 1978.

Sims, Christopher A. (1942–   ). National Bureau of Economic Research; Univ. of Minnesota 1970–   . Influential work on econometric time series analysis; developed tests of causality and exogeneity of economic variables.

Sweezy, Paul (1910–   ). Influential Marxist economist. Editor of the Marxist periodical *Monthly Review* since 1949. Known for his idea of the kinked demand curve in an oligopolistic market.

Tinbergen, Jan (1903–   ). Erasmus University, Holland, 1956–73. Nobel prize 1969. Pioneer in econometrics and theory of economic policy. Contributions to development economics.

Wald, Abraham (1902–1950). Born in Romania. Columbia Univ. 1938–50. Mathematical statistician.

Wallace, Neil (1939–   ). Univ. of Minnesota 1963–   . New classical economist. Collaborator of Thomas Sargent. Research on monetary theory and history.

Weintraub, Sydney (1914–1983). Univ. of Pennsylvania 1950–83. Post-Keynesian economist. Well known for TIP, a tax-based incomes policy. Was a coeditor of the *Journal of Post-Keynesian Economics*.

SELECTED BIBLIOGRAPHY

This bibliography contains articles and books referred to in the preceding text, major publications of the featured economists, and additional relevant literature on new classical economics. The following abbreviations are used: *AER*, the *American Economic Review; JEL*, the *Journal of Economic Literature; JMC&B*, the *Journal of Money, Credit and Banking; JME*, the *Journal of Monetary Economics;* and *JPE*, the *Journal of Political Economy.*

Barro, Robert J. 1977. "Unanticipated Money Growth and Unemployment in the U.S." *AER* 67 (March): 101–15.
———. 1978. "Unanticipated Money Output and the Price Level in the United States." *JPE* 86 (August): 549–80.
———. 1981. *Money, Expectations, and Business Cycles: Essays in Macroeconomics.* New York: Academic Press.
Barro, Robert J., and Herschell Grossman. 1971. "A General Disequilibrium Model of Income and Employment." *AER* (March).
———. 1976. *Money, Employment and Inflation.* Cambridge: Cambridge University Press.
Blaug, Mark. 1980. *The Methodology of Economics.* Cambridge: Cambridge University Press.
Blinder, Alan S. 1979. *Economic Policy and the Great Stagflation.* New York: Academic Press.
———. 1980. "Comment," In Fischer, ed., *Rational Expectations and Economic Policy.*
———. 1981a. "Monetary Accommodation of Supply Shocks under Rational Expectations." *JMC&B* 13: 425–38.
———. 1981b. "Retail Inventory Behavior and Business Fluctuations." *Brookings Papers on Economic Activity:* 443–506.
———, with Stanley Fischer. 1982. "Inventories, Rational-Expectations, and the Business Cycle." *JME* 8: 277–304.
Brunner, Karl. 1969. "Assumptions and the Cognitive Quality of Theories." *Synthese.*
———. 1976. "An Aggregative Theory for a Closed Economy" and "Reply, Monetarism: The Principal Issues, Areas of Argument and the Work Remaining," In *Monetarism,* ed. Jerome Stein. Amsterdam: North-Holland Publishing Co.
———. 1981a. "The Case Against Monetary Activism." *Lloyds Bank Review,* no. 139 (January).

————. 1981b. "The Control of Monetary Aggregates." *Controlling Monetary Aggregates, III.* Boston: Federal Reserve Bank of Boston.

Brunner, Karl, Alex Cukierman, and Allan Meltzer. 1980. "Stagflation Persistent Unemployment and the Permanence of Economic Shocks." *JME* 6 (October): 467–92.

Brunner, Karl, and Allan Meltzer, eds. 1976. *The Phillips Curve and Labor Markets.* Amsterdam: North-Holland Publishing Co.

Davidson, Paul A. 1978. *Money and the Real World,* 2nd enlarged ed. New York: John Wiley & Sons.

Fair, Ray C. 1979. "An Analysis of the Accuracy of Four Macroeconometric Models." *JPE* 87 (August): 701–19.

Fischer, Stanley. 1977. "Long Term Contracts, Rational Expectations and the Optimal Money Supply Rule." *JPE* 85 (February): 191–206.

————, ed. 1980. *Rational Expectations and Economic Policy.* Chicago: University of Chicago Press.

Friedman, Benjamin. 1979. "Optimal Expectations and the Extreme Informational Assumptions of 'Rational Expectations' Macromodels." *JME* 5 (January): 23–41.

Friedman, Milton. 1968. "The Role of Monetary Policy." *AER* 58 (March): 1–17.

————. 1978. "Discussion." In *After the Phillips Curve: Persistence of High Inflation and High Unemployment.* Boston: Federal Reserve Bank of Boston.

Friedman, Milton, and Anna Schwartz. 1963. *Monetary History of the United States, 1867–1960.* Princeton: Princeton University Press.

Friedman, Milton, and Franco Modigliani. 1977. "The Monetarist Controversy: A Seminar Discussion." *Economic Review* of the Federal Reserve Board of San Francisco (Spring).

Gordon, David M. 1981. "Capital Labor Conflict and the Productivity Slowdown." *AER* 71: 389–96.

Gordon, David M., with Richard Edward and Michael Reich. 1982. *Segmented Work, Divided Workers: The Historical Transformation of Labor in the United States.* Cambridge: Cambridge University Press.

Gordon, David M., with Samuel Bowles and Thomas E. Weisskopf. 1983. *Beyond the Waste Land: A Democratic Alternative to Economic Decline.* New York: Anchor Press/Doubleday.

————. 1983. "Long Swings and the Nonreproductive Cycle." *AER* 73 (May): 152.

Gordon, David M., Samuel Bowles and Thomas Weisskopf. 1984. "Hearts and Minds: A Social Model of Aggregate Productivity Growth in the United States, 1948–1979." *Brookings Papers on Economic Activity* 1.

Haberler, Gottfried. 1937. *Prosperity and Depression: A Theoretical Analysis of Cyclical Movements.* Geneva: League of Nations.

Hansen, Lars Peter, and Thomas J. Sargent. 1981. "Linear Rational Expectations Models for Dynamically Interrelated Variables." In Lucas and Sargent, *Rational Expectations and Econometric Practice.*

Heller, Walter W. 1966. *New Dimensions of Political Economy.* Cambridge: Harvard University Press.

Keynes, John Maynard. 1936. *The General Theory of Employment, Interest and Money.* London: Macmillan and Co. Ltd.

Klamer, Arjo. 1981. "New Classical Discourse: A Methodological Examination of Rational Expectations Economics." Ph.D. dissertation, Duke University.

Lakatos, Imre. 1970. "Methodology of Scientific Research Programs." Pages 91–195 in *Criticism and the Growth of Knowledge,* ed. Imre Lakatos and Allan Musgrave. Cambridge: Cambridge University Press.

Lucas, Robert E., Jr. 1972a. "Econometric Testing of the Natural Rate Hypothesis." Pages 50–59 in *The Econometrics of Price Determination,* ed. Otto Eckstein. Washington, D.C.: Board of Governors of the Federal Reserve System.

————. 1972b. "Expectations and the Neutrality of Money." *Journal of Economic Theory* 4 (April): 103–24.

————. 1973. "Some International Evidence on Output Inflation Trade-offs." *AER* 63 (June): 326–34.

————. 1975. "An Equilibrium Model of the Business Cycle." *JPE* 83 (December): 1113–44.

————. 1976. "Economic Policy Evaluation: A Critique." Pages 19–46 in "The Phillips Curve and Labor Markets." Supplement to *JME* 1 (April). Ed. Karl Brunner and Allan Meltzer.

————. 1977. "Understanding Business Cycles." Pages 7–29 in *Stabilization of the Domestic and International Economy,* ed. Karl Brunner and Allan H. Meltzer. Amsterdam: North-Holland Publishing Co.

————. 1980. "Methods and Problems in Business Cycle Theory." *JMB&C* (November): 696–715.

————. 1981a. *Studies in Business Cycle Theory.* Cambridge: The MIT Press.

————. 1981b. "Tobin and Monetarism: A Review Article." *JEL* (June): 558–67.

————. 1981c. "Optimal Investment with Rational Expectations," in Lucas and Sargent, *Rational Expectations and Econometric Practice.*

Lucas, Robert E., Jr., and Edward C. Prescott. 1971. "Investment under Uncertainty." *Econometrica* 39 (September): 659–81.

Lucas, Robert E., Jr., and Leonard A. Rapping. 1969. "Real Wages, Employment and Inflation." *JPE* 77 (September): 721–54.

————. 1970. "Price Expectations and the Phillips Curve." *AER* 59 (June): 342–50.

Lucas, Robert E., Jr., and Thomas J. Sargent. 1978. "After Keynesian Macro Economics." In *After the Phillips Curve: Persistence of High Inflation and High Unemployment.* Boston: Federal Reserve Bank of Boston.

————, eds. 1981. *Rational Expectations and Econometric Practice.* Minneapolis: University of Minnesota Press.

McCallum, Bennet. 1979. "The Current State of the Policy Ineffectiveness Debate." *AER* 69 (May): 240–45.

McCloskey, Donald. 1983. "The Rhetoric of Economics." *JEL* (June): 481–517.

Modigliani, Franco, with Richard Brumberg. 1954. "Utility Analysis and the Consumption Functions: An Attempt at Interpretation." Pages 388–436 in *Post-Keynesian Economics,* ed. Kenneth Kurihara. New Brunswick: Rutgers University Press.

Modigliani, Franco, with Emile Grunberg. 1954. "The Predictability of Social Events." *JPE* 62 (December): 465–78.

————, with Albert Ando. 1960. "The 'Permanent Income' and 'Life Cycle' Hypothesis of Saving Behavior: Comparison and Tools." Pages 74–108, 138–47 in *Consumption and Savings,* vol. 2. Wharton School of Finance and Commerce, University of Pennsylvania.

————. 1977. "The Monetarist Controversy, or Should We Forsake Stabilization Policies." *AER* 89 (March): 1–19.

Muth, John F. 1960. "Optimal Properties of Exponentially Weighted Forecasts." *Journal of the American Statistical Association* 55: 299–306.

————. 1961. "Rational Expectations and the Theory of Price Movements." *Econometrica* 29 (July): 315–35.

Okun, Arthur M. 1975. *Equality and Efficiency: The Big Tradeoff.* Washington: The Brookings Institution.

Phelps, Edmund S., and John B. Taylor. 1977. "Stabilizing Properties of Monetary Policy under Rational Expectations." *JPE* 85: 163–90.

Rapping, Leonard A. 1979. "The Domestic and International Aspects of Structural Inflation." In *Essays in Post-Keynesian Inflation,* ed. James H. Gapinski and Charles E. Rockwood. Cambridge, MA: Ballinger Publishing Company.

————. 1979. "Review of Arthur F. Burns, *Reflections of an Economic Policy Maker."Challenge* (November/December).

Rapping, Leonard A., and James R. Crotty. 1975. "The 1975 Report of the President's Council on Economic Advisors: A Radical Critique." *AER* (December): 791-811.

Samuelson, Paul A. 1947. *Foundations of Economic Analysis.* Cambridge: Harvard University Press.

Sargent, Thomas J. 1971. "A Note on the Accelerationist Controversy." *JMC&B.* 3 (August): 721-25.

————. 1976. "A Classical Macroeconomic Model for the United States." *JPE* 84 (April): 207-37.

————. 1978. "Estimation of Dynamic Labor Demand Schedules under Rational Expectations." *JPE* 86 (December): 1009-44.

————. 1979. *Macro-Economic Theory.* New York: Academic Press.

————. 1982. "Beyond Demand and Supply Curves in Macroeconomics." *AER* 72 (May): 382-89.

Sargent, Thomas J., and Salih Neftci. 1978. "A Little Bit of Evidence on the Natural Rate Hypothesis from the U.S." *JME* 4 (April): 315-19.

Sargent, Thomas, J., and Neil Wallace. 1975. "Rational Expectations, the Optimal Monetary-Instrument and the Optimal Money Supply Rule." *JPE* 83 (April): 241-55.

————. 1976. "Rational Expectations and the Theory of Economic Policy." *JME* 2 (April): 169-84.

————. 1981. "Some Unpleasant Monetarist Arithmetic." *FRB of Minneapolis Quarterly Review* 5 (Fall): 1-7.

Simon, Herbert A. 1959. "Theories of Decision-making in Economics." *AER* (June): 223-83.

————. 1978. "Rationality as Process and as Product of Thought." *AER* 68 (May): 1-19.

Solow, Robert M. 1957. "Technical Change and the Aggregate Production Function." *Review of Economics and Statistics.* (August).

————. 1975. "The Intelligent Citizen's Guide to Inflation." *Public Interest.* (Winter).

————. 1978. "Summary and Evaluation." Pages 203-10 in *After the Phillips Curve: Persistence of High Inflation and High Unemployment.* Boston: FRB of Boston.

————. 1979. "Alternative Approaches to Macroeconomic Theory: A Partial View." *Canadian Journal of Economics* 12:3 (339-54).

————. 1979. "Another Possible Source of Wage Stickiness." *Journal of Macroeconomics* 1: 79-82.

————. 1980. "On Theories of Unemployment." *AER* 70 (March): 1-11.

————. 1980. "What to Do (Macroeconomically) When OPEC Comes." Pages 249-67 in Fischer, ed., *Rational Expectations and Economic Policy.*

Solow, Robert M., with Alan S. Blinder, 1974. "Analytical Foundations of Fiscal Policy." Pages 3-118 in *The Economics of Public Finance.* Brookings Institution.

————. 1976. "Does Fiscal Policy Still Matter." *JME*: 506-10.

Solow, Robert M., with J. E. Stiglitz. 1968. "Output, Employment and Wages in the Short Run." *Quarterly Journal of Economics.* (November): 537:-60.

Taylor, John B. 1975. "Monetary Policy During a Transition to Rational Expectations." *JPE* 83 (October): 1009-21.

————. 1977. "Conditions for Unique Solutions in Stochastic Macroeconomic Models with Rational Expectations." *Econometrica* 45: 1377-85.

————. 1979a. "Estimation and Control of a Macroeconomic Model with Rational Expectation." *Econometrica* 47 (December): 1267-86.

————. 1979b. "Staggered Wage Setting in a Macro Model." *AER* 69: 108-13.

————. 1981. "Stabilization, Accommodation and Monetary Rules." *AER* 71: 145-49.

Tobin, James. 1947. "Liquidity Preference and Monetary Policy." *Review of Economics and Statistics* 29 (May): 124-31.

————. 1958. "Liquidity Preference as Behavior Toward Risk." *Review of Economic Studies* 25 (February): 65–68.

————. 1970. "Money and Income: Post Hoc Ergo Propter Hoc?" *Quarterly Journal of Economics* 84 (May): 301–17; "Rejoinder to Milton Friedman." Ibid., pp. 328–29.

————. 1972a. "Inflation and Unemployment." *AER* 62 (March): 1–18.

————. 1972b. "The Wage-Price Mechanism: Overview of the Conference." In *The Econometrics of Price Determination*, ed. Otto Eckstein. Washington, D.C., Board of Governors of the Federal Reserve System.

————. 1974. *The New Economics One Decade Older*. Princeton: Princeton University Press.

————. 1980a. "Are New Classical Models Plausible Enough to Guide Policy?" *JMC&B.* 12 (November): 788–99.

————. 1980b. *Asset Accumulation and Economic Activity: Reflections on Contemporary Macroecnomic Theory*. Chicago: University of Chicago Press.

Townsend, Robert M. 1978. "Market Anticipations, Rational Expectations, and Bayesian Analysis." *International Economic Review* 19 (June): 481–94.

————. 1979. "Optimal Contracts and Competitive Markets with Costly State Verification." *Journal of Economic Theory* 21 (October): 265–93.

————. 1982. "Optimal Multiperiod Contracts and the Gain From Enduring Relationships Under Private Information." *JPE* 90 (December): 1166–86.

Townsend, Robert M., and M. Harris. 1981. "Resource Allocation Under Asymmetric Information." *Econometrica* 49 (January): 33–64.

Watson, James D. 1968. *The Double Helix: A Personal Account of the Discovery of the Structure of DNA*. New York: Atheneum.